Thought Crime

By

Leigh S. Gettier

ISBN: 0-7596-9725-6 (e-book)
ISBN: 0-7596-9726-4 (Paperback)

This book is printed on acid free paper.

1stBooks - rev. 06/26/02

ACKNOWLEDGEMENTS

Many teachers have contributed to this book. Most influential were Drs. Hall and Mucklow at the University of Richmond, philosophers extraordinaire.

Much thanks goes to cousin and friend, Jim Tucker, Ph.D., for his invaluable assistance with such things as Zwitter ions and electro-chemical adhesion—though all scientific and technical mistakes are mine, and mine alone. Another scientific inspiration has been my brother, Stacy Gettier, Ph.D. He is scientist, engineer, inventor, businessman, and father. His unbounded enthusiasm is expressed in the beneficial application of his considerable skills.

A creative, philosophical, and charismatic presence has been longtime acquaintance Dr. Judith Boice. Author, physician, and healer of the human spirit, she has consistently worked for a better world. To her I wish the best of times.

A good friend is attorney Edward Haas. I trust I can live up to his example.

Thanks to the professors and visiting attorneys and judges at the University of Richmond School of Law who taught a troubled student. Thanks also to a kind and talented law student who helped me with my Russian, so to speak.

DEDICATION

This work is dedicated to the quaint and dying notion of free will.

TABLE OF CONTENTS

Chapter 1

JULY FOURTH

Kelly Kissimmee's bare heels kicked up sprays of brilliant white sand as she leapt high above the volleyball net. Her tanned body, sparkling with sweat, hung weightless in space. Her blond hair swirled in a slow-motion dance of shimmering sunshine. She arched her back and cocked her arm, ready to strike.

Her arm flashed forward. "Whack!" The sharp crack of skin against leather echoed across the yard.

On the other side of the net, two young men dove for the ball that scampered between them. "Tock!" their skulls collided, and they fell unconscious on the sand.

Kelly landed feet apart, ready to repel the next attack. She flung her hair behind her shoulders, revealing brilliant blue eyes and a perfect, Nordic face. White gym shorts separated the square tracks of her tanned stomach muscles from the very long grooves of her muscular thighs. She was six feet, two inches tall.

At the picnic tables, fifty feet away, Irma Laches jumped, whooped, and waived her fists above her head. Goddess Kelly and a flat-chested, skinny, red-haired teenaged girl had just creamed the bigger, stronger college boys. Irma screamed "Go Kelly!" with the crowd, "Awesome!"

Irma shook her head in disbelief, and grinned. There were many men with athletic charisma, but few women. Kelly was one of those few. It was Irma's first experience with what could only be called "Venus envy."

"My God!" exclaimed Charles Chen, festooned in chef's hat and apron, standing next to the grill. "That's Kelly Kissimmee?"

1

"Yes," Lindley Meddlar affirmed, glaring at Irma's exuberance.

Irma smiled in response. "Kelly must be a California Girl. All of that beach volleyball has paid off."

"How so?" Lindley's voice was cold.

The young men were still motionless. A frown flitted across Irma's forehead, but she wasn't really worried. Most men had very thick, very insensitive skulls. The boys would be all right. "Kelly's a wonderful athlete, and she's exceptionally beautiful," Irma explained.

"How does playing volleyball on a beach make someone beautiful?" Lindley persisted.

Irma shrugged off Lindley's cross examination. She didn't feel like dealing with her boss's bullshit—not today. Irma was determined to enjoy her first company picnic.

The groggy boys groaned and started to stir. Kelly and the redhead were quickly at their sides, helping them to their feet. Kelly squatted and, with slender, gentle fingers, brushed sand from each boy's bare legs and backs, and the backs and fronts of their shorts. "Not afraid to touch the enemy anywhere, and in public," Irma silently observed. The young men certainly didn't seem to mind. Kelly was indeed an uninhibited California Girl.

Kelly, the redhead, and the boys walked up the hill— drawn by the ambrosial odor wafting from the grill.

Like a vixen hunting mice, Irma warily circled the picnic tables laden with food.

"See any men you like?" Lindley's voice came from just behind her left ear.

Irma cringed. Lindley was standing too close, trespassing into Irma's personal space. Lindley's eyebrows were raised, commanding a response.

"Well I'm—I'm not looking at men," Irma stuttered.

"Of course not," Lindley sneered. "You can't just stand around. You need to get to know these people."

"I'm getting a hot dog." Irma nodded toward the propane grill where Chen was holding court. "Care to join me?"

"I am going to do my job and make the rounds. Care to join *me*?"

Irma doggedly remained polite. "Sorry. I have a problem with low blood sugar." She would not be dragged around like a mutt on a leash by her boss. Irma deliberately turned away from Lindley and walked to the grill, growling in anger. The only thing she really didn't like about working at Winsome Semiconductor Corporation was Lindley Meddlar. Lindley could go to hell.

"Damn!" Irma thought, immediately impaling herself with guilt. Lindley was right. This was a company picnic. She should have been schmoozing with the engineers. But there was no crime in eating, or having a moment alone, either. Lindley's sarcasm was too harsh. "For Pete's sake, you're supposed to be able to enjoy a picnic!" Irma thought. She angrily jerked the tab on a can of Diet Coke and speared dip with a celery stalk.

As Irma moved toward the grill her anger subsided. She well knew her weaknesses: she was self-conscious about being single and still childishly shy. Lindley had just poked her in both sore spots. Irma shook her head in disgust. Was she that transparent? That weak?

Chen was suddenly in front of her. He held his tongs expectantly above the hot dogs on the grill.

Irma started. "Ch-Charles, it's wonderful for you to do this for the exempts."

"Do it every year, and look forward to it." His eyes crinkled.

Irma looked around. People were scattered on the grass on blankets, eating. She and Chen were alone. She whispered, "Can we talk for a minute or two?"

He put two dogs, grilled to perfection, on her buns, then sat in one of the lawn chairs next to the grill. "Ah. That feels great." He waved toward the chair next to his. "Have a seat."

She sat and relaxed. Chen's one-minute Welcome to Winsome speech when she was hired gave her the impression that he was a man who would rather listen than talk. She had immediately liked him.

This was her first one-on-one with her factory manager. She took a deep breath. "Why was I hired? There are no active legal cases for me to handle, and the Human Resources department certainly seems adequately staffed."

Chen put down his beer and scanned her face. "Is staff size your real concern?"

"Well—no." Irma paused and decided to tell the truth. "Lindley and I are already at odds, and I'm not certain of my role, which makes it worse."

Chen put his hands behind his head. "Want an honest answer?"

"Certainly."

Chen looked toward the far corner of the yard where Lindley was laughing at the center of a group of engineers. "Lindley has worked extremely hard. She is very professional, and seems to treat everyone equally. These are good qualities. That's why she was promoted so quickly. But one month before you were hired four of our oldest, most experienced engineers quit."

"Quit?" Irma was surprised. Winsome was the best employer in New Mexico. No other company—not even the government—could match Winsome's salary and benefits. "You mean they found employment with other manufacturers outside the state and moved?"

"No. I mean they quit. We believe they left without first finding other employment."

Irma thought for a moment. "They quit in anger?"

Chen nodded. "I think so, even though they were too politically correct to express their feelings on their exit interview forms."

Irma wasn't surprised that none had honestly stated their reasons for leaving. They needed Winsome's good will and the recommendations of their supervisors to get employment elsewhere. "Of course," she nodded. "They had to get other jobs to feed their families. Necessity breeds civility."

"Mmm," Chen assented. He, too, understood the ruse. "This sort of thing flies in the face of Winsome policy. We believe in treating our employees well. It takes years and hundreds of thousands of dollars for us to train an engineer. We don't want to donate all of that to competing companies. We have more than enough scientific and business challenges without these defections."

He picked up his beer, took a sip, and lowered his voice. "I met Lindley's parents one day at a Winsome function. They seemed to me to be very poor, very passive, very frightened people. They acted like victims—the exact opposite of Lindley. If anything, she is too self-assured. Now I've had no psychological training, but I would say she is over-compensating for the way she was raised."

Irma responded slowly. "You think Lindley herself, or something she is doing, is somehow causing these resignations?"

"Yes."

"But it's not obvious?"

"No."

Irma raised her eyebrows. "Why would she want to make employees quit? Maintaining good employee relations is her job." Irma shook her head. "I'm not sure I can fix this problem. My degrees are in political science and law, not psychology."

Chen gazed into the distant valley, shimmering in Albuquerque's desert heat. "Irma, let me ask you a few things."

"Shoot."

"What would you do if I fired you right now?"

She tilted her head in surprise. "Why—I would get another legal job."

"How long would it take?"

"Not long. I'm experienced and I work hard. I think I have a good reputation."

"And why are you here?"

"I want to help Winsome avoid legal problems, and to learn the corporate side of employment law."

"Right." Chen paused. "So, you're independent in a way that our regular employees are not. You don't have to work here, and I know that you took a pay cut when you were hired. You're here for the experience, not the money. Frankly, you don't have the scientific or business skills—at least not yet—to have any chance of promotion, so you're not trying to claw your way up the corporate ladder."

"Where does this leave me?" Irma said in a small voice.

Chen spoke quickly and softly. "It leaves you as the best person to ferret out what's wrong in Human Resources. I need someone who is not intimidated by Lindley, and who knows employment law, to find out what's going on. I don't have the time, or the legal skills, to do it myself.

"You were hired by me, not Lindley. She can't fire you. Tell her I've asked you to develop training materials on New Mexico employment law. Consider yourself a secret agent. Call me at home in the evenings." He scribbled his cell phone number on napkin and handed it to her. "It's unlisted. Of course, you'll also handle any real legal issues that arise at Fab 13. Can you do it?"

Irma quickly whispered, "Yes," and shoved the phone number into her shorts pocket.

Lindley was walking up the hill. Chen raised his can of Coors and called out. "Ready for a beer?"

Lindley smiled at her boss, "You bet."

Chapter 2

IRMA LACHES

The next morning Irma stomped around the Winsome cafeteria, splashed steaming coffee on herself, and fumed. Six a.m. was too god-awful early for an experienced attorney to be at work. It was the nightmare of her first days as a legal associate all over again. Seven o'clock, maybe. Eight, okay. But Chen and Lindley, both, had told her to be there at six. "To get a jump on the day shift," they'd said.

She carefully fitted a lid on her extra-large Styrofoam cup, placed her green chile cream cheese, sesame-and-poppy-seed bagel into a white paper bag, then paid for breakfast and hurried down the long sidewalk from the cafeteria to her office building. Even in July the shadows of dawn were cold. She shivered.

Irma had begun her legal career at the old Santa Fe firm of Dallas, Cranch & Wheat. Their forte was workers' rights litigation: suits against employers for sexual harassment, wrongful termination, and discrimination in hiring or promotion based on race, gender, age, or disability. Personal injury was a part of the practice, too, especially wrongful death—where one person died as a result of the negligence of another.

But after five years of working eighty hours a week, Irma had had it with the firm. There were thirty-one partners and one hundred fifteen associates. Half of the associates were female. All of the partners were male. The hypocrisy of a workers' rights firm refusing to promote women made her want to scream. Adding insult to injury, law-office culture precluded lawsuits. Lawyers were just as reluctant as their clients to bite the hand that fed them. They, too, needed the good will of their present employer to get a future job.

And Irma had chafed under the system of assigned cases—boring, run-of-the-mill cases. On the plus side, she had gotten a lot of court time. On the minus, the issues had become old hat. Her professional growth had stopped.

Her personal growth had stopped as well. Her male co-workers seemed fake, and she emphatically did not want to discuss law in her scant free time. She was not meeting new men.

Worst of all, she was gaining weight. Two weekends of careful shopping had yielded a larger wardrobe. But the horror wasn't the cost of the new clothes, it was the realization that the long hours at DC&W (known as D&C—dilatation and curettage—to its female associates) were finally taking their toll.

Recreational tennis and hiking were her college pastimes. But D&C's fourteen-hour days made her too tired for tennis, and it was always too dark and dangerous to walk. Eating and sleeping were higher priorities.

After months of soul-searching Irma decided she was justifiably unhappy. A busy and well-paid existence, and nothing more, was not a life.

At a continuing legal education class (a CLE in the legal world), she met Estee Oppel, Winsome's contract management attorney. Estee told Irma that Winsome paid reasonably well, had good benefits, and most importantly, expected only ten hours a day, five days a week. A permanent vacation! Estee mentioned there was an open position for human resources attorney, and Irma jumped at the chance. She faxed her resume the next day. A little help from Estee, and she was hired.

Irma walked down the main hallway, deep in thought. Strange men still stopped and stared at her jet-black hair, snow white skin, and chameleon eyes—eyes which appeared either gray, green, or blue depending on what she was wearing. Sadly her breasts—perky and enticing to more than one law school fellow—had started to soften and sag.

In her down moments she glimpsed her future as a too-bright, successful, overweight, middle-aged spinster. But at Winsome most of the more than 500 engineers were men. Something was bound to happen.

Irma entered the elevator and punched a button. Even older men were becoming attractive, to her surprise. Throughout her twenties she had seen old men as invariably, "dirty old men."

Just when had that change occurred? Perhaps it was during a court recess. An attorney in his sixties had pulled her gently aside and said, "You know, you're very attractive. You seem honest. I think you need to find a man who appreciates a woman who's honest. That's what went wrong in my marriage: there was a lack of honesty. That's an important quality. Don't lose that. Don't compromise it."

What did psychologists call it when strangers dumped their emotions on others? Irma frowned. "Flashing." That was saying something really personal about oneself to a strange person. It was sudden nudity—sudden emotional nudity.

But the old attorney had seemed more sad than confrontational, and she didn't know what to say. Finally she whispered, "Thanks." He nodded, and left.

Perhaps older men could be more honest than younger men. Perhaps older did mean wiser.

In her cubicle, she pushed the switch on her pc, stretched—long and cat-like—then took a big bite of bagel and a giant gulp of gourmet coffee. They were delicious. She closed her eyes and smiled. The best things about Winsome were its fresh bagels, green chile cream cheese, and coffee. Bootup was a fine time to enjoy them.

Her email held only Winsome's Fab 13 Daily Update: "Most Fab 13 production areas are meeting Gantted projections for a successful startup. Diffusion quals have failed due to high conductivity. Engineering is addressing the problem."

Irma yawned. She had already learned enough about semiconductor manufacturing to know that high conductivity meant that Diffusion was suffering from some kind of contamination. Contamination was enemy number one. But Irma wasn't worried. It wasn't her problem. She couldn't fix Diffusion and Winsome had plenty of engineers who could. She deleted the update.

She placed a yellow pad next to her mouse, and buried herself in a Lexis database search of New Mexico employment-at-will case law. Who had recently sued Winsome, and why? It was her job to know.

Chapter 3

BLOOD

Mary Martinez steered around the tumbleweeds sweeping across Coors Road and smiled. She loved these uniquely western weeds. They were the desert's people—roaming and reproducing in the raging respiration of the earth. They huddled against hillsides and bunched along barbed-wire fences. She expertly avoided the next heaving cluster. These wind-people seldom wrought mischief, except by wantonly withdrawing from their wanderings whenever and wherever they wished—often in her back yard. You could not grow up in Albuquerque without their lighthearted companionship. They were always 'round.

It had been a good July Fourth weekend. She, her husband and their children had enjoyed a picnic in the mountains. The Jemez Wilderness, near Los Alamos, was 4,000 feet higher than their home in the Rio Grande valley and 15 degrees cooler. The day had been filled with laughter, tall pine trees, rocky outcroppings, and a rushing frigid stream. They had even seen the shy little gray mountain stream bird—a water ouzel—cheerfully and miraculously walk under water.

Now sunlight streamed from the Sandias, suffusing the desert in saffron. Two huge rectangular structures—the shoeboxes of a giant, she thought—appeared on the right. Patient monoliths, serene and sharply etched, they rested quietly in the chill morning air waiting for the workday to begin.

One of the boxes was horizontal, the other vertical. She worked in the horizontal box—the largest semiconductor factory in the world, they said—Winsome Semiconductor's Fab 13. The vertical box housed the administrative and support staff who ensured the horizontal box ran smoothly. Mary seldom visited the office high rise.

*   *   *

The red digital clock above Fab 13's security desk read 7:00 a.m.

"Hey Mary. Did you pick up any hitchhiking tumbleweeds this morning?" Sergeant Smith smiled as she passed.

"They didn't have their thumbs out," she smirked in return. Smith was a handsome man with silver hair. Mary suspected he had a crush on her.

Ginny Cotton, Mary's best friend, waited at the foot of the stairs. Mary related Smith's joke to Ginny as they climbed, then added, "I like Smith."

Ginny giggled.

In the gowning room Mary and Ginny pulled on plastic gloves, disposable paper shoe covers, then found their numbered white suits—"bunny suits"—on the racks, and quickly pulled them over their street clothes. Helmets and belts with rechargeable battery-powered filtration units were next.

The reason for the suits, helmets, gloves, and filters was rigorously drilled into every Winsome employee: the manufacturing process was absolutely dependent on cleanliness and purity. Integrated circuits were so tiny that a microscopic particle of skin or salty crystal of sweat could form defects. Defects meant scrap.

Mary entered the air shower—a little hallway with automatic doors at both ends and walls studded with Jacuzzi nozzles. The entrance door closed as a noisy rush of air came from the nozzles, and those inside all turned slowly with their arms up, like chickens on a spit. This dance blew off particles from the outsides of their suits.

"HAVE A SAFE SHIFT," flashed the sign above the exit door, as it opened automatically. Mary and Ginny entered the gleaming, white and stainless steel heart of Fab 13.

They walked quickly through the maze of machinery to Photolithography.

Mary stepped into the darkened room that housed the scanning electron microscopes—the SEMs. This was where she worked every morning. The SEM room was kept dark to enable the operators to see the SEMs' black and white cathode ray tube displays. The CRTs showed ghostly electron images of the tiny lines, spaces, and holes being created on the once-smooth surfaces of the wafers.

Mary scanned the vacuum system displays. All of the little green light-emitting diodes glowed reassuringly, like tiny Christmas lamps. Green indicated that a vacuum pump was on. Mary smiled. Vacuum pumps could seize when turned off. This shutdown they had all been good little pumps—none had seized.

Mary rejoined Ginny at the intersection of the main hallways where Polly Ridley stood, clipboard in hand. Polly, their shift supervisor, was very young and very serious. She had a Bachelor of Science degree in Business Administration from the University of New Mexico.

A small sea of sunburned faces—the day and night shift crews—gathered around her. They laughed, exchanging stories from their pleasant holiday.

"I hope you all had a fine Fourth," Polly greeted them. "Diffusion is having some problems, so we won't be running any first layers. Run whatever back end material you have, and feed as much variety as you can to Etch. Also, prioritize the Lizard hot lots."

Mary knew that during startup one area always lagged behind. Diffusion had vacuum pumps, dangerous gasses, and immense quartz tubes—looking like glass torpedoes—

which had to be frequently pulled and cleaned. It was hard for Diffusion not to have problems.

"Back end" meant wafers that were close to being finished. In her brief tour Mary had noticed that almost all of the wafers on the work-in-progress shelves—the "wip racks"—were back end.

"Lizard" was one of the animal nicknames the engineers gave to new types of chips. They always tagged the first lots as "hot lots" to have them run rapidly. The yield results from Sort were needed to determine if the processing had succeeded, so that problems in production could be fixed.

Mary walked back into the SEM room, read the run cards which showed how far along each cassette was in the manufacturing process, and began sorting boxes of wafers. She quickly found four hot lots and placed them on the stainless steel shelves next to each electron microscope, then sat down at SEM number one.

Its high-vacuum chamber was at ten-to-the-minus-six Torr and its loadlock was vented. Torr was short for Torricelli—the Italian scientist who had first measured air pressure. Ten-to-the-minus-six was a good, "high vacuum." In processing class Mary had learned that at ten-to-the-minus-six there were about the same number of air molecules left in the chamber as there were in near-earth orbit. More air molecules than that would prevent the SEM's electron beam from reaching the surface of the wafer and cloud the image—just as smoke inside an optical microscope could interfere with the light reaching one's eyes.

Mary double-checked the recipe that had been automatically computer-loaded into the SEM. It matched the run card. She pressed the Auto Load button, carefully unboxed the first cassette of twenty-five wafers, and placed it on the automatic wafer handler. As if by magic, the SEM moved the first shiny silicon wafer out of the cassette and into itself. The loadlock entrance door closed with a gentle "chink," and the auto pumpdown sequence began with a quick "shu" of air.

Mary was about to move to SEM number two when an odd sound began on her helmet—a light tapping. For a moment she was completely perplexed. She looked around, but in the dim light could see nothing unusual. She sat and listened. The tapping was getting louder and faster.

A dark liquid ran down her arm. She couldn't believe it. In ten years at Winsome she had never been directly exposed to any of the chemicals. The electron microscope area used none, except for small plastic squeeze bottles of a weak alcohol/water mix, like rubbing alcohol, for wipe downs. Bunny suits were not designed to ward off chemicals—they were too thin.

She quickly moved away from her chair and peered through the dimness at the ceiling. The liquid was dripping regularly from the edge of a rectangular ceiling panel, and it was getting worse. She walked out of the SEM room.

Polly was standing in the aisle. "You're covered in red! Are you bleeding?"

"Red?" Mary held up her arm and stared in disbelief. "It dripped on me from the ceiling."

Polly grabbed her other arm and pulled Mary toward a yellow-curtained shower stall at the end of the aisle. "Get in the shower. Now!"

"Oh no. Oh no!" Mary tried to pull away.

Polly gripped harder. "Its for your own good. You must. We'll get you dry clothes. Stand in the shower for fifteen minutes and take off all of your clothes."

"No…" Mary wailed. Being naked in the fab was too embarrassing to think about.

Polly shoved Mary into the fiberglass shower stall. Water flooded from top and side nozzles as Mary's weight depressed the hinged metal floor grid, opening a valve. Polly quickly closed the curtain.

The water was cold. Mary took off her helmet and dropped it to the grid, then jerked off her suit and clothes. Angry at being forced into the shower, frightened by the red liquid, and embarrassed to be stark naked at work, she crossed her arms over her breasts and began to cry. Her teeth chattered as she stood in the freezing spray.

She felt something in her chest tighten. It must be her anxiety and the cold water, she thought. But it was an odd sensation. She prayed for warm towels and dry clothes. Someone should come soon.

All of the shift supervisors carried radios. Polly grabbed the microphone at her shoulder. "Security, this is Polly. We have an operator in shower twelve in Litho. Do you copy?"

"10-4 on the shower," intoned a deep, fatherly voice. "It's showing up on our status board."

Polly didn't give a damn about the status board. "Get the nurse with dry clothes up here right away."

"10-4 on the nurse."

"And call ERT for a leak in Litho," she commanded.

ERT was the emergency response team, consisting of equipment technicians and shift supervisors. ERT members responded to electrical and chemical emergencies in the fab. In a disaster it was also their job to sweep the building for the unconscious or the dead. Every ERT member was trained in CPR and carried a radio.

"10-4 on ERT."

Ginny walked up. "Can I help?"

"Yes. Mary got some chemical on her." Polly pointed toward the shower. Water was starting to drip from the sides of the curtain onto the floor. "Don't let her out for fifteen minutes, got that? Fifteen minutes. The nurse is coming."

Ginny nodded.

Ellen Rench, a member of the emergency response team, peered curiously up and down the aisle. "What leak?" she said. The ERT call had come through her radio.

"The SEM room. Get the spill cart, now," Polly commanded.

Ellen ran the fifty feet to the service chase where the cart was stored and pushed it rapidly to the SEM room. Three other ERT members were converging on Polly, who peered through the doorway into the dimness.

"The ceiling." Polly pointed.

Ellen cautiously reached inside and flipped the light switch. They all sucked in their breaths simultaneously. "Oh God!" someone said.

Red liquid was gushing from the ceiling, spreading rapidly over the floor.

"Shit. That's not a leak, that's a flood," Ellen observed.

"Dam it up. Dam it up," said Glen, an Etch tech. Etch used dangerous acids. He was their spill expert. He grabbed absorbent pillows from the cart and made a ring around the edges of the spreading red pool.

"Gloves!" Ellen shoved green solvent gloves in Glen's direction. He always wore heavy acid gloves for his regular work in Etch, but in the excitement of the moment, even Glen had forgotten.

"Okay, okay." He was embarrassed.

Polly was on the wall phone with Steve Reddy, ERT shift leader. "We've got a major leak over the electron microscope room in Litho. It's a red liquid—looks like photoresist. It got on one operator, but she's in the shower." She stared at the floor. "It's at least a gallon spill, so far, but I think it's slowing down."

It was indeed slowing. Glen placed white pillows in the center of the pool. The pillows grew red.

Ellen pulled on a green glove, kneeled, and deliberately placed a finger into the red liquid. She lifted her face shield and carefully sniffed her finger.

"What the hell are you doing?" Glen yelled.

Ellen was thoughtful. "No solvents. This smells like blood."

17

"Blood?" the other techs asked, in unison.

Polly was hanging up the phone. She turned to Ellen. "Steve wants someone from Litho. He's going to meet you in the interstitial to find the source."

Ellen held out her glove. "This smells like blood."

Polly blinked, hesitating only a second. "You still need to meet Steve. Can you do it?"

Ellen raised her feminist hackles, which were usually kept well hidden. She was one of the few female technicians at Winsome Semiconductor. She snapped, "Of course," and strode out.

Chapter 4

INTERSTITIAL

The emergency exit was the closest route to the stairs and the interstitial space twenty feet above. Ellen pushed the door open. Then, unzipping the shoulders of her suit, she deliberately climbed the stairs.

The interstitial was a windowless attic the size of a football field just under the roof of the fab. Electric motors turned blowers, air whooshed, and galvanized steel plenums accumulated the pressurized air. A thousand flexible ducts, like tentacles, squirmed downward, directing the air into the filters that formed the clean room's ceiling far below.

Ellen had a nightmare after her last dreary assignment in the interstitial. A giant squid grappled her naked body with painful suckers and she was pulled, screaming, into the blackness of the ocean's depths.

She well knew the genesis of her dream: the lighting sucked. Sparsely, as if by afterthought, a few tiny lamps clung precariously to the steel trusses twenty feet above the interstitial's meandering, suspended catwalks. It was a place of black shadows, gray steel, and demonic swirling air.

She stood indecisively on the large landing at the top of the stairs, reluctant to open the steel fire door to the interstitial. She keyed her mike, "Ellen to Steve."

"It's Steve. I'm almost at the top of the stairs. You there?"

"Waiting for you."

Steve opened the stairwell door and stepped onto the landing. "Do you know what the liquid is?" he said as he clipped his microphone onto his shirt.

"It smelled like blood." Ellen spoke slowly and distinctly.

Steve paused. "You're kidding."

19

"No kidding."

They both looked at the gray fire door. The area above the electron microscope room was on the other side, only twenty feet away.

"A lot of blood," said Ellen.

Steve Reddy was forty years old. He had supervised every area of the fab at one time or another. He hardly ever looked like he was taking anything too seriously. Ellen couldn't think of anyone who didn't like Steve. Now he was dead serious.

He frowned at Ellen, "Are you sure you want..."

"Let's go," she interrupted.

Steve swiftly opened the fire door wide and stepped from the concrete landing onto the steel catwalk. Ellen was close behind.

"Oh!" they both said, as if they had been punched in the stomach. Time stopped. The fire door hissed shut behind them, sealing them in.

A girl was suspended in the rushing air of the interstitial, and she was spinning—spinning slowly. The figure slowly twirled in the air currents; a slender, beautiful ice skater in a white jumpsuit, doing a graceful spin, arms stretched over her head, as if reflected on mirroring ice, upside down.

Then Ellen understood. There was a girl in a bunny suit upside down. She was tied to a roof girder by a rope attached to one foot. The other leg was bent at the knee, gracefully. Blood was dripping off of the girl's long blond hair.

"Someone's cut off her hands!" Ellen blurted in a hoarse whisper. She covered her mouth with the back of her hand. Saying it made it worse.

Steve saw the bloody stumps. Both hands had been severed at the wrist. They were gone.

A small voice from the past spoke inside Ellen's head. Don't touch anything at a crime scene. Don't touch . . .

don't touch . . . Winsome's training of the ERT teams was thorough.

Adrenalin surged through her body as fear screamed in her brain. Ellen whirled into a steel beam, bruising her shoulder, flung open the fire door, grabbed Steve's arm, and viciously yanked him back to the landing. The door hissed closed. She pawed for her shoulder mike.

Steve got to his first. "ERT leader to base."

"10-4 ERT leader. Go ahead." Sergeant Smith's confident voice was distinctive.

"We've got a dead girl hanging from the rafters in the interstitial above Litho near the back stairs. Send the nurse right away . . . " he trailed off.

"Ah, that's a 10-4." There was a surprise and hesitancy, both, in Sergeant Smith's voice.

Steve dropped his microphone. "Dammit! . . . Use the phone! . . . Shit!"

They all knew everyone these days had scanners. Every human being living in Albuquerque, Santa Fe, and the Rio Grande valley had just been alerted to the fact that a gruesome murder had occurred at Winsome Semiconductor. Ninety percent of the population of New Mexico lived within a seventy-mile radius of the plant, including network TV stations and newspapers.

"Shit! Shit!" Steve slammed his palm into the wall.

Ellen had never seen Steve so vexed at himself. She leaned back against the wall and stared at the closed fire door. The vision of the pirouetting ice skater, spinning, spinning slowly, was still in her mind. She crossed her arms and closed her eyes. Tears streamed silently down her cheeks.

Steve viciously grabbed the wall phone handset and punched in the emergency number. He barked at Ellen, "Do you know her?"

Ellen opened her eyes. "No. I don't think so." It sounded like someone else was speaking. The mechanical, dead voice that spoke her words could not be her voice.

"Smith here," said the phone.

"Get the nurse, Drew, up here right away. Right away."

"She's on her way to Litho with dry clothes for Mary."

"Back stairs! Tell her now!" Steve shouted. He had unnerved himself with his mistake with the radio.

Ellen felt sorry for Steve. He was a good guy. She reached out and put her hand on his shoulder. "She has to be dead. All of her blood is down in the SEM room. She has to be dead. The nurse can't help her."

Steve looked up. He was calmer. He nodded grimly and spoke into the phone again. "Smith . . . "

"Go ahead."

"Tell Drew the girl's dead, so she doesn't kill herself getting here."

"10-4 as to Drew."

"Listen, Sergeant. We need to secure this area. However you want to do it. Seal off the doors to the interstitial. Notify facilities to pull out their techs so we don't have anyone just wandering through. This is a crime scene, right?"

"We're already sending our people up to secure the doors. We've just told facilities."

"The police are coming?"

"On their way."

"You need me, I'm at this phone. Extension . . . " Steve paused, looked at the phone, and gave Smith the number.

"10-4."

Steve hung up the phone and shook his head. He still couldn't believe his mistake with the radio.

*   *   *

Jamie Wright, Irma's paralegal, was talking on her telephone headset and typing at the same time. She squealed "Oh my God!" and quit pecking.

Irma leapt up and looked over her cubical wall, "What is it?"

"Someone's died at Fab 13!"

"An accident?"

"I don't know!"

Irma didn't hesitate. She needed to be there. This was going to be a legal issue. "Where should I go?"

"Try Chen's admin, she'll know what's going on."

Irma slammed her hard hat on her head. Usually she thought her pink hard hat was incredibly funny, but today it was an automatic gesture. She grabbed her leather valise from her desk and walked briskly to the front door of the office building. Fortunately there was a shuttle waiting. The Fab 13 office building was physically separated from the clean room building. The site was so large that Winsome aptly termed it the "Fab 13 Campus." Walking was impractical if you were in a hurry, thus the shuttles.

* * *

Chen was gone, but Sally Sue, Chen's administrative assistant, was in her cubicle, next to his.

"Outrageous" was the word everyone used for Sally. Over six feet tall, she wore tight jeans, cowboy boots, had a soft low voice, a mysterious grin, long dark hair, spoke Texan, and drove men crazy. She'd been divorced twice. She kept in shape by country-western dancing.

Irma and Sally were the same age, and Sally didn't know a writ from a rat, but she knew how to relate to men. "Better than me," Irma thought. It was funny seeing Chen the scientist with Sally the cowgirl at meetings. But even men who were shorter than Sally asked her out. "Non-threatening to men," Irma said to herself. "That's the difference. What you see is what you get with Sally." What was that acronym? WYSIWYG. Sally was WYSIWYG.

"Where's the body?" Irma asked.

"It's in the interstitial, up the back stairs. Do y'all know how to get there?" Sally drawled.

"Actually, yes, from the fab tour when I was hired. Does this sort of thing happen often?" Irma had been at Winsome for four weeks. Sally had worked at Fab 13 since day one, and even prior to that, during its construction, she had worked in one of the contractors' trailers. She would know the number of fatalities.

Sally looked sad. "The first one," she said, softly.

"Thanks," Irma nodded and quickly turned away, marching through the maze of cubicles toward the back stairs.

Chapter 5

SEXY HUNKS

Ellen and Steve leaned glumly against the wall on the landing outside of the interstitial, next to the phone, and waited for the nurse. The fire door was closed.

Drew Goode burst through the stairwell door, breathless. "Show me!" she panted. She wore a radio, an orange backpack, and carried a huge red and white toolbox.

Steve moved in front of the fire door. "Slow down. This is a crime scene. You can't just barge in there. She's already dead. She has no hands and is hung upside down." His voice was hard.

"I say when someone is dead!"

Steve spoke more softly, "Drew, don't barge in. We'll open the door. But stop and think if there's any way she could be alive without hands and all of her blood down in Litho. Take off your stuff. We'll hand it in if you need it."

"Dammit! Arteries can self-seal. It's one of the effects of shock."

Steve put his hand on her shoulder and turned her away from the door. He looked her hard in the eyes. "There's more than a gallon of blood in Litho. She's got to be dead."

She glared at Steve. Steve—a man with almost no medical training—was trying to prevent an RN with twenty years of ER experience from doing something stupid.

She abruptly set down the first aid kit and yanked off her backpack. Somewhere along the way she, too, had learned about crime scenes. And Steve was right about the blood. "Open the door," she commanded.

Steve pulled open the door. Drew looked at the bloody stumps at the wrists and the blood on the hair. She had seen the blood in Litho. More than a gallon, she had also estimated. "You're right, she's dead." She let the fire door close without stepping through. Drew wasn't fazed a bit.

Ellen was suddenly angry. "How can you be so cold-blooded?"

"There's about an ounce of blood for every pound of body weight. I'd say that girl is tall enough to weigh 128 pounds. That's 128 ounces—one gallon. It looks like she bled out more than a gallon. Steve's right. No blood. No life."

Ellen stared at Drew, eyes flashing. How could Drew—a nurse—not care?

Drew read Ellen's thoughts. Right out of nursing school, twenty-five years ago, she had seen a car spin off the road into a snow bank. She pulled onto the shoulder and ran over as fast as she could. There was a teenaged boy inside. His head broke the car's side window and the glass sliced open the carotid artery in his neck. Drew opened the door, pulled him out of the wreck and was placing pressure on the artery within minutes of the injury, but he was dead already. It was his only wound—just one deep cut under the chin at the side of his neck. He was handsome and young, and the accident wasn't even that bad. But once the blood was out there was no way to put it back in. Drew sat on the snow and rocked the dead boy's body until the police came. Then she cried for two weeks. It was too unjust.

"I'm not cold-blooded." Drew explained calmly, "I've just seen it before. I've had to learn to feel responsible for what I am responsible for. And I'm not responsible for this girl's bleeding to death. I do wish it hadn't happened. But I could get another call this minute to go help someone else who's still alive. They have to be my priority."

Chen and Sergeant Smith rushed through the stairway door together. Steve and Drew gave them the rundown, opened the fire door, and showed them the girl.

*　　*　　*

When Irma got to the top of the stairs, she was surprised to see everyone in street clothes—no clean room bunny suits. She had been told in orientation that there was a strict clean room protocol requiring booties, gloves, and a hairnet even in the interstitial, to keep dirt from falling into the clean room. But no one was wearing any of that. And then she remembered they had said, "except during emergencies."

Irma looked under Chen's arm and through the open fire door. First she saw the blood on top of the plenums and duct-work. She thought she smelled the blood—the sticky, sweet, musky, nauseating smell of blood. She saw the hair hanging down. It didn't make sense—dark red blood on sunny golden hair. The figure slowly turned. She saw the face above the hair. "Oh God!"

Chen turned quickly and looked at Irma. Recognition flashed in his eyes.

Irma silently mouthed the words, "Kelly Kissimmee."

Chen's eyes assented. He spoke loudly, over the sound of the rushing air and electric motors. "They're sending the Lifeguard helicopter. The medical examiner is on the way, and a detective from Albuquerque. We'll let Lifeguard move her."

Irma cupped her hands in front of her mouth and spoke into the ear of the tall, thin female technician in the plaid work shirt and jeans. "What happened here? How could this happen?"

"It looks like someone cut her throat and wrists." Ellen's voice was hoarse.

Chen said to Smith, "We have other problems today. I'm going to let security take care of this. You need the nurse and who else?"

Irma spoke up. "I should be here for the questioning by the police."

Chen stared at her. Irma guessed his thoughts: he was unsure of her expertise. She spoke authoritatively. "We are near confidential areas of the fab, and we don't want the police to declare the entire building a crime scene. The questions asked of Winsome employees should be within what is reasonably needed by the police."

Irma knew it was time to take charge. She raised her voice. "Let's have everyone who is here stay, except for Chen. I'm sure they will want to talk to all of you." She hoped she appeared cool and confident.

She knew that from Chen's point of view this had nothing to do with running the factory. He was interested in the scientific detective work of solving the process excursions which were right now threatening to wreck startup; he would rather be thinking about the diffusion furnaces, racking his brain for possible sources of contamination. Dead bodies were in the category of a "human resources issue." The HR attorney—Irma—was the right one to handle it.

Chen gave Irma a quick nod as he walked out through the stairway door. Irma nodded curtly in reply. She and Chen were on the same wavelength. This was a very good thing. She was lightening his load. She was doing her job.

Steve, Ellen, Sergeant Smith, and Irma waited in silence—the men leaning against the walls with their hands in their pockets—the women with their arms crossed over their chests. The fab was too cool for summer clothes, and it was too much effort to yell over the sound of the blowers. There was enough to think about.

Irma reflected. Law school hadn't trained her to stand around dead bodies. But she was surprising herself. She was taking it well. She hadn't gone to pieces. Maybe it was the picture of the decomposed body that she had to look at while she was taking Evidence. Maybe it was studying the murders, the tortures, the horrible crimes against children. Maybe it had hardened her. She knew it could be worse.

She didn't know Kelly, not really. That would be worse. She had to admit she was excited.

She had to work fast. There was a yellow pad in her valise. She pulled it out, huddled the group around her, wrote down their names, then asked how they had been notified of the body and when they had arrived on the scene.

It took a full minute for her to work up the courage to open the door and stare at Kelly still dancing gracefully in the air currents. Disjointed sentences appeared on her pad describing the blood on the air handlers and the traces of the rivulets where it had flowed down into the clean room below. She sketched a stick figure, hanging by a rope threaded through a pulley high above, one end tied around Kelly's ankle, the other to a nearby railing.

"This is a real life game of hangman." Irma thought, sadly, as she sketched. Then, "I am cynical, cynical, cynical." She shook her head.

Law made you cynical. You saw too much and heard too many lies. It was the curse of knowledge, of knowing both sides. She even had two sides to herself; the superego side of her lawyer's brain always ready to interrupt her productivity and equanimity with self-criticism. Was she schizophrenic?

Irma meditated furiously, "You have the power, you have the power, you have the power," and ordered herself, "No! Stop thought." She bit her tongue and forced her hand to move. Her pen flew across the page. She estimated distances: the heights of the pulley and Kelly's shoulders above the catwalk, and the distance from the catwalk down to the clean room ceiling. Kelly's beautiful, thick blond hair had to be three feet long, extending well passed her wrists.

Irma stopped writing and stared. Blood was still dripping from the stumps of Kelly's wrists and off of her hair. The drops fell lazily onto the box plenums. Irma visualized the drops impacting the steel in slow motion, forming halos of microscopic droplets. These tiny specs of red were quickly swept away by the tornado flow of interstitial air and rushed passed the paddles of a giant blower, through the black funnel of a flexible duct, and forced down toward the pleats of a filter, only to stick onto its meticulously manufactured, bleached-cellulose fiber media. None of the aerosol droplets of life made it into the clean room. They were just red particles, undesirable in a world of clean steel.

Biology—life—was trapped, drying out. Kelly's life was still ending; her blood cells still dying. Irma wondered, "How many? How many blood cells are still alive, crying out for sugar, oxygen, warmth, and the symbiotic companionship of their sister cells?"

She suddenly felt ill, turned away, and found her nose buried in a muscular male chest. Irma pulled her face out of an orange jump suit reeking of Old Spice deodorant.

The Lifeguard crew had arrived.

Drew Goode was talking with a very handsome, dark-haired young man whose orange suit was embroidered "Doc Jones" over its right pocket. Drew gave him the facts about the blood. "So there's at least a gallon down in Litho, and she's got to be dead," Drew concluded.

Doc Jones looked troubled. "Normally we get the victim out right away, if there's any chance . . . "

Drew interrupted, "The radial and ulnar arteries in both wrists are wide open. It also looks like she bled from the neck, so at least one of the carotids was cut as well. They didn't self-seal. There's no chance that she's still alive."

Sergeant Smith stood, guarding the open fire door. He spoke to the paramedics. "No one goes in until the detective arrives. We want to get whoever did this."

Irma raised her eyebrows. Here was a confrontation between a Winsome guard and the Lifeguard crew. Sergeant Smith was clearly on Winsome's side, and on the side of the police, but against Lifeguard. "What's the usual protocol?" Irma wondered. Do the docs always trump the detectives?

Does Lifeguard get to trample every crime scene in the name of the welfare of the victim, even when the victim is likely to be dead? Was this a borderline situation? How do you instantly balance these interests? In the law, balancing competing interests was the job of a judge, not a security guard.

Irma analyzed the arguments. "If there is any chance of life." Did that mean any chance from the point of view of the reasonable doctor; any chance from the point of view of the reasonable layman; or from the God-like perspective of twenty-twenty hindsight? And what was "any chance?" One in a billion, one in a trillion, one in a quadrillion? How could one calculate the odds? Weren't incalculable odds meaningless? Wasn't "any chance" a figure of expression, a rhetorical device, not science?

The girl had to be dead, didn't she? All of her blood was down in Litho, just like Drew said. But suppose her brain was still alive, still viable? What then? Irma closed her eyes. She imagined beautiful Kelly's consciousness trapped, helpless, in a lifeless body. "Oh God. Oh God."

Irma hated her brain. It was unerringly, indefatigably, inevitably, incessantly, irrepressibly, mercilessly, and she thought, sometimes maliciously, analytical. "Stop it!" she screamed at herself. "Stop it! Turn it off! Turn off the thesaurus. Shut the book. Shut it. Stop thought, stop thought, stop thought." Irma imagined the slow, slow closing of a giant book, and her racing thoughts slowed. She focused outside of herself. She watched the Lifeguard crew. They were impossibly orange, young, and slender. They were sexy hunks. She must not become caught in a mental maelstrom of her own making.

A Winsome security guard came through the door at the top of the stairs, with a group of outsiders close behind. The large landing was getting crowded.

A tall man in the new group looked around and raised his voice. "I'm detective Larry Softhousen." Softhousen pointed at a young fellow, "This is forensics technician Evan Dinst, and this is Albuquerque's Medical Examiner, Mercedes Easter." He nodded toward a woman who was so short that Irma could only see the top of her hair behind the shoulders of the men.

Irma evaluated the newcomers. Dinst was a nerd, she thought. His blond hair was crew cut, his pants green Dockers, and his white dress shirt adorned with a red bow tie and a pocket protector filled with writing implements.

"Pocket protectors went out in the sixties!" This glimmer of humor lifted, only slightly, Irma's mood. She noted this skinny kid's nervous energy and enthusiasm. She guessed him to be twenty-five.

Softhousen said, "No one leaves," his voice a weathered, slow, western drawl.

Irma surreptitiously surveiled the detective. A good ol' Texas cowboy. Irma knew the type. They grew up on a ranch, riding fence and branding cows. They joined the Army when they were eighteen and won medals saving their buddies. They were lanky, blond, strong, and shy. She predicted that at some point Softhousen would say, "Ah, shucks."

She noted that the detective was aging, but not badly— just becoming wind-blown—his face tanned and lined. Almost-worn-out brown Rockports had replaced the cowboy boots on his feet. "Archetypal detective," Irma thought.

Softhousen, Dinst, and Mercedes took turns looking through the fire door at the dead girl.

Steve explained that no one had touched her yet; no one had been more than two steps passed the fire door.

Mercedes quickly put on Tyvex booties and latex gloves. Softhousen held the door as she carefully walked along the catwalk to the body, then gently placed her fingers on the girl's neck. "No pulse."

The detective, standing at the fire door, pulled out a little notebook. He wrote down the date and time, and, "No pulse per ME."

Mercedes looked at a digital instrument in her hand. "Ambient temp's 72.8."

"Yeh," Softhousen acknowledged.

Mercedes leaned over the railing and placed a hand on Kelly's shoulder, turning her slightly. She inserted the tip of the infra-red digital thermometer into Kelly's ear. "Head temperature, 90.3 degrees." Mercedes shook her head sadly.

"Got it," said Softhousen, scribbling on his pad.

Mercedes walked out to the group, retracing her steps. "She's smart and tough," thought Irma. Mercedes looked like the kind of woman who could amputate her own leg, without anesthetic, if she had to.

Irma admired doctors, especially the women. They had the same mental toughness, the same concentration as lawyers. They could put aside their own cares, their own pains. They did it for the sake of themselves, for their work, and for others. They had disciplined their minds and attempted to master the infinite science of the body just as lawyers had tried to master the equivocations of the Byzantine linguistic labyrinth of the law. Good doctors and good lawyers knew they could not know it all, and, even if they could, their disciplines would not hold the answers to life's ultimate questions.

Irma remembered her first weekend in law school, roaming the law library. Cases, millions of cases, federal and state, in thousands of volumes. Then she ran upon the shoals of the Admiralty Law shelves. There was a picture of an old schooner in a storm on the wall nearby. The law of the sea. Thousands more cases, from around the world. She'd had no idea this legal specialty existed.

The law library annex was filled with England's laws, and England's cases, going back 500 years. And there were foreign laws, foreign cases, foreign compilations and foreign commentaries in foreign languages. Shelves in the basement held thousands of law journals. The library stacks groaned under the volumes of the now-defunct older laws of the fifty states and the U.S. territories—the superseded code. Billions of pages and trillions of words. All of it was relevant sometime, somewhere, to someone seeking justice. No one—not the most brilliant, well-bred, well-read, well-educated student with the most photographic mind could ever know it all.

Mercedes wore loose, faded blue jeans, scuffed white leather shoes, and a doctor's green scrub shirt. "The privilege of power," thought Irma. "She gets to wear what she wants, and it's comfortable."

Irma was instantly envious. Lawyers emphatically did not get to wear what they wanted, and it was often uncomfortable, especially for the men. Irma would not own a tie. Her male attorney friends hated those awkward, expensive little appellations of prestige. And female attorneys hated heels; especially standing around in court, all day, in heels. Irma called them "Hells."

Mercedes had greying blond hair and grey eyes piercing Benjamin Franklin, gold, wire-rimmed glasses. She radiated energetic competence—she bore down, focused, and did what had to be done. Cutting open a decayed, maggot-ridden corpse was only a necessary chore, a tool in her quest for forensic knowledge. If only the criminals in New Mexico could see the kind of person they were up against. Doctor Mercedes Easter was a woman to be feared.

Irma referred to her pad and introduced the Winsome personnel.

Softhousen asked if she had captured everyone who had been involved in the incident on paper.

Irma nodded.

He turned to the group. "I need to talk to you all. I appreciate everyone's help. The girl's dead and we'll eventually take her to the morgue. Lifeguard can leave. The crime scene will take us the rest of the morning, and we'll begin interviews."

The Lifeguard crew walked, single-file, down the stairs.

"Who was here first?" Softhousen asked.

Steve and Ellen raised their hands.

Softhousen took a step toward them and lowered his voice. "Give me the short version."

Ellen explained how the red liquid had dripped on Mary in Litho, then Steve described how the two of them had found Kelly.

Dinst said to Softhousen, "Sounds like we might have a decent crime scene for once. I'll get my floor samples, then the pictures, and you and Mercedes go last."

Evan opened up his sampling kit and put on booties, latex gloves, a hair net, and kneepads. He carefully got down on his hands and knees at the open fire door, and began examining, with a magnifying glass, the expanded steel catwalk leading to the body. Occasionally he lifted debris with pieces of clear tape. He put the samples in pre-numbered baggies, and recited into a headset plugged into a tape recorder clipped to his belt what he saw, where he was sampling, and the numbers on the bags. Mercedes helped him place the baggies in a sample case.

Meanwhile, the police photographer selected a short zoom lens for his 35 mm camera and plugged an industrial-sized flash unit into a battery pack slung over his shoulder. He stood carefully behind Evan, taking pictures of everything.

Evan spoke to Mercedes, "Blood samples?"

"There should be plenty of blood left inside her," Mercedes replied, "but it can't hurt—especially on the railings. Whoever did this may have cut himself."

Evan gradually worked to within ten feet of the body, then spoke toward the door, "The area's pretty clean. There are some fibers on the grating. I'll do the railings last."

Softhousen wrote down everyone's names and said, "Except for the folks who discovered the body and the nurse, if you don't have to be here, leave. We need one Winsome guard to secure the area." Smith, standing by the phone, waived his hand. The detective turned to Irma. "Where can we go to do interviews? A meeting room?"

Irma said, "Follow me," and proceeded down the stairs with Ellen, Steve, Drew, and Softhousen close behind.

Chapter 6

INTERVIEWS

Irma's group stood outside the open door of a small meeting room.

Softhousen announced, "I'll make this go as quickly as possible. I'm going to interview everyone separately. I'd like you to stay in the cafeteria until I get to you. Do not discuss the case. Whenever there is a very emotional event, even the best observers can have differences, and those differences can help us solve the crime. So it's very important that we get everyone's impressions just as you remember them, without your trying to compare them with anyone else's. Also, this investigation is completely confidential. Don't say anything to anyone about what you saw this morning."

"This is standard police procedure," Irma confirmed. She thought to herself, "At least I think it's standard." Secretly, she was terrified; she had never been involved in a criminal investigation. Criminal law was sleazy. She was afraid of criminals. She had never done a police ride-along, had never been present at a police interrogation, and only vaguely remembered the general principles of the Fourth Amendment search and seizure cases she had been forced to study in school. She had been planning on going into anything but criminal law all the way through law school. Yet, here she was, with a new job, in the middle of a murder.

Softhousen motioned to Steve. "Mr. Reddy? You first."

Steve sat at the table as Irma closed the door behind them. He related to Softhousen everything he could remember, including his mistake with the radio.

Softhousen was sympathetic. "Well, maybe we'll get lucky. Maybe no one heard it." He asked Steve, "Have you had any trouble with the law?"

Steve turned red.

Irma blanched, and stated in a hard voice, "That question is improper, detective, and you know it. Winsome doesn't hire criminals. Everyone gets a background check. If you want to ask self-incriminating questions, Mr. Reddy is going to want to have his own lawyer present."

"You're present." Softhousen was firm.

"I'm not Mr. Reddy's attorney."

"Then why are you here?"

"I represent Winsome. It is in Winsome's interest not to have our employees harassed by the police and to know their rights. So you might say I only represent Mr. Reddy in a limited sense—through Winsome's eyes. But I am not a criminal defense attorney, and Mr. Reddy has not employed me to represent him. I'm telling you that as Winsome's legal counsel I object to your question. And I'm telling Mr. Reddy that he doesn't have to answer it without his own attorney present. Is Mr. Reddy a suspect?"

Steve looked at her with grateful eyes.

"Right now everyone's a suspect. It's in Winsome's interest to catch whoever did this, you know."

"Yes it is, but not by intimidating our employees. I'm sure you can obtain criminal records through official channels, if you need them. Let's move on." Irma was proud of herself. After being hired by Winsome she had reviewed the rules of professional conduct relating to corporate counsel. They were coming in handy. She was sure of her responsibilities.

Next Ellen, then Drew recounted their involvement with Kelly that morning. Irma heard no substantial inconsistencies. Nor were there any more objectionable questions from Softhousen.

Then Softhousen and Irma were alone. "Detective, where do we go from here?"

"Yeh, but it's Larry," he said quietly.

Irma thought she had impressed him. She knew she had kept her cool and hadn't said anything stupid, yet. "Okay, Larry. Please call me Irma."

"Irma. When did you get to the scene?"

"Fifteen minutes before you did. Just before Lifeguard arrived."

"And before that?"

"I was in my office in the other building. Am I a suspect, too?" She asked.

"Yeh, well, we need to narrow this down. The blood dripped on," he checked his notebook, "Mary Martinez at approximately 7:45 a.m. So for starters, we need to know the names of everyone who was in the building at that time."

"That's during shift overlap. And we still have outside contractors in the building doing shutdown work." Irma shook her head, slowly.

"So, how many?"

"In this building alone, a wild guess—about 500 people. On site—2,000. We can get lists."

"Christ! I can't interview 2,000 people."

"Look, it had to be someone familiar with the area above the clean room. That means a fab or facilities technician, an engineer, or possibly a contractor." Irma was surprised at herself. For a neophyte to semiconductor manufacturing she thought she was doing fairly well.

"So who have we eliminated?" Softhousen frowned.

"We can tentatively eliminate office workers because most of them stay away from the mechanical areas of the building. We can eliminate operators—the people who just run the machines in the fab. They don't normally go up into the interstitial. We may be able to eliminate any oncoming people who gowned, say, up to a half hour before the blood started."

"Why?"

"Because it takes five to ten minutes to gown up and get into the fab, and it had to take some time to string up Kelly, right?" Not to mention the time to cut off her hands, Irma thought. "Isn't what we really need the information from the medical examiner? Was Kelly tied up before or after she died? Did she really die from blood loss? How long was she dead when we found her? It might be easier to narrow things down that way, rather than by questioning 2,000 Winsome employees."

Softhousen answered carefully. "We will get the ME's report. Who are the other possibile suspects?"

Irma nodded. It sounded like Softhousen had suddenly realized he was going to need Winsome's—Irma's—full cooperation. "Well, the night shift techs, engineers in the fab and any extra workers. Kelly was wearing a bunny suit. That means she must have been working in the fab."

"Where's the night shift now?"

"Most are probably at home, asleep. They have to be back here in about nine hours. They work twelve-hour shifts."

Softhousen looked away, lost in thought. "Okay. Today we need to make a good start. How can we find out if anyone saw anything unusual? Someone acting suspicious who wasn't supposed to have been here? Can we see if someone who was here last night is absent from work tonight?"

"The guard desk in the lobby and Sergeant Smith are a good place to start. They are supposed to notice who enters and leaves the building," Irma replied.

"You don't track who's in the building? They don't have to scan in and out?" Softhousen sounded surprised.

"No they don't. They only scan to get into the clean room and a few other secured areas." Irma's voice was hard.

"This isn't jail. People can come and go freely. Engineers and techs get called in at all hours of the day and night to work on problems. The guards only check to make sure everyone who enters and leaves is wearing a Winsome badge."

"So we may never know for sure who was here."

"That's right."

"What about the victim? Who is she?" Softhousen's eyes narrowed.

Back to basics, thought Irma. "Kelly Kissimmee, a summer intern."

"Summer interns, too? You mean college students?" It sounded as if Softhousen wished he had chosen the July Fourth weekend to begin his summer vacation.

"Look—" Irma was sensitive to being overwhelmed by the size of the factory. She had felt that way for the past four weeks. "—I think we should talk to Charles Chen, the factory manager. This is a rotten time for this to happen, in the middle of startup, but I think we can convince him to call meetings with all of the supervisors. I'm sure he will let you talk to them. You can ask about unusual occurrences last night, tell them about the victim if you want, and tell them what you want them to look out for with their employees. Right now, it's just the front end day shift folks who are here. We can set up more meetings to cover the other shifts."

"How many shifts?" Softhousen's voice was wary, dreading the answer.

"Four for the fab personnel. They work twelve-hour shifts, alternating three and four days a week. Plus, there's a regular Monday through Friday day shift for the office workers and engineers. The contractors and construction workers have their own, separate schedules."

"And it could be someone from an off shift?" Softhousen was scribbling in his notebook.

"Yes. Extra people come in for shutdown from all shifts. But we have a list of those." Irma had studied the shutdown procedures and had gone to the shutdown planning meetings. She was on firm ground.

Softhousen looked up from writing. "July Fourth shutdown ended this morning?"

"Yes, at 8:00 a.m."

"Get me that shutdown list, and who worked last night, including the contractors. Let's get Kelly's file. Set up those meetings with the supervisors. But first let's check with Dinst and Easter."

Irma quickly scribbled Larry's requirements onto her yellow pad. "A quick call to get this started." She punched numbers into the speakerphone centered on the table.

"Sally," said the speakerphone.

"It's Irma with detective Softhousen. We need to get Kelly Kissimmee's file and to set up a short meeting with all the day shift production and facilities supervisors this afternoon. Can you run it by Chen?"

"Already done," Sally was pleased at having anticipated their request. "At 1:00 p.m. in 307. I'll get Kelly's personnel file and the shutdown list."

Irma continued, "Also, we need the list of people who worked during the shutdown."

"You betcha," Sally drawled.

"Thanks," said Irma. She punched off.

Softhousen was impressed. This was a big place, but it was organized and the people were smart and worked fast —even the Texans.

Chapter 7

VAMPIRES

Irma did not want to see Kelly again. But she had done well thus far, she thought. She might as well see it through. And Detective Softhousen was not a Winsome employee; he had to be escorted at all times.

Irma guided Softhousen back through the maze of hallways and up the stairs to the interstitial. Mercedes and Evan were placing the last of the plastic evidence bags into large black sample cases stenciled ALBUQUERQUE POLICE. Sergeant Smith stood next to the phone.

Mercedes looked up and announced, "We're finished. I've called for the morgue van and a couple of officers to help us carry down the body." She motioned toward the closed fire door and glanced at Softhousen, "She's still there, if you want to see her."

Softhousen nodded back, and he and Mercedes walked onto the catwalk. The fire door slowly shut behind them. Irma stayed outside, on the landing. A police investigation was confidential. She did not expect to be privy to their conversation.

As the door clicked into its frame Mercedes grinned at Softhousen. She was fifty-something and he was forty-something. "Alone at last," she said.

"With a stiff." Softhousen wasn't in the mood to kid around. He put on latex gloves, then gently turned the body so he could see Kelly's face.

He let out a low whistle. "What a babe. She could be a model."

Mercedes said, "You mean 'could have been.' Yes, she's beautiful. It's a shame."

"What have you found?" Softhousen asked.

"Like the nurse said, the carotid was transected—that's cut completely through—on one side of the neck." Mercedes was clinical—detached.

"Believe it or not, I know what 'transected' means." Softhousen scowled.

Mercedes ignored his irritation. "There are no obvious signs of a struggle; her hair is bloody, but not tangled. And that's strange—you would expect her hair to be a mess.

"It looks like the neck was initially punctured with a small, sharp knife, almost like a scalpel. The arteries at both wrists also bled freely. I can't tell right now whether the neck was cut before or after the wrists. Her hands were cut off in the vicinity of the scaphoid, lunate, and triquetral bones. A knifelike object was applied with some force to the wrists. There is some bruising on one side from the pressure."

"On one side." Softhousen spoke to himself.

"Yes. And I think whoever did this wanted to drain her body of blood."

"Yuk. It's those damned vampires again." Softhousen said it with a straight face.

Mercedes looked disgusted. "Just when I was beginning to think you could be civilized. We found her helmet down in those air hoses next to the catwalk."

"Ducts." Corrected Softhousen. "All of that medical training, and you don't know a duct from a hose."

"Whatever. Ducts. Evan wants to lower her down and take the rope and pulley as evidence."

Evan opened the door and came out onto the catwalk, carrying a black plastic body bag. He wore gloves and a face shield.

"This girl's not likely to have AIDS," said Softhousen.

Evan shrugged. They knew he was afraid of getting AIDS from dead bodies. He carefully began to untie the knot on the railing.

Evan stopped, then bent closer and examined the knot. "Hello, here's something. Get me an evidence bag. Whoever did this left us a present." He grinned behind his face shield.

Mercedes gave him a bag. Softhousen helped to loosen the knot while Evan used tweezers to carefully extract a yellow piece of latex glove which had been pinched in the knot. He delicately placed it in the bag and looked significantly at Softhousen. "We may have a fingerprint here. I'll check it out back at the lab."

"So now we know maybe the killer wore gloves," Softhousen observed.

They gently lowered Kelly onto the catwalk.

Chapter 8

BLOODY GLOVES

Irma's curiosity finally got the best of her. She opened the fire door and glimpsed Kelly's golden hair as the body bag was zipped shut.

Softhousen walked up to Irma. "I want your trash."

"What?" Irma was completely mystified.

"The killer may have worn gloves, bloody gloves, and put the gloves in the trash somewhere."

"Oh, okay." How did the factory handle its trash? She had no idea. Her eyes asked Sergeant Smith for help.

Smith read her expression and said to Softhousen, "You really want all of it? This is big factory. How about the dumpsters out back? He could have gone there."

"Dumpsters?" Softhousen again looked overwhelmed.

"Big, industrial size dumpsters. They're full right now. Most of it is construction debris—cardboard, wood from crates, plaster, stuff like that. There's also acid waste."

"Acid waste?" asked Evan.

"Yes. You'll need to wear acid aprons and acid gloves with face shields to look through it. It's in yellow bags," Smith explained.

Softhousen and Evan looked at each other. They both hated looking through trash, especially a lot of trash, especially trash with acid in it that could hurt you.

"Evan," Softhousen faked a diplomatic tone, "suppose you go look at the dumpsters on your way out, just to see if there's anything there. Construction debris we don't need. Let's have the other trash all brought out and we go through it outside. Bloody gloves should be pretty obvious."

Smith said, "I don't mean to rain on your parade, but Litho has a lot of red stuff—photoresist—in its waste. Looks just like blood on the gloves."

"Do the best you can." Softhousen was tired of being intimidated by this huge factory. It was Evan's turn. "I'll have the extra officers stay to help."

"Yeh. Well. Thanks." Evan was thrilled.

"I'll drive the morgue van back," Mercedes cheerfully volunteered. She had driven out with Softhousen in his unmarked car.

Smith got on the phone and ordered the factory's trash collected and delivered to the back dock. "I'll get you acid gear, too," he said to Evan.

Evan looked depressed.

Two Albuquerque police officers arrived with an aluminum-framed stretcher. Softhousen, Evan, Mercedes, Irma, and Sergeant Smith watched as the black-uniformed officers strapped the body bag to the stretcher and carefully carried it downstairs. They followed quietly.

"Can we take her out at the back dock?" asked Irma.

Sergeant Smith smiled, "Way ahead of you. The morgue van is already there."

They only saw a few workers during the walk from the stairs to the dock, and none of the workers asked questions. Apparently word of Kelly's death had already gotten around the factory. As the officers loaded the body into the black van, Mercedes turned to Softhousen and Irma, "I'll get back to you with a preliminary report as soon as possible."

Mercedes slowly drove away and Irma heard the faint thwishing sound of a helicopter. Perhaps it was Lifeguard leaving.

Softhousen, Irma, Evan, Smith, and the two officers walked along the dock until they came to three tractor-trailer-sized trash containers. Maintenance people from inside the factory were already placing plastic bags full of trash on the dock nearby. They could see inside the clear bags there were hundreds gloves and cloth wipes with red stains on them. The acid bags were opaque yellow.

Softhousen said to Evan, "See if you can find out when this stuff was placed in the bags. Prioritize what you look through. Do the best you can for the rest of the afternoon."

Evan and the officers were not eager to start. "Look," Irma said to Smith and Softhousen, "is there any way Winsome can help? Suppose we get a Litho technician to help with the red waste? He may be able to differentiate between blood and photoresist. Could this cause a chain of custody problem for you?"

"Not as long as he's supervised," Softhousen replied. He turned to Evan and the officers. "Can you guys supervise?"

They actually smiled. Irma brightened. Things were beginning to look less hopeless. "I'll arrange for a couple of technicians to help you." She looked at her watch. "The cafeteria is just inside. I'll treat you to lunch before you start. The trash will still be here in an hour."

"Much obliged, ma'am," said the tallest, and Irma noted, the most handsome officer.

"Yes, thanks." Evan chimed in.

Irma looked at Softhousen and Smith. "We can discuss what to say to the supervisors while we eat. Sergeant, will you do us a big favor and bring the new hire and summer intern photos to the cafeteria so we can look at them? Could you check and see if anyone has reported an employee missing to security, as well?"

"I'll be there in ten minutes," said Smith over his shoulder, already heading toward the guard desk. "Glad to help."

Chapter 9

HAMBURGERS

Irma led the way into the cafeteria, where she and Softhousen quickly picked up hamburgers and found a small table in the corner.

Irma took a bite of burger and looked at Softhousen. "Winsome tries to be very honest with its employees. I think we need to approach this meeting with the supervisors from that perspective," she said.

"Police investigations are confidential," he replied.

"Yes. I know that. But look—you'll be publicizing her identity eventually. It would be better if our employees heard it here first. You need their help. You need their trust. I'm not telling you to disclose any confidential details, but we need some of the basics out in the open."

Softhousen thoughtfully chewed. "One of the supervisors could have done it. Right now we have no leads."

"What choice do we have? Whoever did it is going to know the police have found out by now," Irma's eyes flashed.

"You're right about that." He sipped his Coke. "I can say we found a murdered girl above where?"

"Kelly Kissimmee. Above Lithography . . . "

He scribbled in his notebook. " . . . Lithography at 7:45 this morning. We don't need to say much else. No gory details. We want to know if they or any of their employees noticed anything suspicious this morning. If they noticed anyone missing or acting strangely. If anyone had blood on them besides . . . "

"Besides Mary, the Litho operator," Irma interrupted.

"Yeh, besides her."

Irma was suddenly worried, "And, we don't want to start a panic."

"I can't be responsible for the morale in this place." Softhousen looked around the cafeteria.

To Irma it seemed much more quiet than usual. Occasionally employees eating at other tables stole glaces at the two uniformed officers seated with Evan at the next table.

Softhousen continued, "But I can say this appears to be an isolated event."

"Would it be a good idea for our employees to pair up?" Irma asked.

"Yeh, sure. And they can let each other know where they are at all times and how long they expect to be away, if they have to leave their work station."

'Work station.' Irma noted that Softhousen was picking up Winsome's idioms. She nodded, "I guess that's the best we can do."

Sergeant Smith sat down in the empty chair at their table. He looked tired and hungry.

"Do you have the photographs?" asked Softhousen.

"Right here." Smith pushed a bulky brown expandable file into the middle of the table. "Do you mind if I get something to eat and join you? I'm starving."

"Please do." Irma smiled. She liked Smith. He was helpful, polite, and unobtrusive.

As Smith walked away, Softhousen said, "Nothing like a nice gory murder to work up the old appetite."

Irma gave him a sour glance and pulled the file toward them. "Let's look." She wiped her hands, then pulled out a stack of photographs and divided the pile in half. "You check these." She pushed the bottom half-pile toward Softhousen.

It was the very top photograph in her pile. Irma stopped and stared. She thought, "A California Girl." It was Kelly wearing a very tight, ab-revealing tee shirt. Undulating over Kelly's beautiful breasts, the shirt read:

$$E=mc*2$$

Cal Tech Engineers
Have Good Figures

Irma imagined Kelly walking into the factory straight from a morning of surfing. She was glowing, radiant, and unbelievably healthy. Kelly's a foxy grin displayed a mouth of brilliant white teeth. Her sea-blue eyes were surrounded by golden hair. Irma shook her head sadly. Kelly was awesome. The bottom of the photograph was labeled, "June 15, 2000. Kelly Kissimmee, Summer Intern, Safety Engineering." The description did not do her justice.

Irma said, her voice even, "Here's Kelly's," and passed the photo to Softhousen.

He only took a second to reply. "Yep. I'd say so. And she was just about a ten, too."

Irma said to herself, "Men! All hormones and no brains!" Kelly was so bright and beautiful in her picture that Irma wanted to laugh and cry at the same time. Just seeing Kelly's photograph was what psychologists called a "peak experience." Grimly, she wondered if Softhousen was inspired to think of Kelly only as a sex object. But, she thought, giving him the benefit of a doubt, perhaps Kelly was a peak experience for him as well. It was a mistake to see men as one-dimensional.

Irma said, "Now what? She was probably renting an apartment here, alone, or possibly with another intern."

"I need to find out what she was doing last night and interview whoever she was working with—also her supervisor," said Softhousen. "Get me her personnel file, and emergency contacts. I'll take care of notifying her next of kin."

Irma got up and made a quick call to remind Sally. "She'll meet us at the meeting with Kelly's information in," she looked at her watch, "ten minutes."

Smith came back with his food and they showed him the photo. He simply nodded. Irma had no doubt that Kelly had attracted the carnal attention of the guards as well. That's why her photograph had been on top.

Irma pushed her irritation toward men aside, and brooded. Why would anyone attack and kill a summer intern, a college student, from out of state? California was a long way from Albuquerque. How could Kelly possibly have made an enemy who worked for Winsome in New Mexico, while she was attending college in California? It seemed highly unlikely. Most college students were so wrapped up in their studies, their social circle, and sports, that there was no time for serious interpersonal conflict.

But Kelly was so incredibly attractive—could it be a jealous boyfriend? Maybe an upperclassman who had graduated and was now working for Winsome? Irma made a note on her pad. "Ex-boyfriend, Cal Tech, at Winsome?" It would be easy enough to get one of the HR admins to do a sort of recent hires in the Excel database based on university. But college students might go to national science conventions, might be in touch with anyone anywhere on the internet. "Not conclusive at all," Irma thought. There were too many possibilities. Looking for another Cal Tech student was probably a long shot, but it was worth a try.

This was a strange crime. Hanging someone upside down in order to drain their body of blood and frighten the people below. Why do that? A psychopath might. A guy who obsessed on women. A man who hated pretty women. Perhaps Kelly reminded this guy of his abusive older sister, or his mother, or the girlfriend he never had. Maybe it was someone like the Texas tower killer, here at Winsome, at this moment stalking through the dark, windy interstitial for his next victim. Irma shivered.

"No stereotypes!" Irma chided herself. What about women—Lesbian relationships gone bad, jealous female lovers? Anything was possible these days. And there were other motives besides jealousy. People killed for insurance proceeds; they killed for the thrill of the ultimate control over another human being; and they killed because of political, religious, and philosophical beliefs.

And there was hatred of technology. It was a perfect fit. Winsome was a world leader in the design and manufacture of large-scale integrated circuits—computer chips, micro-controllers, chipsets—whatever you wanted to call them. People hated computer technology for all sorts of reasons—a phone bill which was too high, a paycheck lost, an invasion of privacy. Irma could only imagine a few of the possibilities.

She felt herself at the edge of a downward spiral into depression, but realized she was doing it to herself; overwhelming herself with possibilities. The remedy for depressing thoughts was to stop them. Irma willed her mind to take another tack involving action. Even a simple action would do the trick. She looked at her watch. The meeting with the supervisors was about to start.

Chapter 10

GASEOUS GOLD

The windowless, cave-like meeting room normally held 300 people. It reminded Irma of deep underground in Carlsbad National Caverns; from the dark corners she half-expected to hear the eerie rustle of bat wings. The dozen front end day shift supervisors were appropriately somber as they sat in the front two rows of seats, beneath a single bank of lamps, surrounded by gloom.

Irma and Softhousen stood to the side on a low wooden stage. Chen stood in the center, facing the supervisors. "Thank you all for being prompt." His voice echoed softly from the back wall. "We need your assistance in addressing the incident which happened this morning. Detective Larry Softhousen," Chen nodded in Softhousen's direction, "is the lead investigator for the Albuquerque Police Department. Irma Laches," he indicated Irma, "our new site human resources attorney, will be Winsome's coordinator for the investigation." Chen looked at Softhousen and moved aside.

Softhousen took center stage. "As you all probably have heard, one of Winsome's female employees was found dead in the interstitial this morning. Some of her blood dripped through the ceiling into," Softhousen quickly checked his notebook and hesitated with the unfamiliar word, "Lithography. We don't know the cause of death yet, but believe there was someone else involved. The other party may have worn a pair of the same latex gloves that you all wear in the fab. The gloves may have blood on them. Please tell your employees keep their eyes peeled for a pair of bloody gloves."

One of the supervisors raised a gloveless hand. Softhousen nodded for him to speak. "We heard she died from blood loss. Is that correct?"

"We're waiting for the autopsy results," Softhousen explained. "As you would expect, autopsies cannot be done instantly. Time-consuming laboratory tests must be performed. I'm sure you are all also aware that a death is not always as it first appears. There can be multiple causes, one cause can mask another, and an accidental death can even look like a homicide."

"So you don't know what killed her?" asked another supervisor.

"That is correct. We do not." Softhousen spoke easily. It was the truth. "Have any of you seen any people who shouldn't be in the fab, or in areas where they wouldn't usually work?"

The supervisors all looked at each other. Their unspoken answer was "No."

The same supervisor raised his hand. "How about the dead girl? Do you know who she is?"

Softhousen nodded. "Almost everything from now on in the investigation will be kept confidential. We know the girl's identity, and will release her name after notifying her next of kin. Please do not speculate."

He paused for more questions. There were none. He continued, "Have your employees pair up, notify others of their whereabouts, and ask them to tell you how long they expect to be gone before they leave the clean room."

Irma was impressed. Softhousen's confident, informal manner was putting the supervisors at ease. She added, "You can always call Security the very second you suspect anything is amiss."

"And keep the rumors to a minimum," Chen ordered. "We need to stay on track here. We want to catch this person, but we also have a factory to run. Emphasize to your folks that this appears to be an isolated event, and that we need everyone's help. You can tell them what we've told you. Let's all take the common sense precautions.

"All information needs to funnel through Irma. Tell your folks to report anything or anyone unusual directly to her. But 'unusual' does not mean emergencies. For emergencies, always, without exception, call Security," Chen concluded.

Irma put her desk phone number, pager number, cell phone number, and home number on the white board next to the stage. The supervisors dutifully copied them into their day planners. They left quietly, with no cheerful banter. Chen, Irma, and Softhousen remained.

Chen put his hands in his pockets, and waited for the door to close behind the last supervisor before he spoke. "Because of the murder I was late for a meeting this morning with Louise Glasser's diffusion excursion team.

"Normally we have a few excursions during startup. So, it wasn't unusual to have a tube or two fail in Diffusion, but that should have been all. However there have been additional failures since this morning. In fact, all of the Diffusion tubes tested today—more than a dozen—have failed.

"We are getting other unusual failures. Etch, Thin Films, and Diffusion—every area of the fab except Lithography and Sort is failing in at least one major parameter. Most of the vacuum equipment won't even pump down." Chen stopped.

Irma knew what Chen was saying. In orientation they had explained that identical production machines, redundant support systems, emergency generators, stringent maintenance, and the awareness of contamination that was instilled in every Winsome employee; all were to prevent catastrophic failures from happening. The engineer teaching the contamination portion of the training had said that it was impossible for all of the equipment in the fab to go down. He had even said it was absolutely impossible. "Everything is down?" Irma asked.

"Except Litho and Sort." Chen closed his eyes for a second. Irma knew there was something he did not want to say. Then he said, very quietly, "This is a fab crash."

"That means . . . " Softhousen started to ask.

Chen interrupted. The consequences were obvious to him. "That means we can't run a single wafer. Production has been completely stopped. Because so many of the production areas are testing abnormally, we have no confidence that any of our equipment can run good product.

"Our disaster protocol is in place: first, engineering must identify and prove at least one clear cause which fully explains each and every failure occurring in each area; second, no production wafers can be run until a full series of tests over a forty-eight hour period shows that a majority of the equipment in every area is repaired and is able to run normally. My guess is that we will be lucky to get the fab back up in a week, if then."

"Could it possibly be related to Kelly?" asked Irma.

"We won't know until a pattern emerges from whatever is causing the failures. They can't all be failing for the same reason."

"Could the blood dripping into Litho have caused this contamination?" Irma asked.

"That's impossible," Chen stated, flatly. "For instance, there is no way for a liquid dripping from the ceiling in Litho to miraculously cause sealed stainless steel or quartz vacuum chambers, several bays away—the ion implanters, barrel ashers, sputtering equipment, and diffusion furnaces—to fail to pump down or fail their other quals.

"In addition, there are no common facilities systems which could cause pump-down problems. Most Litho equipment is connected to solvent exhaust, which is a completely separate system from the scrubbed exhaust used by the rest of the fab. There are no common ducts, no common blowers, no common vacuum pumps, and even if there were, there is so much airflow inside the ducts that airborne contaminants cannot possibly go against the flow.

"Even if it had not been cleaned up, a gallon or two of liquid cannot possibly run that far across the clean room floor, which is flat. And the spill was contained in the SEM room. It was cleaned up quickly. It is physically and chemically impossible for the blood to have contaminated the machines in the other areas of the fab."

"Isn't the air throughout the fab all mixed together up in the interstitial?" Irma asked.

"Well, that's a good point," Chen was surprised at Irma's grasp of the fab's design. "However the main blood gases are nitrogen, oxygen, and carbon dioxide, which are already in the air, anyway. None of those would cause a problem. On top of their being non-toxic, the volatility of blood gases is tiny. Blood quickly equilibrates when exposed to air, and actually absorbs oxygen. But even there, the amount of O2 absorbed from the air in a gallon of blood is minuscule in comparison with the volume of oxygen in the fab. Also, none of the fab processes use ambient oxygen. Though the pump-down characteristics of the most sensitive vacuum equipment might infinitesimally change, it would be so small that it would not affect processing.

"These same factors apply to the moisture—the water vapor—which is released to the air as blood evaporates. It is nothing in comparison with the volume of air in the fab. The effect is the same as mopping a small area of the floor, and that has no effect.

"Even if some of the blood dried and some of the blood cells were swept into the air, they would all be filtered out by the HEPA filters. Blood cells are so large, relative to our level of filtration, that they would all be trapped. There is simply no physical or chemical mechanism for contamination by blood to occur fab-wide."

Softhousen suddenly spoke, "If not the blood as a cause for the failures, how about a power failure? Isn't electricity common to all of the machines?"

Chen explained patiently, "Of course, you are right, electricity is common to all of our equipment. A conservative estimate is that we have 2,000 computers on site: personal pc's, equipment controllers, servers, safety systems, and our process control system mainframes. A serious voltage spike could destroy every single one of them. We would be down for weeks. So power is one of our main concerns.

"Line voltage monitors are installed throughout the buildings. We have our own power substation out in the yard with the best equipment we could put in it. Critical production machines are installed with uninterruptible power supplies—UPS's—or power conditioners that filter out spikes and sags. We have high capacity emergency backup generators to keep the most power-hungry, critical fab machines, emergency lighting, and safety systems in operation in case there is a total blackout, earthquake, grid failure, airplane crash into a power transmission line, or some other disaster.

"We have banks of batteries and invertors which kick in instantly to fill in for the few seconds it takes for the backup generators to come on line. We have a dedicated landline and a microwave link to the Four Corners Power Plant, in Farmington—the closest high capacity commercial power station.

"However, even with all of these systems functioning perfectly, when we lose power for only a second most of the equipment in the fab goes down. That means we can end up scrapping a hundred thousand dollars worth of wafers, and lose a million in potential profits—a huge loss from just a one second power failure. That's how important power monitoring is to us."

Larry couldn't reply. He was probably kicking himself for asking such a stupid question, thought Irma. Only, it wasn't a stupid question. "It sounds like we don't have enough backup capacity," she observed.

"True, we don't," admitted Chen, "but we can't. This place uses so much power that it isn't cost-effective. We've done feasibility studies. It would cost hundreds of millions to build the generating capacity to do a full backup. The only fab equipment that it is cost-efficient to back up with emergency generators are the diffusion furnaces, which are batch-processing systems. A single furnace can be processing a thousand wafers at once. The furnaces are heated electrically. If the power shuts off, the diffusion tubes start to cool down immediately and every wafer must be scrapped."

"Why?" Softhousen was following Chen's explanation intently.

"You need a little background to understand this," said Chen. "We grow precisely doped layers of glass on the surfaces of the wafers in the diffusion furnaces. It's analogous to that little experiment children perform in order to grow sugar crystals: you super-saturate boiling water by dissolving as much sugar in it as possible, then you pour the water into a glass and let it cool. Crystalline sugar precipitates out of the liquid, and will form on a seed crystal on a string. We super-saturate the furnace tubes with the gasses necessary to form doped glass, which is mostly silicon dioxide. The silicon surfaces of the wafers themselves are the seed-crystals upon which the glass grows.

"The wafers must be flat at all stages of processing. In order not to create physical stresses resulting in cracks in the glass, or bending of the wafers, the layer being grown must be maintained at a constant temperature, then very slowly allowed to cool. After a power failure and rapid cooldown the wafers come out of the furnaces bent just like potato chips; they are worthless scrap. The bending is caused by the enormous stresses in the glass surface caused by uncontrolled cooling."

All of the wafers Irma had seen in the factory had looked perfectly flat. She could not imagine one looking like a potato chip. What were those shapes called—the saddle shapes formed by potato chips and soap films? She stretched her mind back to high school geometry: minimal surfaces.

Chen continued, "Also semiconductors require regular crystalline structure in order to have consistent electrical and chemical properties. Even if the wafers don't warp, rapid cooldown destroys crystalline uniformity and drastically changes those critical electrical and chemical parameters."

"How does irregular crystalline structure change the chemical properties? Don't crystals of any size contain the same chemical elements?" Irma asked. Chen was a fantastic teacher. She might as well take advantage of this opportunity to learn from the master.

Chen nodded, "Good question. Every layer that is formed on the wafer gets etched, so etching follows every furnace deposition. Etching means chemically eating away areas of the new layer. Etching is necessary to form the transistor gates and junctions, the contacts, and the other structures we want on the surfaces of the wafers. The etching equipment—etchers—are precisely controlled as to time and temperature. Since different faces and edges of crystals present different numbers, configurations, and surface energies of atoms, those different surfaces will etch at different rates. Different-sized crystals also etch at different rates for the same reason. If the crystalline structure of the deposited films changes, our normal etching recipes will be wrong. The etchers will either over- or under-etch."

"Can't the recipes be adjusted?" Irma was fascinated.

Chen thought for a moment. "Yes, of course. But how much? When we intentionally change an etch recipe we will run dozens of experiments over a range of etch temperatures, etch times, and other parameters, in order to be sure we can etch away exactly as much glass as needed. We can't make good product by guessing at what recipe changes to make. A power failure during diffusion makes the film that was deposited a completely unknown quantity. Someone, someday, may be able to look at a botched layer of glass with an electron microscope and figure out how to fix it, but we aren't there yet. The technology doesn't exist. We must have a known, consistent layer of glass going into the etchers in order for them to perform properly."

Irma could think of no more questions.

Chen turned back to Softhousen, "There is one more, hidden issue in backing up electrical systems. It's the classic problem of diminishing returns in redundant systems.

"Ultimately, Winsome probably can't run a small power plant any better than they run the enormous generators at Four Corners. The more complex we make our factory power systems—with backup breakers, backup lightning arrestors, backup generators, backup high-capacity switches, backup transformers, backup grounding, and backup surge and sag protection—the more likely it is that something in the system will fail. Our own power plant would be just as likely, perhaps even more likely than any large commercial plant to have glitches and outright failures. We must accept the fact that we are going to have occasional power failures, whatever source of electricity we choose.

"But we know our present excursions are not due to a power failure. Power failures are obvious—they show up on our monitoring equipment, we get alarms, and I have never seen a significant failure where the office lights didn't flicker. Every engineer in the building runs into the fab to check his or her production equipment when that happens."

Softhousen nodded. He was learning a great deal about high tech manufacturing.

Chen refocused the conversation. "What do we know about Kelly?"

Irma spoke up. "Remember the volleyball game on July Fourth? She was a summer intern from Cal Tech, working in safety engineering. She had only been here three weeks." She handed Chen Kelly's picture.

Chen looked at the photo, and nodded. "Of course I remember her—a fantastic athlete. What a shame. How could she make an enemy here so quickly?"

"Well, she didn't necessarily need one." Softhousen nervously tapped his notebook with his pen. "This is looking like a crime of terror, not personal animosity." He paused and spoke softly. "Keep this is confidential. It looks like there was no struggle. Kelly may have already been dead or unconscious when she was strung up."

"Which means she didn't necessarily bleed to death!" interrupted Irma.

Softhousen looked surprised. He had only just thought of that himself. "Yeh. Mercedes—the medical examiner—will determine the cause of death." He paused. "Another odd thing, we couldn't find Kelly's hands, or the knife or whatever was used to cut off her hands."

Irma spoke excitedly, "And I noticed that she had no Winsome i.d. badge on her suit. Whoever killed her had to know we would figure out who she was fairly quickly, so why did he take her badge?"

"To slow us down?" speculated Softhousen.

"It could have fallen off," Irma suggested.

Chen said, "We can easily disable her i.d. on the security system so no one else can use it."

"No. Don't do that," Softhousen ordered. "There's an off chance the perp will use it. Keep Kelly's badge enabled. Is there any way to flag me right away if it's used?"

"I'll check on that." Irma scribbled a note to herself on her yellow pad, at the end of the dozens of notations she had already made.

Chen looked far away. Suddenly his face darkened, frighteningly. He reached for the speakerphone. Irma stared at him quizzically. As he punched buttons he explained, "I'm paging Louise Glasser." Seconds after he finished Louise rang back.

"What's up Charles?" said the speaker phone. There was tension in Louise's voice, Irma thought.

"Do you have update on the contamination in Diffusion?" Chen asked.

"I was reaching for the phone to page you when you paged me." Louise sounded exhausted. "We EDX'd the first wafers."

"And?" said Charles.

Chen had explained EDX to Irma at the barbecue. She had pretended as hard as she could to look interested. Now she remembered: he had used electron diffraction x-ray analysis, or EDX, extensively when he was a student at MIT. It was an analytical tool commonly added to electron microscopes. The SEM's electron beam was used to excite the electrons on the surface of the wafer. A liquid nitrogen-cooled germanium-lithium sensor sensed the x-rays which were given off as the excited electrons fell back to their original shells. The energy levels of the emitted x-rays gave a 'fingerprint' for each element present. EDX was very sensitive. The fab used it to find small amounts of contamination on the surfaces of the wafers.

"You won't like this." Louise sounded afraid.

"What?" Chen was impatient. He didn't like to play games.

"We got a gold peak," Louise said in a small voice.

Irma knew what that meant. During weeklong orientation classes Winsome had drilled into all of the new hires that the worst contaminants in the fab were sodium from the sodium chloride—the salt—in sweat, and gold. You could wear gold rings in the fab. But, you must, underscore <u>must</u>, wear the latex gloves on your hands at all times to prevent any possibility of gold contamination.

Winsome's fear of gold was elemental: it was an almost perfectly inert, soft, and electricity conducting metal with a low melting point. This meant that once gold had contaminated a machine it was almost impossible to clean it out. Most acids wouldn't touch it, and gold was so malleable that physical removal—scraping—would only spread it around and make the contamination worse.

Gold's low melting point meant that it could evaporate in a vacuum. This phase change from a solid to a gas without becoming liquid was called "subliming." Gaseous gold! Irma had been amazed. She had not known that such a thing was possible.

At the very end of the manufacturing process, in their own little clean room, Winsome had machines called gold evaporators whose job it was to evaporate tiny amounts of chromium and gold onto the back sides of the wafers, forming both a ground plane and an adhesive layer. At another facility, Die Attach, the gold/chrome-coated chips were placed into ceramic packages and heated. Utilizing another amazing chemical event, the gold and chrome melted together at a lower temperature than either would melt individually, forming a gold-chrome "eutectic" alloy. This provided the needed physical and electrical bond between the die and the gold preform in the ceramic package without heating the chips to a temperature high enough to destroy them.

But this was after the chips were finished, after all of their internal structures had been formed, and after a final layer of glass—the "passivation layer"—had sealed the chips' top sides from harm.

Prior to passivation the chips were extremely vulnerable to contamination. Inside a diffusion furnace's quartz tube the tube's hot wall and vacuum would cause a spec of gold to vaporize and coat everything inside. Everything: the quartz tubes; the front, back, and sides of the wafers; and the slotted glass fixtures which held the wafers upright inside the tubes—the "quartz boats;" everything inside would acquire an invisible, microscopic gold coating. Then after diffusion, the gold would physically rub off from the wafers onto the other machines and contaminate all of the succeeding processing steps. Eventually every processing chamber in every machine in the fab would become gold-contaminated.

Since gold was an excellent conductor of electricity its presence in the wafers would short out everything: transistors would no longer switch current on and off and memory arrays would no longer remember. A gold-contaminated wafer would be completely ruined; it would have "zero die yield."

"How many wafers?" Chen was cold, clear, analytical.

"Forty-eight. Every one was from the test runs this morning."

"From how many different tubes?"

"Twenty-four. Two from each tube."

"How many tubes were brought up this morning?"

"Thirty-six. We are still testing the last twelve tubes."

Chen closed his eyes. This was a semiconductor factory's worst nightmare: gold in the diffusion furnaces! Thank God they had only run test wafers, and not product, he hoped.

"Shut it down!" Chen commanded.

"What?" said Louise.

"Pull every technician and operator out of diffusion right now. They are not to touch any more wafers. Not a single wafer. Tell the other areas to keep their people out of diffusion. Have ERT put yellow 'DO NOT ENTER' tape across every diffusion entrance. Pull all of the quartz techs out of the fab as well." Chen thought for a second. "Have you had lunch?"

"No." Louise was surprised by the question.

"First page your leads, get them to pull everyone out of diffusion, give them a break to eat, then have everyone meet in 307 at . . . " he looked at his watch, "14:30 to come up with a game plan to deal with this. Everyone. Call our quartzware vendor and tell them to send a manager to the meeting, too. Got it?"

"Right away." Louise hung up.

Softhousen looked bewildered. Things he didn't understand were happening too fast. "What's going on?" he asked Chen.

Chen looked furious. "Sabotage. Was Kelly wearing any jewelry when you found her?"

Irma said, "I don't remember seeing any. Her hands were gone." She looked at Softhousen.

"This gold could be from her jewelry," said Chen.

"I was going to page her supervisor, Perry Nerrid," Irma suggested.

"Now." Chen whispered.

Irma was frightened. She had not know that Chen could exhibit cold fury. She pulled out her Palm Pilot, found Perry, and started punching numbers into the phone. She got lucky. Perry was at his desk. "Meeting with Chen in 307," was all Irma needed to say.

"On my way." Perry slammed down the phone.

Irma realized, belatedly, that as safety engineering manager Perry had probably been wondering why he hadn't been involved with the murder sooner.

Chen called Sally and told her to round up all of the area engineering managers as soon as possible.

He turned to Irma and Softhousen. "We need to catch this guy. In round figures, every hour this factory is idle, we loose ten million dollars. That's a combination of lost profits, wasted upkeep for the buildings and equipment, and salaries. My guess is we're looking at a minimum of five days' downtime to clean up this mess, and maybe ten million in equipment replacement costs. Five times twenty-four times ten plus ten is," it took Chen less than a millisecond, "one billion, two hundred ten million dollars."

Irma thought about saying "A million here, a million there—it really adds up," but wisely did not.

Chen continued, "It's possible that whoever did this is using Kelly's jewelry to contaminate this factory—to bring it to its knees."

Softhousen was surprised. He had never, in twenty years of detective work, had a case of industrial sabotage. "But how does jewelry . . . ?"

Irma whispered to him, "I'll explain later."

Perry burst in and slowed to a stop in front of Chen. Perry was 45 and lifted weights. He was the most energetic adult Irma had ever seen.

Chen looked at Irma. It was her turn to speak. She nodded and said calmly, "Bad news, Perry. The girl that was killed was Kelly Kissimmee."

Perry stood still.

"We have to run the autopsy," said Softhousen, "but she looked just like her picture."

Irma handed the photograph to Perry. "We're sure," she said.

Perry barely glanced at the photo. It had never crossed his mind that it could be Kelly.

Irma could tell that Perry obviously liked—really liked—his intern. What were the five stages of grief? According to Dr. Elizabeth Kubler-Ross they are shock and denial, anger, bargaining, depression, and acceptance. "He's in shock and denial," she thought. "Stage one."

The first area manager walked into the room. Chen immediately began an intense but quiet conversation with him.

Irma said to Softhousen, "Let's go to a smaller room and talk to Perry." She took Perry's arm and led him out into the hall.

"Thanks, Mr. Chen," said Softhousen.

Chen interrupted his conversation with the area manager. "Please let me know the cause of death as soon as possible, and about the jewelry."

Chapter 11

PERRY NERRID

In the small conference room which they had used previously for interviews Softhousen and Irma stared at Perry, and he stared straight ahead, at neither of them. His skin was pale.

Irma began, "Perry, this isn't your fault. Are you okay? Can I get you a cup of coffee? A Coke?"

Color began to come back into Perry's face. He looked at Irma. "Thanks . . . just had lunch. I can't believe . . . How can this happen? We screen everybody. Maybe a contractor . . . "

Softhousen copied Perry's name into his notebook from the Winsome badge hanging on his collar. "Mr. Nerrid," Softhousen's voice was kind, "I need to ask you about Kelly."

Perry nodded.

"What was she doing in the clean room?" Softhousen began.

Perry shook his head to clear his mind. "Uh, projects . . ."

Irma felt sorry for Perry. He didn't know where to begin.

"Projects?" prompted Softhousen.

"Yes." Perry paused. "All the summer interns are assigned projects. We try to give them at least one short-term project they can complete in ten weeks, and involve them also in long-term projects. We want to give them a feeling of accomplishment with the short project—something they can write up for school—something they can accomplish by themselves. The long projects are more like what really goes on around here—usually participating in something we've already got going. They get to interact more with the operators, techs, engineers, and managers on those."

"Alright," said Softhousen, "so what was she working on this morning?"

"Her short-term project. It was to do an audit of all the O2 sensors in the building, to determine if they need any maintenance, to develop . . . "

Softhousen stopped writing, bewildered. "Wait. Back up. What's an oh-two sensor?"

Perry was getting his confidence back. "Sorry. When I come into the building I switch into techno-babble. We have a number of areas in the building where we use liquid nitrogen. We call it LN2. It's very cold. When it warms up it evaporates, turns into nitrogen gas, and can displace the oxygen in the air. There was a fatality at another company several years ago from a guy walking into a room where liquid nitrogen was used. He suffocated from lack of oxygen. We don't want that to happen here. So, we check the liquid nitrogen locations continuously to see if the oxygen level is normal."

"So, oh-two is oxygen?" Softhousen asked.

Perry nodded.

"Why didn't the guy who died just walk out?" Softhousen was trying to understand.

Irma was sympathetic. Science wasn't her strong suit, either.

Perry explained, "Nitrogen, N2, is colorless, odorless, and tasteless. Air is seventy-eight percent nitrogen and about twenty-one percent oxygen. So you're breathing seventy-eight percent nitrogen right now. This guy had no way of knowing he was breathing too much nitrogen."

"Seventy-eight plus twenty-one is ninety-nine percent. What's in the other one percent?" Irma broke in. At least she could add, she thought, even if she was a lawyer, not an engineer. In the next instant she realized that she was putting herself down. She didn't expect any of the engineers in the plant to be familiar with the national reporter system for legal cases—something every lawyer in the country knew by heart—so why should any of the engineers at Winsome expect a lawyer to know the composition of air?

Perry explained, "That one percent is mostly argon, then carbon dioxide. There are also about a dozen trace gasses down in the parts per million. Let's see," Perry closed his eyes and thought for a moment, "in order, from greatest to least: neon, helium, krypton, sulfur dioxide, methane, hydrogen, nitrous oxide, xenon, ozone, nitrogen dioxide, iodine, carbon monoxide, and ammonia. That's for clean, dry air at sea level. In polluted air the levels of sulfur dioxide, methane, nitrous oxide, ozone, carbon monoxide, and ammonia are higher."

"How do you remember all that?" Irma was astounded by the vast world of engineering knowledge, previously unknown to her, to which she was being exposed every day at Winsome. She would never, in a hundred lifetimes, learn it all.

"I've been working in safety and environmental engineering for twenty-three years," Perry smiled sheepishly, "and I was looking at an air composition table this morning."

Irma liked Perry. Any guy who could get embarrassed about knowing the composition of air was humble—and humility was high on her list of desirable qualities in men. "That's cheating," she chided.

Perry grinned. "I guess it is." He spoke to Softhousen. "But back to your question. Nitrogen is basically inert and you don't know you're breathing it. This guy had no way of knowing he was breathing almost pure nitrogen. Your body only knows when too much waste carbon dioxide, CO_2, builds up inside you. Too much carbon dioxide and you feel like you're suffocating."

"Yeh, but he was still making CO2 inside his lungs, wasn't he?" Softhousen was remembering something from one of Mercedes' autopsy reports.

Perry answered, "Well, CO2 is made mostly in the muscles and is carried to the lungs by the blood stream. But, you're right, he was still producing CO2, except he was breathing in an out normally up until his death. Every time he breathed out he was getting rid of CO2, so the level of CO2 in his body was normal. His CO2 wasn't building up. His body just didn't tell him he wasn't getting enough oxygen."

"So, he just died?" Softhousen persisted.

"No. He passed out, fell to the floor, then he died. If there had been more oxygen at the floor, he might have lived. But since LN2 is cold, it produces cold nitrogen gas. Cold gas is dense, so it settles. There was even less oxygen at the floor, so he died from lack of oxygen."

"That could happen to anyone?" Softhousen was shocked.

"Everyone's body works the same way. We just don't have very good oxygen sensors. At high altitude you do get headaches from reduced oxygen. Also pilots without enough oxygen experience tunnel vision." Perry put his hands to his face and made raccoon eyes. "But, those effects happen too slowly to have helped the fellow who died."

Irma smiled at the raccoon eyes. She also remembered Perry's patience and humor from the "Intro to Safety at Winsome" course he had taught when she was a new hire, a month before. The students had all liked Perry.

"It sounds like we're all defective," Softhousen commented.

"Not really. There is nowhere on earth where it is cold enough to naturally make liquid nitrogen. Oxygen pervades earth's atmosphere, so our bodies had no reason to develop an oxygen sensor to combat this problem until the twentieth century. There was no evolutionary reason to develop one.

73

Technology is confronting us with a whole new set of hazards."

Irma had a question. "How about gas in mines?"

Perry laughed. "There's always an exception. Sure. You can also die from breathing pure methane in a mine—or in a septic tank, by the way. It works the same way, physiologically. The methane displaces the oxygen, and you can't sense it because methane is colorless, odorless, and tasteless, just like nitrogen. That's why miners carried canaries. The canaries have faster metabolisms—are more sensitive to low oxygen then we are—and they die first. But we can't have canaries in the clean room. So we have oxygen sensors."

"Septic tanks aren't odorless—they stink!" Irma sniffed.

"It's the mercaptans," said Perry, "sulfur-containing hydrocarbons—other gases that are mixed in. The methane alone is colorless, odorless, and tasteless."

Softhousen said, "Thanks, Mr. Wizard."

Perry smiled. "So Kelly was, first, developing a procedure for checking the oxygen sensors' accuracy; second, trying to determine the life left in the oxygen sensing modules; and third, writing up a complete maintenance spec and recommendations for improvements based on her findings."

"That's a short-term project?" Softhousen was impressed.

Perry nodded. "A little ambitious, but doable. She could also refer to the manufacturer's specs and telephone the OEM—original equipment manufacturer—as needed. Much of the information is probably already available. It was her job to pull it all together and put it into our online spec format. Sometimes manufacturers are way too conservative in their specs. Stuff can last a lot longer in a clean room because of the cleanliness and constant temperature. We don't want to waste money replacing parts that don't need to be replaced."

Irma's ears twitched. Perry was being defensive. She had picked up something subtle in his voice, body language, or both.

She could rarely explain exactly what triggered her warning system, but Irma's male colleagues were always astounded at her ability to pick up witnesses' emotional nuances in court. Psychiatrists labeled this sensitivity a mental defect—they called it "hypervigilant hyperarousal"—but Irma had made this "defect" work to her advantage. In fact, she thought of it as a gift. The shrinks were wrong.

Softhousen always asked one more question. "So these oxygen sensors. They can go bad?"

Now Perry looked really uncomfortable. "Well—yes."

Irma jumped in, "But they're all hooked into the security computer, right? So you know when they go bad? You get an alarm?"

"Not exactly." Perry paused. Both Irma and Softhousen stared at him until the silence became awkward.

"They're—they're not hooked in." Perry stammered. "They were installed after the other company's fatality. There is a lot of airflow in all of the areas where we have liquid nitrogen. The gas can't collect. We never thought we would have the same problem. The company where the fellow died had a small room, with a black plastic curtain around an electron microscope. The curtain contained the gas and made it worse . . . " he trailed off.

"What alarm do the sensors have?" Irma cross-examined Perry.

Perry spoke softly, "They give off a built-in tone. A Mallory Sonalert, solid-state, piezoelectric . . . "

"But the fab is noisy!" Irma interrupted.

"You can hear the Sonalerts within twelve feet of the sensors. I checked myself." Perry affirmed.

"You mean like a beeper?" Softhousen asked. He hated the sound of his beeper. He had launched the damned thing into a wall on more than one occasion.

"Yes, I suppose so." Perry looked defeated.

Irma and Softhousen looked at each other. There were lots of situations where you couldn't hear a beeper. Even the sound of a washing machine could drown out its feeble bleat.

Irma had an uncomfortable thought. Perry was covering his ass for doing a poor job with the original installation. He had probably hoped Kelly would discover the problems, and then recommend louder alarms and a tie-in to the central alarm system. It would save him the embarrassment of recommending that his own installation be upgraded—a tacit admission that he had done an inadequate job the first time. It would be an improvement, and make Kelly look good too.

Softhousen fiddled with his little notebook. "What time was she scheduled to work?"

"She could work whenever she wanted within the time windows Gantted for the engineers to be in the fab. No one was supposed to be inside during the planned power outages," said Perry.

"Gan-Ted?" Softhousen scribbled as he spoke.

Irma had sat in on the shutdown planning meetings because she wanted to learn how the factory really worked. She explained, "A Gantt chart, G-A-N-T-T, is a big sheet with lots of separate time lines for all of the different projects. It's the only way to make sure the projects don't interfere with each other—like if you had welding going on at the same time the fire sprinkler system was disabled for maintenance, you would have a fire hazard and no way to extinguish it." That issue had arisen in a meeting. "And no one was supposed to be in the fab when the lights were out."

"Did Kelly know all of this stuff?" asked Softhousen.

"She wasn't at any of the shutdown meetings I attended." Irma remembered those meetings well. All of the other Winsome employees there had worn shutdown garb—tee shirts and jeans—even the engineers. In her nice lawyer outfit she had stuck out like a sore thumb.

"I . . . I'm not sure if she knew about the Gantt chart," said Perry.

Irma concluded that Perry had thought Kelly so bright and personable that he had assumed she would find the facilities shutdown coordinator, figure out the Gantt chart, and then work out her own schedule.

"So we don't know when she came in," Softhousen verified. "Did she have a roommate? Anyone else here we can check with? A buddy?"

Perry shook his head, "No. On the O2 project she worked alone. I don't know about her friends. She was probably renting a furnished apartment for the summer. We give a pretty generous stipend so the interns will have enough money to live comfortably. I guess she could have had a roommate," he shrugged.

Irma closed her eyes. Perry had no idea what Kelly was doing with her free time. Winsome was so work-oriented that it was gauche to speak of life outside the plant. This was just the tip of the iceberg, Irma thought. There were probably people who had worked at Winsome for years and no one knew who they really were. At D&C it had been even worse.

"We should check with her new hire orientation classmates to see who she hung out with. I'll get the list." Irma volunteered. All of the new hires were excited and insecure. They looked to each other for support. In orientation beautiful Kelly had certainly made some friends.

"Get those names." Softhousen flipped his notebook closed. "I would like to see where Kelly could have been working—those oxygen sensors."

Chapter 12

ALL-AMERICAN GIRL

There was a knock at the door and Sally Sue sauntered in. She handed a manila envelope to Irma. "That's Kelly's personnel file," Sally drawled. "Sorry it took so long. They weren't filed properly. Most of the human resources staff are on vacation . . . "

"No problem," Irma interrupted. Sally was good.

Sally's cowboy boots breezed out. Softhousen stared midway down the closed door. "No shortage . . . " He stopped.

" . . . of?" asked Irma, eyebrows raised.

" . . . beautiful women around here," he finished stubbornly.

Irma and Perry exchanged embarrassed glances. Winsome had a strict policy against any form of sexual harassment, and that included comments about anyone's appearance—even compliments. Softhousen's observation didn't conform to Winsome culture.

"Let's look at this." Irma changed the subject. She opened the envelope and gave Softhousen half of Kelly's file. He laboriously read each page. Irma quickly scanned her pile then patiently waited for him to finish.

"Whew!" said Softhousen, looking at Kelly's resume. "The All-American Girl. She was an All-American basketball player at Cal Tech—and a straight-A student . . ."

" . . . in engineering," finished Irma. "And she was taking a master-class on the cello. Kelly's parents in California are listed as emergency contacts."

"Should we call them?" asked Perry.

"Here?" Irma was apprehensive.

"Yeh, why not." Softhousen had done this a hundred times. "How do you work this thing?" He nodded at the speakerphone on the table.

Irma punched in the numbers. The phone on the other end began to ring.

"Let me handle this," Softhousen warned.

"Hello? This is David Kissimmee," answered an older voice.

"Mr. Kissimmee, this is Larry Softhousen with the Albuquerque Police Department."

"Is this about Kelly?" There was an edge of fear in Mr. Kissimmee's voice.

Softhousen waited a moment. "I'm afraid so."

Mr. Kissimmee paused. "Let me get my wife on the other line."

In the background, they could hear Mr. Kissimmee say, "Susan, it's about Kelly. Please pick up the other phone."

Irma thought, "My God, this is awful."

"This is Mrs. Kissimmee."

Mr. Kissimmee said, "I'm back."

"This is Detective Larry Softhousen of the Albuquerque Police Department. I'm at Winsome Semiconductor Corporation on a speakerphone with Irma Laches, their legal counsel, and Perry Nerrid, Kelly's boss. I'm sorry to have to inform you that Kelly has apparently been the victim of a murder." He stopped.

There was absolute silence on the other end. "At least they live in peace and quiet. They have better things to do than to watch the soaps on TV," Irma thought. Then she chided herself for being so vapid. Lots of her friends in law school liked soap operas. She was employing a subconscious psychological strategy to avoid thinking about what the Kissimmees were going through.

"She's dead?" Mr. Kissimmee's voice was tremulous and broke as he said it.

"I'm afraid so, sir," said Softhousen.

"How…" Mrs. Kissimmee trailed off.

"I'm sorry, we're not completely certain what happened. She was found dead at Winsome this morning. We will let you know as soon as we know…"

"Perhaps it wasn't murder." Mr. Kissimmee interrupted. His voice was firm and angry. Irma looked up as if stung. All along she had thought it was murder.

"I'm sorry, we don't know," said Softhousen.

"You will let us know." Mrs. Kissimmee paused, then her voice broke. "Was she hurt?"

Softhousen avoided the truth. "We don't know yet. But we do have some questions you may be able to answer which could help in our investigation."

"You'll have to excuse me." Mrs. Kissimmee put her phone down. They could hear her crying softly in the background.

Mr. Kissimmee's voice strained, "Go ahead."

"Did Kelly have any friends or a roommate in Albuquerque?" Softhousen asked.

Mr. Kissimmee paused. "Kelly told us that she had rented an apartment for the summer, alone. She mentioned friends named Troy and Tracey, I believe, during her last phone call."

Softhousen and Irma wrote down the names.

Softhousen continued, "What else did she say?"

"She was excited about working for Winsome Semiconductor, since it was where she wanted to work after graduation. Kelly liked Perry, and she was enthusiastic about getting an early start on her special project during the July Fourth shutdown."

"Did she wear any jewelry?" asked Softhousen.

"She liked to wear two gold rings, a gold necklace, gold bracelet, a gold watch, and gold earrings."

Both Irma and Softhousen wrote furiously as Mr. Kissimmee described each of the items in detail.

"She died inside the Winsome Semiconductor factory, is that right?" asked Mr. Kissimmee.

"That is correct, sir." Softhousen spoke softly.

Mr. Kissimmee stated, "I want to fly out there."

"With me." Mrs. Kissimmee came back on the phone.

"We don't need you to do that," said Softhousen, firmly.

Perry could identify her body, Irma thought.

"We'll be there tomorrow," said Mr. Kissimmee.

Irma's eyes closed. This was not going to help. But she couldn't possibly advise them not to come. First, she wasn't their lawyer. Second, if Kelly were Irma's daughter, Irma would do the same thing.

Softhousen gave them his office and pager numbers.

"Mr. Perry?" asked Mrs. Kissimmee.

"This is Perry Nerrid."

"Oh, excuse me, Mr. Nerrid. Does Winsome Semiconductor have a position on what killed Kelly?"

Irma spoke, "This is Irma Laches. We are assisting Detective Softhousen in determining that. We don't know either."

"Why does Winsome have a lawyer involved so soon?" asked Mr. Kissimmee.

"It's my job to represent Winsome during any law-related activity on this site. That includes assisting with police investigations." Irma stated, simply. "We need to know what happened to Kelly as well."

"Kelly is my top priority," said Softhousen. Irma nodded furiously and pointed at herself. "Winsome's priority also. We should know more soon."

"I should hope so!" said Mr. Kissimmee, angrily. The Kissimmees' two phones clicked off together.

Irma, Perry, and Softhousen sat in silence. Irma turned off the speakerphone.

"Damn," said Irma. This was one of the reasons she had not wanted to go into criminal law. What do you say to the parents of a beautiful, brilliant girl who just died needlessly? "Now what? They think there's a cover-up. Damn."

Softhousen spoke. "Look, they had to know where she was found. I realize that Winsome may have had nothing to do with this; Winsome hasn't necessarily done anything wrong."

Perry looked slightly relieved.

Irma said, "I'll get you that list of employees." She punched up Sally's desk phone number and explained that they needed a list of Kelly's new hire classmates.

Perry tore a clean sheet from Irma's yellow pad and began listing the locations of the oxygen sensors in the fab.

Softhousen picked up the wall phone and entered Mercedes' number at the morgue.

"Mercedes Easter," she answered.

"Mercedes, Larry. Anything new on the girl – Kelly Kissimmee?"

"I don't think she died from blood loss. She is generally cyanotic—like she would be if she either choked or drowned. But her airway's clear and she doesn't have water in her lungs. There's no pulmonary edema. And there aren't any ligature or finger marks, petechia, or areas of ecchymosis on her throat."

Softhousen summarized, "So, she's blue, but didn't choke, drown, or bleed into her lungs, and there is no bruising or local hemorrhaging on her neck."

"That's what I said." Mercedes snapped. "Suffocation is still a possibility. But there are no signs of a struggle, and no bruising anywhere on her body, which is strange. You would think she would have fought with someone who was trying to suffocate her. Her body is perfect."

"Yeh," said Softhousen.

Mercedes shot back, "You're too old to think like that. Her stomach was empty. She hadn't eaten for hours. The blood gases don't show carbon monoxide. In fact, her blood shows nothing unusual. Preliminary gas chromatography indicates she was free of toxins. It's very odd."

Softhousen looked at Perry who was still busy listing the oxygen sensors. He suddenly had an idea. A scientific idea. "How about nitrogen suffocation?"

Perry and Irma looked up.

Mercedes paused. "Air is…"

"…seventy-eight percent nitrogen." Softhousen finished her sentence.

Mercedes barked out a laugh. "How on earth do you know that?"

Softhousen smirked. "Classified. Kelly was working on a project with liquid nitrogen. Could she have died from breathing pure nitrogen?"

A long moment of silence passed before Mercedes replied. "That would fit with all of my results so far. Though why would someone open her carotid artery and cut off her hands if she were already dead?"

Softhousen did not answer her question. "Did she have any jewelry?"

"Once we got her suit and clothing off, there was a simple gold necklace," said Mercedes. "Her ears were pierced, but she wore no earrings."

"And nothing else?"

"No."

Softhousen hung up. He turned to Perry and Irma. "Nitrogen suffocation is a possibility, and her rings, bracelet, watch, and earrings are missing."

"We'd better tell Chen." Irma called Sally and left a message. Then she walked across the hall to the large meeting room. Chen was just inside the door, watching an Etch engineer at the white board trying to figure out how to remedy gold contamination.

"Charles," she began.

He gave her his full attention.

She whispered, updating him on the missing jewelry and the possibility of nitrogen suffocation.

"So, her death could have been an accident, not murder?" Chen asked.

"Yes."

"And possibly Winsome's fault?"

"Possibly."

"Wow." Chen looked pained. There was no way he could have anticipated this. Winsome constantly stressed safety. Chen smiled grimly "Its a good thing we hired you."

"Someone still had to cut off her hands…"

"…and sabotage the equipment," finished Chen. "Keep me posted."

Irma went back to the small meeting room. Perry was holding his face in his hands. He was probably wondering if Kelly's death could have been his fault. He had assigned the O2 sensor project to Kelly.

"Listen, Perry," Irma said gently, "wasn't the airflow turned off in the fab during shutdown? Don't they put up a lot of plastic to cover things?"

Perry put his hands on the table. "Well, yes."

Softhousen and Irma looked at each other, significantly.

"So, maybe the nitrogen was trapped by the plastic sheets, just as it was by the plastic curtain, and her death was an accident?" Irma speculated.

"And maybe someone disabled one of the oxygen sensors," said Perry, "and set her up."

Softhousen was impatient. "There are still too many maybes. Let's see if they've found anything in the trash, get Evan, and check out those oxygen sensors."

They met Chen in the hall. He quickly approved clean room access for Softhousen and Evan.

Chapter 13

ONE MINUTE MANAGER

Irma knew it was time for a real conversation with Charles. She could tell he had read that stupid "One Minute Manager" because every conversation she'd had with him at work had been less than a minute, and that was not enough. She nodded to Perry and Softhousen. "You two go on ahead. I'll meet you out on the dock."

"Charles," she began, and boldly put her hand on his arm, leading him across the hall to the little meeting room. He sat and looked at her expectantly as the door closed. "Charles, you need to level with me in order for us to be able find whoever did this."

Chen looked surprised. "Of course," he paused, "but I think that's what I've been doing."

Irma sat down directly across from him. "I need to know what your suspicions are—whether there are any secret goings-on here at Winsome. Has anything else happened which could result in someone being angry, jealous, or whatever, at you, at Kelly, or with Winsome in general?"

Chen was stumped. "I don't know..."

"You mentioned employees quitting for no apparent reason." Chen was too positive, thought Irma. He focused on the real problems of the factory. He blotted employee rumors, backbiting, and slander from his mind. That's why he was such a good manager. He was concerned with what was important. Gossip was usually worse than useless—it was manipulation—intentional manipulation of other people. Gossip wouldn't speed production, reduce defects, fix broken machines, train employees, boost morale, or reduce costs. Gossip was verbal waste.

But now Irma needed to know the gossip. "Listen, Charles. I know how good you are at rising above the rumor-mill, and usually that's the right thing to do—but could you please try to feel out some of the area managers on this? Can you get Sally Sue to tap into the admins' grapevine and see what's on it as far as who might have been able—and angry enough—to hurt both Kelly and Winsome?"

"Why can't detective Softhousen just interview these people?" asked Chen.

Rumors really were not Chen's style, Irma thought. He was probably opposed to them on philosophical grounds, too. Chen's religion, his philosophy, was science. Rumors were not scientific. She had to convince Chen to change his personal style—in effect, his religious beliefs—beliefs which had been spectacularly successful for him.

She looked him straight in the eye. "Sure, detective Softhousen is going to work day and night. But Charles, this is unusual. Larry told me that in spite of his twenty years of experience, this is the first case of industrial sabotage he's ever had. We aren't talking about the normal list of suspects: the deceased's friends and acquaintances. We are talking about the two thousand employees in this factory. Every one of them is a suspect. Detective Softhousen and the entire Albuquerque Police Department can't possibly interview them all.

"In addition, Winsome is a high-profile company. We are a leader in high technology. We are the guts of the computer industry, and that makes us an enormous target. It means that anyone could have done this for any reason: personal, professional, political, or philosophical—even for some religious reason, for God's sake, and God knows there are enough strange religions out there. It could be someone from another state, even from another country. There are too many possibilities. We have to get a sense of what's going on. This is not a top-down management situation.

This is bottom-up. Rumors may be our best source of information."

Chen looked at Irma without speaking, collating data. "I'll call a special meeting with the managers," he said. "We can brainstorm the rumors…"

"Listen Charles," Irma interrupted, "you can't brainstorm rumors—you'll have group dynamics. There are leaders and followers in groups. The followers will jump on the bandwagon. A group consensus will start to develop. You won't get a true, individual picture of what everyone thinks.

"I think you need to take some time, some real time—not just one-minute updates—to talk to the managers one-on-one. Talk to each manager for at least fifteen minutes. Be friendly, ask them how they feel about Kelly's death. Admit to being afraid yourself. Show them that you can put yourself in their shoes. Establish a person-to-person connection before you ask anything about their employees. Then ask them about their guesses—their intuition as to what's really happening here. Ask them if anyone has recently quit in anger. Ask them about the loners and the workaholics."

"Workaholics—that includes almost everyone in engineering!" Chen laughed. "That's about all we have."

"Okay," Irma smiled, "delete workaholics. But you know what I mean. Someone who has gotten their attention for some reason. Someone they don't feel right about."

"This is going to be a new experience," said Chen. "In my entire career I have never asked an engineer to tell me his feelings about the people that report to him. It's Winsome's official policy to care about performance, not politics, at work. We want people who can get things done, who can get the equipment back up and running, who can qualify new processes and troubleshoot defects, and who can lead teams to do those things."

Irma agreed, "I know. I know this is somewhat intrusive of the managers' privacy, and in a sense, it's intrusive of their direct reports' as well. There may be some negative fallout. Be discrete.

"I don't want Winsome to violate federal laws by perceiving people as being disabled just because they don't have outgoing personalities. I am not advocating that we sink collectively into a morass of soul-searching. We just need to tap into something we usually don't use—people's intuitions about each other. Charles, I wouldn't advocate this sort of thing unless I thought it was absolutely necessary. Normally I don't believe in using rumors either."

Chen folded his arms across his chest. "What happens if someone starts telling me their personal history—you know, how they were beaten or raped as a child?"

"Boundaries," Irma answered immediately. "Boundaries. I'm not telling you to destroy all interpersonal boundaries. All I'm saying is to widen them a bit in one area. If someone starts dumping all of their insecurities and fears on you tell them you're not comfortable listening to those personal revelations. Tell them you're not a shrink and that's not what you were asking for. Use body language—you know, get up, move toward the door—to indicate you are going to terminate the session if they continue talking about that stuff."

"And if they persist?" asked Chen.

"Cut off the interview. Leave."

"Leave? You mean, walk out?"

"Exactly," Irma affirmed.

Chen shook his head.

He was too much of a gentleman to walk out on anyone. But you had to know how to handle people. Irma knew that boundaries were the foundation of civilized society. She had heard too many stories from lawyer friends about clients whose boundaries had vaporized—clients who had verbally, and even physically, attacked them.

Criminal prosecutors were especially persecuted. Either the victim was dumping on them because they didn't hang the defendant from the highest tree, or the defendant was whining about malicious prosecution, or the defendant's family was pitifully pleading for the return of their loved one who was now rotting in jail.

Often every conceivable option pissed off someone. In doing their best to be objective and play by the rules, lawyers were accused of being heartless, emotionless, and greedy. Irma had concluded that the glory and the glamour of the law was simply to stay sane and to do one's best to stick to the rules—rules that the public either didn't know, didn't care to know, or reviled. No wonder so many lawyers ended up either loving the law or loving alcohol. In the end, lacking public respect or admiration, it was all they had.

Right now it was Irma's job to catch the fiend who had done this to Kelly, and to do it by the rules. "I'm not telling you to break the rules, Charles, just to gather information. It won't kill you or anyone else to know that you're human, that you have feelings, that you can be afraid. It won't hurt for people to know that you need their opinions *in extremis*. You are not dumping on them, and they should not dump on you. You are just lowering the barriers a little bit. I know you can do it."

"Can't you…?" he said.

"No Charles, I can't," Irma interrupted. "I'm new here. People don't know me and trust me the way they do you. I have no actual or virtual authority, which is made even worse by the fact that I'm an attorney. I know I'm going to be perceived as a professional cynic even when I'm voicing my truest, innermost feelings. I am definitely the wrong person to ferret out management intuitions as to what may have happened.

"You are respected. And I don't want to go too far down this road, but, in Freudian terms, you are a father figure—someone people will turn to when things really get rough. This is one of those times. You must try."

Chen sighed deeply and stared at the ceiling.

Irma stopped talking. Charles needed to think.

Finally, he said, "Okay. I'm sold." He looked at Irma and crinkled his eyes in a small smile. "I wondered when all of this touchy-feely stuff would catch up with me. It finally has."

"It's not a disaster," Irma smiled back. "Just pull them aside and talk to them when it's convenient. Look upon it as learning a new management skill."

Chen pushed back his chair and stood up. "Thanks. We'll see what turns up from my interviews, and I'll ask Sally Sue to do the same with the admins."

Irma nodded, and Chen walked out. She smiled to herself. It had gone well, she thought. It was uncomfortable for her to be assertive with her boss, but perhaps she was already beginning to make a difference, for the better, at Winsome Semiconductor Corporation.

Chapter 14

OXYGEN SENSORS

Perry and Softhousen walked onto the loading dock and leaned back against a shaded wall.

Evan, the policemen, and the two Litho techs were sorting trash in the sun. Heavy blue plastic aprons, thick orange acid gloves, and pivoting clear face shields covered them from head to toe. Under large areas of the translucent aprons their clothes were black with sweat. The temperature was 108 degrees, Fahrenheit.

The procedure was to break open a trash bag, strew its contents on the dock in front of a dumpster, then go through it one piece at a time. Any obviously non-bloody trash was thrown into the dumpster, and any remaining red material was carefully compared to photoresist-coated samples determine if it was blood-soaked.

Irma strode into the searing sunshine. "Any luck?" she asked Dinst.

Evan slowly straightened, then raised his face shield. Sweat poured off of his face and ran down his apron. When he tried to wipe his eyes with the back of a gloved hand, the sweat just smeared. Squinting miserably from the salty sting, he said, "Not yet. We're about halfway through."

Softhousen came over from the shade. "Good time for a break guys. Go inside and get some Cokes."

*   *   *

Evan scrubbed his face with handfuls of wet paper towels in the restroom and soaked his hair with cold, fresh water.

In the cafeteria, feeling better, he bought an extra-large Coke, loaded with ice. He slowly sucked on his Coke as he listened to Perry explain the O2 sensors. "So you think Kelly was in the clean room, working at one of these O2 sensor locations before she went up into the interstitial," Evan summarized.

Irma nodded, "And that's why she was wearing the bunny suit."

Evan's Coke gurgled. He was down to the dregs.

"Ready?" asked Softhousen.

*   *   *

They picked up clean room badges from the guard desk and walked upstairs to the entry airlock of the gowning room. Irma helped Evan clean everything in his evidence kit, and his camera, with alcohol-and-water-soaked lint-free wipes. Everything brought inside the clean room had to be wiped down.

Perry convinced Softhousen to take off his tie. He wouldn't need it under his bunny suit.

Irma felt like an old high-tech hand watching Softhousen and Evan struggle into their Goretex suits. Tight elastic at the ankles, wrists, waist, and shoulders made it unexpectedly difficult the first time. The second time would be much easier.

The suits transformed Softhousen and Evan into self-conscious, space-suited snowmen. Since everyone wore the same suits, and hairstyles couldn't be seen, you recognized people in the clean room by their eyes and their body shapes. It was an obscene transformation.

They danced their way through the air shower—Softhousen and Evan very reluctantly.

Perry led them through the maze of white walls, computer keyboards, color monitors, racks full of wafers, and stainless steel machines. Softhousen grumbled, to no one in particular, "There's no shortage of computers in here."

A few more turns and they arrived in front of a sprawling control console with a vertical, periscope-like stainless steel tube towering above it. A large white tank perched at the top of the periscope. A layer of frost coated the top of the tank.

They huddled around Perry. "It's a SEM," he said.

"A what?" asked Softhousen.

"A scanning electron microscope. We use it to check the size of the features on the integrated circuits and to look for defects." Perry explained.

Evan pointed to the tank. "And what's in there?"

"Liquid nitrogen." Perry reached up and rubbed off some frost.

"Since when does a SEM need liquid nitrogen? The one at the forensics lab doesn't use it." Evan commented.

"It's for an attachment. The x-ray fluorescence detector…"

Softhousen's tired voice interrupted, "We'll take your word for it."

Irma shared his feelings. All of this technology was wearing her down, too.

Perry pointed. "This is it."

It looked like a blue lunchbox. It was mounted to the wall behind the liquid nitrogen tank, and its display read "21% OXYGEN."

"She had to have taken the cover off of the O2 sensor unit," Perry said.

"So there might be gouging from a screwdriver on the cover, or some tools lying around?" Evan asked, bright-eyed. He was in high-tech heaven.

"Exactly."

"How about a clipboard for taking notes?" Irma spoke up. Engineers and operators in the clean room carried around clipboards with special blue paper—plasticized not to shed particles.

Perry nodded. "Maybe also a clipboard."

They all looked, but there wasn't much to see. The walls and floor of the clean room were immaculate. Perry effortlessly dropped into pushup position and peered under the SEM and the wall. "Nothing," he said, getting up. "Let's do a quick check, first. If we need to we can come back."

Evan spoke to Perry, "If she had left some tools or a clipboard, wouldn't they have been cleaned up by now?"

Perry frowned. "Possibly, but the operators do the cleaning. Generally they won't touch a tech's tools. At the meeting with the night shift we can ask if they saw anything."

Perry guided them deeper into the sparkling maze. They arrived at a sliding glass door. He explained, "There's another LN2 tank in this chase."

"Do a lot of people go back in there?" asked Softhousen.

"No, just the techs, and they go into the service chases only when they need to."

"There's no buddy policy?" asked Evan.

Perry answered, "Only for electrical troubleshooting. The work in the fab is mostly routine maintenance. It's basically safe. The techs are extensively trained. We have glass doors and panels in the chase walls so people can see if someone's hurt."

"But not everywhere," Evan looked through the door. "This chase has a dead end which is invisible."

Perry sighed. "You're right. Some parts of some of the chases can't be seen."

Irma remembered a law school discussion. No place was ever perfectly safe; people could paralyze themselves turning over in bed. She empathized with Perry. Even the most unforeseeable of accidents were his responsibility. It was his job.

This was something they had in common. No matter what the outcome of a trial, it was the attorney's fault— even after advising their client that winning was a long shot.

"The power of projection," she thought. Taking responsibility for one's own actions was the very last option for most people—only to be adopted after all other sources of blame were exhausted.

"I'll wait here." Irma looked at Perry. The chase was tight, and she was claustrophobic. The snug suit, helmet, and gloves weren't helping, either.

Perry addressed Softhousen and Dist, "Go inside. The O2 sensor is to the left."

The automatic glass door hissed open. They disappeared from view and the door hissed shut.

Irma and Perry were alone. Irma leaned close to Perry's helmet and spoke just over the airflow. "Shouldn't the O2 sensors have been hooked into the security system?" She had wanted to ask him that question for the last hour.

He folded his arms across his chest, put his head down, and thought before answering. "There are lots of safety systems which aren't hooked into the master alarm system. An individual machine may have a dozen sensors: over and under temperature; low and high exhaust; low water pressure; fire, smoke, and gas detectors; and sensors for various electronic problems. We cannot monitor all of them. It would be thousands of inputs. And, as often as the techs work on these machines, it would a nightmare to frequently enable and disable the master alarm. We would get dozens of false alarms every day, and that would defeat the alarm's purpose. We want people to react instantly, not to stand around thinking it's just another false alarm. So we only monitor the most life-threatening things with the master alarm system: the condition of the fire sprinkler system, the fire alarms, and the toxic gases."

"Why the gases?"

"We use Hydrogen Fluoride, Phosphine, Boron tri-Fluoride, and di-Borane. They are all killers. They are so toxic that by the time you smell them, you're either dead or seriously injured. The leak-detection equipment for the toxics has dedicated battery backup. It works even in a complete power failure." He pointed to a large yellow lamp in the ceiling. "If there's a poison gas leak that goes off. It's the signal to get out—no questions asked."

"And the oxygen sensors aren't hooked in?" Irma confirmed.

"Nitrogen isn't toxic. As I said, the airflow in the fab is sufficient…"

Softhousen's head poked out of the chase door. "Y'all want to see this."

Perry and Irma's both frowned as their eyes met. They squeezed passed Softhousen.

Evan lay on the floor next to a screwdriver, a voltmeter, and a clipboard. He illuminated part of the steel rack which supported the LN2 tank with his flashlight.

"What've you got?" asked Perry.

"There is some white plastic on the rack near the floor. It looks like the same plastic that's used in the suit helmets," said Evan. "Acrylo-nitrile butadiene styrene, ABS, I believe."

Evan, the nerd, fit right in at Winsome, Irma thought. "Did you see a gouge in Kelly's helmet?" she asked.

"No, but we weren't looking for one, either," Softhousen demurred. "We'll check when we get back to the morgue."

"So she could have fallen and hit her head on the metal strut…" Perry started to explain.

Irma interrupted, "Wouldn't the helmet have protected Kelly?"

"From suffocation? How could it?" Perry snapped. "The suit just filters the air. There is no oxygen supply."

"Yes, but the helmet may have protected her physically, a little. I'll speak to Mercedes—the Medical Examiner— about bruises under her hair." Softhousen directed Evan, "Let's collect her tools." Then he asked Perry, "Where's her toolbox?"

Perry replied. "Engineers generally keep a few tools at their desks outside the clean room, and just carry them into the fab as needed."

"So maybe there are fingerprints," Softhousen speculated.

"Not if she did a good job of wiping her tools down," said Perry. "Let's ask the night crew if anyone saw her working here."

"I'm freezing!" Irma interrupted. She hugged herself. The hurricane inside the chase was chilling her to the bone. The spookiness of the investigation didn't help, either.

Perry glanced significantly from Irma to Softhousen. "See what I mean about the airflow. The chase serves as an air return. The air from the ceiling HEPA's moves down, across the fab floor, then up through the chases and back to the interstitial to be filtered and returned to the clean room. There is too much air movement for nitrogen to become stagnant and suffocate someone." He looked straight up. "There's the interstitial."

Irma looked up. In the dimness high above she made out, vaguely, the grey steel of a catwalk and girders.

Softhousen spoke to Perry. "But you said the air handlers were turned off during parts of the shutdown..."

"Yes. That's right."

"...and the power was out and all of the lights were off..."

"For part of the time."

"...and the walls, floors, and air vents were covered with plastic..."

"They could have been."

"...so she could have suffocated right here."

Perry's shoulders sagged and he said softly, "Alright, yes, she could have."

"We need that schedule, what did you call it?" asked Softhousen.

"The Gantt chart," Irma interjected.

"Yes. The Gantt chart showing when the power was off," Softhousen concluded.

Irma was puzzled. "But how on earth did Kelly get up into the interstitial if she accidentally died here? It doesn't make any sense." She watched Evan pull floor samples with scotch tape for a moment. When noone answered her question, she looked up at Softhousen. Then she answered her own question. "Someone had to carry her."

"Yup," drawled Softhousen. He looked at Perry. "How far is it from here to where we found her?"

"Well, if you put a ladder right here and got onto that catwalk," Perry pointed straight up, "it's about seventy-five feet that way." Perry pointed to his left.

"Pretty doable, I'd say." Softhousen replied. "Were there ladders in here during shutdown?"

"Probably a half-dozen or more inside the fab."

"Extending all the way up into the interstitial?"

"Yes. Depending on the type of work, often the workers need to go up and down," said Perry.

Drew had estimated that Kelly weighed 128 pounds, thought Irma. She visualized a white-suited figure holding Kelly, using a fireman's carry, climbing a ladder.

She shuddered again—this time with fear—and said, "What motive? Why go to the trouble of carrying a dead girl up a ladder, stringing her up, and then cutting her hands off? Why do that?" Irma tried to place herself in the psychological shoes of a mutilator of dead bodies, and could not. She could not see how anyone could have found a beautiful young co-worker like Kelly slumped on the floor and then...

Softhousen's voice was calm. "People go nuts. They don't like something: their job, their parents, their girlfriend or boyfriend, gays, Lesbians, prostitutes, policemen, women, themselves, modern art, abortionists, you name it."

"But why mutilate a corpse?" Irma was still bewildered.

"The guy who did this hung Kelly upside down so her blood would drain down into a dark place in the fab to scare people, right?" said Softhousen.

"Do we know it's a he?" asked Perry.

"Good point. We do not. A strong woman could also have carried Kelly," Softhousen admitted.

"But why frighten people? What's the point?" Irma asked.

Softhousen explained. "A possible motive here is dislike of something about Winsome Semiconductor and revenge through terror."

"Or paid sabotage," said Perry.

"That, too," Softhousen tried to put his hands in his pockets, but could not. The bunny suits didn't have pockets. He crossed his arms over his chest.

"But why wouldn't they just quit working here? Why become a criminal?" Irma was still perplexed.

"You're assuming it's a Winsome employee, which is only one possibility," Softhousen explained. "Maybe they think Winsome has done something criminal, like Ted Kaczynski. You know, maybe they think technology is criminal—that one criminal act deserves another. Also, if Kelly died accidentally, it wasn't murder. And that widens the range of suspects considerably; it's not just murderers. Our list should include every wierdo with a grudge."

Perry was troubled. "Why would someone who hates technology work here in the first place? Why would they go to the trouble of acquiring the skills?"

"You're assuming it's a technician or engineer, then," said Softhousen.

"Well, mostly techs work back here and up above, not operators."

"Got a print!" Evan shouted. They all turned to look at the screwdriver in Evan's extended hand. "On the shaft—a clear partial, right through the center of a whorl. Could be a thumb. She must have missed a place on the shaft when she wiped it down. It's enough for a match. No problem."

"Except we don't have her hands, remember?" Softhousen furrowed his brow. He said to Irma, "I need to call the Kissimmees back and ask them if they did one of those child identification things with Kelly. Maybe they have her fingerprints."

Evan quickly snapped a dozen photographs. Softhousen bagged Kelly's tools.

*   *   *

While Perry and Evan went to check on the trash Irma and Softhousen returned to the little room with the round table. Softhousen dialed the Kissimmees' number.

"Hello?" queried a sad, old voice.

"Mr. Kissimmee, it's Detective Softhousen again. I'm with Ms. Laches."

"Go ahead." Mr. Kissimmee suddenly sounded alert.

"We've found a fingerprint…"

"…of Kelly's?" Mr. Kissimmee interrupted.

"Well, we're not sure. Did you ever do that child identification procedure where you got a set of her fingerprints?"

"Yes, I think so." There was a pause, then he asked, "Why can't you get her fingerprints…directly…?"

Irma thought, "He doesn't want to say, 'from her body.'"

She and Softhousen looked at each other. Irma doodled "Oops" on her legal pad.

Softhousen was tired. They were all tired. He said, "Her hands were," he paused, uncomfortably, "damaged. If you could bring those prints it would really help."

Mr. Kissimmee choked back a gasp. Irma had a sudden urge to put her fingers in her ears. Instead, she put her head in her hands.

"What the hell happened to our daughter?" Mr. Kissimmee yelled.

Softhousen used his most diplomatic tone. "Mr. Kissimmee, we still don't know. We're getting closer. Giving you our latest speculations won't help. Can you please bring the prints tomorrow? Better yet, if you could take them to the local police station right now and ask them to fax them to me as soon as possible, that will help us out greatly. Could you please do that?"

There was less anger. "Oh—sure—right away."

"Thank you. Have you found a flight?"

"We'll be there before lunch tomorrow."

"All right sir. We'll meet you," Softhousen looked at Irma. She pointed down at the table, "here at Winsome Semiconductor. They can give you directions at the airport car rental." Irma nodded vigorously at Softhousen and gestured with her fingers as if she were picking something up off of the table. "It might be better...We will send a cruiser to pick you up."

Irma wanted to offer to pick them up herself, but she hesitated. She couldn't do it, ethically. It might be construed as having an appearance of impropriety: direct communication with an opposite party. And since Irma represented Winsome, she was the enemy. They would probably rebuff her kindness, anyway.

"Thank you." Mr. Kissimmee spoke through clenched teeth.

"Yes sir. Thank you for the trouble about the fingerprints." Softhousen gave Mr. Kissimmee his fax number, got their flight number, and said goodby.

Irma expelled a sigh of relief. She wondered what it would be like—meeting the Kissimmees, in person. She panicked internally: it would certainly be much worse! As a little girl she had hid under her bed from vicious New Mexico thunderstorms. She wanted to hide under her bed now.

"Pretend it's court," she said to herself. "Pretend you're dealing with angry witnesses. Detach. Don't empathize. Don't be overwhelmed by the Kissimmees' emotions. It's not your fault their daughter's dead." Irma saw herself, in court, in charge. Her breath slowed. She was in control. Her panic subsided.

"If the trash is finished, we're done here for the time being," said Softhousen. He closed his little notebook.

Irma looked at her watch. Four o'clock! It seemed as though she had been staring at Kelly's lifeless body hanging from the rafters only minutes ago.

A shrill chirp interrupted. They both reached for their pagers.

"Me," said Irma and entered the number on the display into the speakerphone.

"Irma, it's Drew," said the phone. Drew's voice was strained.

"I'm here with Detective Softhousen. What's up?"

"Mary Martinez just died." Drew stopped speaking.

Softhousen opened his notebook automatically, "Who?"

"How?" Irma's voice held panic.

"Hypothermia, we think. While I was upstairs talking to you and Detective Softhousen, she was in the emergency chemical shower in Litho. They wouldn't let her out—and it was too long! With all the excitement about Kelly I didn't get back in time." Drew fought back tears. "The water was too cold. She collapsed inside the shower and her heart stopped. Noone could see her behind the curtain. When I got there I started CPR, and she's been on a respirator at the hospital all this time, but she never regained consciousness. Finally…there must have been some damage to her central nervous system that…" Drew stopped speaking.

Irma tensed. She could see the headlines: WINSOME EMPLOYEE FREEZES TO DEATH! This was the hottest day of the year, so far. Albuquerque was in the desert. Another irony.

Drew continued, "We follow OSHA guidelines. They require a minimum of 15 minutes in the shower."

"So we blame OSHA?" Irma raised her eyebrows. This was a defense she had never heard of.

Softhousen scribbled on his pad. He said sadly, "The cure was worse than the disease."

"The police have already been notified," said Drew. "I think they sent an officer to the hospital."

"I won't be doing the report on her. But this could make Kelly a felony murder—eh counselor?" Softhousen looked at Irma.

"Isn't mutilating corpses a misdemeanor?" replied Irma.

"What are you talking about?" asked Drew.

Irma explained, "Felony murder is where a lesser crime is turned into a charge of murder because the crime somehow causes someone else to die. Even if the cause is indirect—like where a store owner in a holdup dies of a heart attack—the underlying felony is still converted, legally, into an additional charge of murder against the criminal."

"You can do that?" Drew was amazed.

"It's fairly common," said Softhousen.

"But if all we have here is mutilation of a corpse—which I believe is only a misdemeanor—it will be misdemeanor manslaughter, not felony murder," Irma explained.

Irma's brain was churning. What a mess! As a means of punishment some U.S. prisons had shackled unruly prisoners, naked, under cold showers. It was cruel and unusual punishment. Mary's accident was both foreseeable and unnecessary.

However, it was not in Winsome's best interest for Drew to fall apart. Irma had to be a corporate attorney. "Don't worry Drew. Accidents happen. Healthy people don't have heart attacks in cold showers. Just send me a copy of Mary's medical data, and your own written report of the entire incident as soon as it's convenient." Irma looked expectantly at Softhousen, but he had nothing to add. "We'll get together later and talk about this," Irma finished.

"Okay." Drew was exhausted.

Irma hung up, then called Sally to get the shutdown Gantt for Softhousen. Last she called Jamie and asked her to begin gathering information on Mary Martinez.

Chapter 15

WATER PEAKS

When Softhousen and Irma walked through the door to the back dock, Perry, Evan, the two policemen, and the Winsome techs were cleaning up the last of the trash and tossing it into the dumpster.

The handsome cop straightened, "No luck, sir."

"Well—kind of a long shot." Softhousen was philosophical.

"He'd have to be dumb to leave bloody gloves lying around," Evan observed.

Irma thought of a famous Hollywood murder trial.

The dock door opened. Irma was surprised to see Chen. He motioned for Irma, Evan, and Softhousen to move into the shade, close to the wall of the building.

Irma told Chen what they had seen in the clean room.

Chen waited until the technicians and police officers had left the dock before he started to speak.

"You know, it started with the gold contamination in the diffusion furnaces this morning, so we stopped running the furnaces.

"Next, we sampled the VTW's. Oh, sorry—" Chen looked at Softhousen and Evan, "—the vertical tube washes. They are machines in the QCR—the quartz clean room— which spray hydrofluoric acid up into the furnace tubes to clean them. The acid is pumped from bulk delivery, 330 gallon totes."

Softhousen scowled. As usual, he was having trouble following the technical jargon, but was gamely trying. It was all part of the crime. He pulled out his little notebook and wrote down "VTW" and "bulk delivery" as Chen spoke.

105

Evan interrupted, "I thought acid was always delivered in gallon bottles."

"It used to be that way," said Chen. "But, the entire industry has converted to totes. Bottles have to be rinsed and thrown into the landfill. Since totes are sent back to be refilled there is less waste. Also, instead of having to hand-pour gallon bottles 330 times, a single tote can be moved into place in the pump room by one person with a pallet jack. There is much less chance for accident and injury."

"And the contamination?" Irma urged. She had heard about the totes in orientation.

"Someone could have opened a tote and put in gold. The gold would have been pumped, along with the acid, to the furnace tubes during their last cleaning in the VTW's."

"Wouldn't gold dust just sink to the bottom and stay there?" asked Evan.

Chen nodded, "Good point. The analysis came back showing the acid in the tote has traces of gold, nitrogen, oxygen, and chlorine in it. So it's possible that this person mixed up some aqua regia—nitric acid and hydrochloric acid together which dissolves gold—then added part of Kelly's gold jewelry, and finally poured the whole mess into the hydrofluoric acid tote, contaminating the hell out of it."

There was a painful expression on Chen's face which Irma could not quite interpret; possibly a mixture of sadness, anger, and grim determination.

"The totes aren't padlocked?" Softhousen was incredulous.

Chen replied, "No. The fill and drain port caps just screw on." He paused. "So, diffusion, which relies on bulk HF and the QCR for clean tubes, is totally down. But, we have a plan. We buy new tubes and flush out the bulk delivery system with pure aqua regia. It will take forty-eight hours of downtime, minimum, to get diffusion back up. If that doesn't work, we will have to replace all of the tubing, the nozzles in the VTW's; everything.

"Next we checked bulk sulfuric. Same thing, only worse. In addition to sulfuric acid totes, we have a sulfuric recycling system which filters and reconstitutes the acid to an exact concentration. It's a very expensive system, but it also saves money."

Chen closed his eyes. "Now the whole sulfuric system is contaminated with gold and chlorine. All it takes is a trace of gold. Sulfuric recycle has to be shut down, disassembled, and either replaced or thoroughly cleaned—we're not sure. We called the company that made the recycling unit. They are sending their engineers and a full crew of techs with replacement parts. We're estimating a week to get it back up. Again, we may have to replace all of the wetted parts. That's about a million dollars for new parts and labor."

Softhousen wrote down, "Sulfuric recycle $1M."

Chen looked up at the serenely blue New Mexico sky for a moment. "And it gets worse. All day the Thin Films crew has had a heck of a time pumping down the sputtering systems, evaporators, and ion implanters—all of our high-vacuum machines. Their vacuum chambers were vented during shutdown for routine maintenance. The slightest contamination, especially anything with water in it, and the chambers won't make it back down to base pressure—that's the degree of vacuum they must reach in order to qualify to run product."

"RGA's—residual gas analyzers—are analytical tools attached to the vacuum systems. They show what gasses remain inside. The RGA CRT AMU graphs were showing a major peak at AMUs sixteen, seventeen, and eighteen—hydrogen and oxygen—H_2O. We call it having high water peaks."

"You just left me in the dust," said Softhousen.

"The RGA screens display a graph of the residual molecules inside the vacuum chambers. Periodic table atomic mass units are on the x-axis, and intensity is on the y. It gives a wavy line. Water has a distinctive series of peaks. Does that help?" Chen was patient.

Evan nodded enthusiastically.

Softhousen said, "No, but thanks anyway."

"The etch team has had similar problems with the RF plasma etchers and the barrel ashers. We opened every vacuum chamber that had been vented during shutdown and checked for contamination." Chen hesitated. He looked uncomfortable. "What we found is in the walk-in refrigerator in the cafeteria."

Softhousen suddenly looked up. "What?"

Chen answered slowly. "Every system that was vented as of shift change this morning had what looked like parts of someone's fingers inside. While you were checking for clues on Kelly, we just about had a panic. We've had about two dozen techs and operators see Kelly's—what do you call them?" He thought for a moment. "Phalanges. The segments of her fingers."

Softhousen and Irma tried to speak at the same time. Softhousen won. "Jesus! Why didn't you page us?"

"What you were doing was more important," said Chen simply, "so I handled it. We baggied the phalanges, cleaned out the chambers, and got the systems back up and running. Everyone wore gloves. Kelly's phalanges aren't contaminated."

Softhousen looked at Irma with angry expectancy. She said, timidly, "Chain of custody?"

Softhousen nodded, furiously. "You should have called us. Do you have a record of who found which phalange, where? Did the people who found the fingers initial and seal the baggies with some kind of tape?"

"I don't think so." Chen looked worried.

This was the first time Irma had seen Charles exhibit less than 110% self-confidence. Her mind sorted through criminal law information from the bar exam. Interfering with a police investigation—obstruction of justice—was a criminal offense which carried jail time. Chen could go to jail. She responded quickly to Softhousen, "But the location of the body is the main source of evidence, right? That was well preserved…"

Softhousen scowled at Chen, ignoring Irma. "Was the reefer locked? Do you have the only key?"

Chen sighed and said quietly, "No, I don't think it is locked. If it were, the cafeteria manager would probably have a key, and maybe some of her staff. I left specific instructions that the baggies were to be left alone. They are on an empty shelf. What's the problem?"

Softhousen glowered at Irma, "Tell him."

"Charles, there must be an unbroken chain of custody in order for evidence to be used in court. Anything less leaves open the possibility that someone could have tampered with the evidence. It sounds like a number of people have access to the refrigerator, which leaves open the possibility of tampering. And without labeling, we cannot connect the phalanges to the machines in which they were found. They cannot be used in court."

"I didn't know," Chen said defensively. "We needed to get that equipment back up and running."

"Yeh, but if we need to make a case for industrial sabotage, you have just seriously weakened it. You have also weakened our case for murder." Softhousen snapped.

Chen looked thoroughly deflated.

"Look," Irma said to both of them, "let's just not do it again. Every scrap of evidence about the contamination, or anything having to do with Kelly, needs to be documented: who found it, when they found it, where they found it, and the surrounding circumstances. This includes any testing here at Winsome, any visual indications of contamination, anything related to what's happened. It would be best for every person involved to write up and sign a very detailed report immediately, so they forget nothing. There is no telling how many years in the future we might need their testimony at trial. Contemporaneous writings are allowed in to refresh a witness' memory. Also the scene where anything of Kelly's is found needs to be sealed off and checked by the police. That includes Kelly's cubicle."

"I'll get her cubicle sealed off right away," said Chen. "I didn't know about the chain of evidence…"

"Custody," Irma corrected.

"…custody. I'll get the word out right now, to the managers, and have them pass the word to all of the engineers and technicians about that and the reports."

"One more thing, Charles." Irma pretended she was counseling a client, and tried not to show any judgmental emotions. "Don't the implanters use solid-source arsenic?"

"Yes."

"Placing arsenic-contaminated body parts in a refrigerator in which food is stored is probably both an OSHA violation and a violation of New Mexico Health Department regs."

Chen shook his head in dismay, "Damn. I knew that."

Irma was conciliatory, "I doubt anyone will know, or care to report it."

Chen nodded. "But it won't happen again. I'll contact APD immediately next time."

There is nothing like kicking your boss when he's down, thought Irma. But she trusted Chen. It was an honest mistake, made in the heat of the moment. He wouldn't do it again. She changed the subject. "So, this person was running around the clean room sabotaging equipment this morning while we were in the interstitial with Kelly?"

"It would seem so," Chen admitted.

"But wouldn't the technicians and operators notice someone strange touching their machines?" Softhousen asked.

Chen leaned against the wall. "I've been thinking about that. First of all, everyone is extremely busy with startup. Second, if it were a stranger who looked unusual—very tall or short, fat or thin—people would notice. So it's someone with an average build. Someone who fits in. Maybe even someone who should be here: a tech, engineer, supervisor, or field service technician. Someone who is comfortable around vacuum systems and knows how to open them up. Often there is no one around watching the equipment. The techs and operators move from one machine to the next and take breaks. The machines aren't guarded."

Evan butted in, "So it's someone who works this shift?"

"Not necessarily. Folks from other shifts come in to help with startup."

"So, who have we eliminated?" asked Softhousen.

"Just the construction workers," said Chen. "Most of them left first thing this morning. Also, I doubt any of them know how to sabotage these machines. Not too many operators know how to open the vacuum systems, either, or else they would be working as techs. Techs get better pay."

"So it's techs and engineers," said Softhousen, writing on his pad. He shook his head sadly.

"Or field service engineers or managers," added Irma.

Chen nodded.

Irma shared his malaise. Why would someone with an education, with a great job at Winsome, do something like this? Not for money, surely. Surely not for money.

"What is the total actual damage at this point?" Softhousen's pen was poised over his notebook.

Chen stared at the Sandia mountains, hazy and blue in the distance. "Let's say essentially five days' production lost, plus cleanup costs. God, I don't know." He paused. He waived his hands in frustration. "We're just going to have to wait and see what the total is after everything is back to normal. There are also intangibles, like damaged morale, employees who end up quitting because of this, stock prices, things like that."

"And Mary Martinez' death," said Irma.

"Yes, I heard. Her death too." Chen looked at Irma. "Mary's death is not an intangible."

Softhousen turned to Evan. "Will you go with Mr. Chen and check out Kelly's cubicle?"

*　*　*

Irma and Softhousen stood inside the gleaming Winsome cafeteria kitchen. Irma held a large freezer bag open while Softhousen dumped double handfuls of ice into it. Then he carefully placed the small baggies containing Kelly's phalanges on top of the ice. Last, he dumped two more double handfuls on top of the smaller baggies. Irma watched through tired eyes.

"Want my job?" Softhousen took the freezer bag from Irma and sealed it.

"Let me think about that for a second or two," Irma said with a weak smile. "No."

She chided herself, "Now I'm joking about body parts! This must be that glamour and prestige they told us about in law school." She was, indeed, turning into a cynical old maid, she thought.

They placed the large baggie into a white plastic trash bag.

"I'll go with you to security," said Irma. "Normally, they would insist on searching the bag."

"Yeh. Thanks."

At the security desk Softhousen signed out and Irma vouched for the contents of the trash bag. The guard insisted on having a look anyway. "Ugh," he said. But it wasn't a wafer, diskette, or machine part—those were the items that were not allowed out—so he let them go.

Irma thought grimly that a person's hands—that most amazing, useful, and delicate part of the human body—were of less value to Winsome than machine parts. "You idiot!" she shrieked at herself. This was the kind of irrational newspeak one heard from activists—conservative and liberal. "It's ownership! Winsome doesn't own Kelly, or the parts of her hands. Of course they are valuable!" No Winsome manager, CEO, or stockholder would ever think that Kelly's hands weren't valuable. The guards were quite properly concerned with securing Winsome property. It was their job. She vowed to have fewer new age conversations with her neighbors.

She and Softhousen walked out of the building together, with Kelly's phalanges.

He placed the bag in the trunk of his car, and then seat belted himself in. She spoke into his open window. "See you at the meeting at 10:00 o'clock."

"I'm going to be at the forensics lab until then." He wrote the phone number on one of his cards and handed it to her.

Irma gave him her best tired smile. She said, "Thanks, Larry," as he drove away.

The sunset created glorious orange-streaked clouds under a deep blue sky, but neither of them noticed.

Chapter 16

CORRALES

Irma drove her little Miata back to her adobe house. She drove slowly. There didn't seem to be anything to say about the pieces of Kelly's hands except "Yuk," and she and Softhousen had already said that. She decided to think about something pleasant—something she really liked.

Corrales was a small, quiet, historic Spanish town, nestled between a bluff of Albuquerque's west mesa and the Rio Grande. Because it was so small, and the folks in the post office knew everyone by name, the homes had no numbers, only street names. Irma's address was: Señorita Irma Laches, Calle Ocho, Corrales, Nuevo México, Estados Unidos.

She smiled to herself. She had just lied. It was New Mexico, not Nuevo México; and it was Ms., not Señorita. In fact, most New Mexicans spoke English quite well. English was their first language. There seemed to be more transplants from other states than there were native New Mexicans. Even so, you could still find little enclaves here and there, mostly in rural areas, where the residents spoke nothing but Spanish.

Her adobe home suited her. She had purchased it just after starting with Winsome. She wanted a change—a BIG change. Most lawyers would sneer at her mud and straw home with its tiny, naturally landscaped yard and single old algodones, or cottonwood, tree. But her house felt right, her yard felt right, and Corrales felt right. She wanted her personal space to be as quiet, restful, and as different from work as possible. After years in a condo—just a glorified label for "apartment," she thought—having her very own house and yard, however small, was a magnificent luxury.

Western was the only style in which to decorate her adobe hacienda. Irma had happily gone to Santa Fe and purchased Pendleton blankets, a rough-hewn four-poster, and Native American woven-reed wastebaskets. She had even indulged herself by carefully selecting a magnificent Navajo blanket hand woven by the legendary Navajo weaver, Bessie Manygoats. Its muted, naturally dyed, blue, yellow, white, and red patterns now adorned her living room wall.

Besides Bessie's blanket Irma's favorite decoration was her huge, fluffy, totally artificial, white bearskin rug. She had placed Mister Bear invitingly in front of her tiny fireplace. She still giggled every time she walked into the room. There would be some wonderful evenings to come, with some handsome man...

Saturday mornings in Corrales were a time to visit, to have tea, to talk about southwestern cooking, children, schools, and share neighborhood gossip. She liked her neighbors. They were slender women. They were artists and mothers and doctors and single and married. They wore hand-woven cotton clothing: puffy white blouses and blue Navajo skirts with leather sandals in the summer. They read books, and discussed their sex lives, sex abuse, men, psychology, politics, and the changing roles of women. They were young and liberal and believed in hypnosis, acupuncture, massage therapy, crystal healing and herbal remedies. They were older and conservative and kind, cultured, and exceedingly polite.

They looked to Irma for advice. Women were needed in the law. It was a matter of power and oppression. Being unmarried and childless did not matter. Irma's choices were hers—a career was important, and it was not too late for her to have children if she wanted them. And there were ways, without getting married and without having to demean herself, to have children. It was a wonderful option. Irma smiled. Corrales was where she belonged.

Chapter 17

MORGUE

Softhousen arrived at the morgue and presented Mercedes and Evan each with a Coke, a twenty-piece box of Chicken McNuggets, and red sauce. Evan slurped, dipped, and munched his nuggets, while staring at the baggies with the bloody little pieces of Kelly's fingers.

Softhousen dunked his first cold, greasy McNugget, and mumbled, his mouth half-full, "This is delicious." Then he consulted his notebook. "The fingers were found in the Winsome clean room, inside machines which have vacuum chambers."

"How did they know they were there?" Evan asked as he watched Mercedes carefully arrange Kelly's bloody phalanges on a stainless steel tray. The tray rested on Kelly's very flat, and very naked, stomach.

Softhousen again consulted his notebook, "Residual Gas Analysis water peaks were what clued them in."

Mercedes laughed derisively as she stripped off her bloody gloves and dipped her first cold McNugget.

"Now what?" snarled Softhousen.

"Oh, nothing," Mercedes giggled. "You said that perfectly, and you had no idea what it meant!"

"Go to hell," Softhousen shot back.

Evan licked his fingers and got busy taking closeup Polaroid photographs of Kelly's finger tips. Then he and Mercedes took prints from each distal phalange.

Evan excitedly shuffled photos and sheets of fax paper and pointed. "All of the prints match, too. The phalanges match the prints that were sent by the Kissimmees, which also match the one on the screwdriver. It's a right thumb print."

Softhousen nodded and stared at Kelly from his stool at the foot-end of the examination table.

Mercedes followed his stare. "Necrophiliac pig!" she hissed like a snake.

Softhousen shrugged. "You get to look at dead naked men all day. I'm not surprised you hate men. This is a rare treat for me."

"Looking at dead naked men?"

Evan moved in between them, chewing another McNugget. "Come on, guys!"

Softhousen angrily dunked his last McNugget.

Mercedes found the only remaining straw in the McDonald's bag and viciously stabbed it into her Coke. After she sucked up a mouthful, she calmed down and gestured at the tray. "It looks like everything matches. All of the parts fit together."

"Yes, they do," Softhousen deadpanned, deliberately continuing to stare between Kelly's long, muscular legs.

Mercedes gave him a withering scowl, moved the phalange tray from Kelly's abdomen to a wheeled cart, and covered Kelly's torso with her lab coat.

Evan addressed Softhousen. "Just before you got here we determined that the gouge in the helmet and the piece of plastic also match perfectly."

"So now we know she was there…" started Softhousen.

"…and she suffocated probably, and fell, hitting her helmet on the steel strut," Evan finished.

"How did you match the gouge?" asked Mercedes.

Evan smiled. He loved his work. "We used the same technique we use for matching fingernails. First we sputter the plastic to decorate the sample with gold, and then use a dual-field comparison microscope to look at the micro-grooves in the scraping and the helmet which were caused by tiny burrs in the strut. The grooves matched."

Softhousen hated to urge Evan to even greater detail, but he remembered something. "Is this the same 'sputtering' thing Chen was talking about at Winsome?"

"Yes. We have a little laboratory sputtering machine the size of a suitcase. The ones they have are monsters. But it's the same principle."

"I'll take your word for it," Softhousen sighed. "Do we have a time of death?"

"Based on the head and ambient temperatures, and her height and weight, the charts which show heat loss after death say she died at 7:00 a.m., plus or minus ten minutes."

"Plus or minus ten minutes! With all of your medical training is that the best you can do?" Softhousen sneered.

Mercedes took a deep breath, smiled maliciously, and pounced for the kill. "Actually, heat loss can be an extremely precise way of determining time of death. Heat from the human body is transferred, and therefore can be lost, by conduction, evaporation, convection, and radiation.

"If we were to measure the actual wind direction and speed at, say, five hundred points evenly spaced around Kelly's body, and hire an aerodynamicist to determine the regions of laminar, that is, non-turbulent, and non-laminar, meaning turbulent, airflows at the surfaces of her clothing, taking into account the effects of the textures and wrinkles in the clothing and their interactions with the various airflow vectors, including the penetration of the airflow into and insulating value of the fabrics, then use integral calculus to determine a weighted average for air movement around her clothing, we would be able to meaningfully modify the convective component which is factored into the standard heat loss table. The table I used for Kelly is for an average female body wearing light cotton shirt, pants, underwear, sneakers, and socks, lying on dry earth, in still air, at STP."

"What's STP?" Even gazed worshipfully at Mercedes. Softhousen's face held an expression of being slowly and exquisitely tortured.

Mercedes nodded and smiled. "STP stands for Standard Temperature and Pressure, that is, zero degrees Celsius and 29.92 inches of mercury, as I said, in still air. However, convection can be speeded up considerably by air movement. That is why the tables contain additional axes and curves to correct for wind and various amounts of humidity. However, the air in the interstitial was not only moving, it was swirling, which amplifies the cooling effect considerably. Kelly's body was also slowly spinning—another complicating factor. So, as you can understand, aerodynamic studies, though complex, might considerably improve the accuracy of the tables.

"Obviously, we would also need to factor in the other ways in which Kelly differs from the average female body. She is taller, more slender, more muscular, and therefore has a lower percentage of body fat than the female bodies used in deriving the table. These factors can be compensated for, either through further experiments or extrapolation from the differences between the heat losses of male and female bodies. Kelly's body is likely to be more toward the masculine side. Mathematically extrapolating a new curve, that is, a mathematical model, for her body type, from the existing data, is certainly a possibility.

"Kelly's clothing is also different than the clothing in the model. Here it might be a good idea to hire a thermodynamicist to determine how the thermal conductivity of the clothing and bunny suit Kelly was wearing differ from the cotton clothing used in deriving the table. In addition to testing the particular fabrics Kelly is wearing individually, it will be necessary to test them together. Trapped air, as I'm sure you know, is an insulator. Air can be trapped between layers of clothing, thereby synergistically enhancing the each layer's insulative properties.

"In addition, Kelly's clothing, her skin, and her hair could have different emissivities than those of the cadavers

119

used for the table. Emissivity, as you know, is the ability of a certain texture, color, or type of material to emit infra-red radiation—that is, radiant heat. The standard of comparison is, of course, the black body. Black objects generally have the highest emissivities—they emit the most heat. They also absorb the most heat. It is a direct relationship. But, in this case, because of the lack of external sources of heat, such as heat lamps or the sun, there was no appreciable heat for Kelly to absorb. Therefore all we are concerned about is Kelly's emissivity. Because Kelly's bunny suit was white, her emissivities are likely to be quite low. Also, as I recall, Teflon itself has an extremely low emissivity. The Teflon coating of the fabric may have considerably modified its normal properties.

"A very direct approach to the problem would be for us to run experiments using Kelly's body, clothed as it was. We warm her with electric blankets to 98.6 degrees Fahrenheit, then hang her as we found her and measure the declining temperature of her body at, say, ten second intervals. My guess is that those numbers would be extremely accurate.

However, there would still be unknown factors. Such an experiment could not duplicate her evaporative heat loss due to perspiration, and the heat loss caused by her loss of blood. And, even after the brain ceases to function, there may be some residual metabolic activity in the cells of the body, generating heat at low levels.

"As you know, evaporative heat loss is the cooling which we all experience from perspiring. We don't know hard she was working—how many calories she was burning in her muscles and how much she was perspiring—just before she died. So we have no way of determining, or duplicating at this point, exactly how damp Kelly's clothing and skin were from perspiration. That must remain an unknown.

"Blood, of course, has thermal mass. Generally, in thermodynamic equations, thermal mass is a constant. With Kelly it is a complex variable because the flow of blood out of her body changed over time. The blood coming out of Kelly's body rapidly increased in volume until a certain point, and then gradually decreased. At least a first order differential equation would be necessary to mathematically describe the characteristics of the heat outflow from her body due to her blood loss.

"As I mentioned, the residual metabolic activity left in Kelly's cells after death is an unknown, which is further complicated by the blood loss. Given the number of cells and the different availabilities of the residual blood supply to them, and the different oxygen needs of the different cells, this may be an extremely complex problem to work out analytically.

"A cell physiologist might be able to help. However, given the complexity of this problem from an theoretical standpoint, my guess is that an empirical approach would be best; that is, a series of experiments in which sensitive temperature probes are placed in the various organs and muscles of recently-dead cadavers in order to determine which of them may be generating heat, and for how long they continue to do so. A series of heat-loss curves could be constructed from the temperature probe data, and compared with a second set of losses, after the cadaver is re-warmed, say, a week later, when all of the cells could be assumed to be completely dead. The differences between these two sets of curves would indicate residual metabolic activity. Of course, Kelly's case differs from these research subjects, again, due to her blood loss and musculature.

"Couldn't you drain the blood from the cadaver by cutting the hands off, puncturing the carotid artery, and hanging it upside down?" asked Evan.

"Of course," Mercedes smiled, "and that would improve the applicability of the experiment to Kelly.

"Also, as you are aware, recent physical exertion can have quite a lasting effect on body temperature. Even on a very cold day, exercise can produce both subjective and objective warming of the body which lasts for an hour or more. Unfortunately we have no idea, and there is no way for us ever to know, how hard Kelly was working during the hour before her death.

"Because of the data reduction and mathematical modeling, it might be a good idea to include a mathematician in this research project. So, by diligently applying aerodynamics, thermodynamics, mathematics, cell physiology, and with a month or two of experimenting with Kelly's body and recently dead cadavers, we might be able to get the time estimate down to plus or minus ten seconds. You understand, this ten-second estimate arbitrarily places the experimental error at plus or minus three standard deviations. That is a 99.6 percent confidence interval.

"Lastly, in Kelly's case I believe conduction can be safely ignored. Her only physical contact with a solid was the rope around her ankle. As the thermal conductivity of dry hemp is, I'm sure, extremely low, and as the surface area of contact was small and far away from the body's central core, and not close to major arteries, any heat loss because of contact with the rope would be minimal."

"Goddammit!" Softhousen exploded, "You know I don't need to know all of this crap!"

Mercedes smiled sweetly. She consulted a computer printout. "I've double-checked the blood gases. We don't even test for nitrogen. It's inert and hard to test for. The partial pressure of gaseous nitrogen in the blood is directly related to its partial pressure in the atmosphere. The relationship is based on the physics of gases and their solubility in liquids, not on any bio-chemical activity of the body. So as soon as Kelly was removed from the area of lethal nitrogen, even if there had been some slight N_2 elevation in the blood, it probably would have returned to nominal levels prior to sampling. The same sort of equilibration is demonstrated by the phenomenon that scuba divers sometimes experience called the bends."

"Do you mind translating that for us dummies?" Softhousen gave up and closed his eyes in pain. He could not, and would not, ever get the scientific upper hand with Mercedes.

"There is no way of getting any direct evidence of nitrogen suffocation."

"Why didn't you say so? Anything else?"

"She also had exceptionally low cholesterol levels…" Mercedes smirked.

He took the bait. "Really? Will my high cholesterol cause my hands to fall off?"

"As your body rots after death." Mercedes slowly raised her eyebrows.

Softhousen sighed. He had just been intellectually skewered again. "What do we know about what cut her throat and severed her wrists?"

Mercedes resumed a professional tone. "Different weapons, no doubt about it. A sharp small knife for the throat. The carotid was actually cleanly punctured, not completely transected. The epiphysis of the left ulna was completely transected by the blade of a different tool. The blade polished the bone in a semi-circular arc."

"An arc?"

Mercedes showed Softhousen the photographs. "Also, there is a ridge," she pointed at the photograph, "right there, as though the blade stopped, and then continued to cut. So, it looks like some sort of machine tool did this. There is no uneven hacking as you would have with a handheld knife, machete, or axe."

Softhousen was mystified. "Have you ever seen anything like this? A saw maybe?"

"No," Mercedes responded. "The kerf of a saw has distinctive striations from the saw teeth. Here there were none. I also checked the secure FBI database to which we have access on the Web. There were no matches."

"We'll have to ask at Winsome whether they have some sort of special tool for severing wrists," Softhousen suggested.

"Exactly," said Mercedes, refusing to smile.

"How about bruises?" prompted Softhousen.

"I looked carefully for bruises on her face and under her hair. There were none there or anywhere else on her body, except on one side of her wrists. Whoever carried her was careful not to bang her around. There is a ligature mark around her right ankle from the rope. Since the lividity is extremely localized, I would say that injury occurred post-mortem. There is no evidence of recent sexual activity or rape."

"Thanks," grunted Softhousen, scribbling.

"The helmet," began Evan, "wasn't bloody at all. Apparently it was removed before Kelly's throat or wrists were cut. There were no cuts in the cloth parts of the helmet. There were two blond hairs inside, along with a hair net. We haven't requested DNA analysis of the hair, but under the comparison microscope they look to be a perfect match to Kelly's own hair. She used no dye or peroxide."

"How about the bunny suit?" asked Softhousen.

"There were just a few tiny flakes of orange paint and pieces of aluminum on the outside of the elastic at both wrists, in a swath across the fabric. Whatever cut her wrists may have left the paint and aluminum. It also microscopically tore at the outside of the elastic material. The tool had a rough surface, at least on one side."

"Orange paint, aluminum, tearing, one side," Softhousen mumbled as he wrote in his notebook, mystified. "Could the tool have picked up bits of the cloth from the elastic wrists?"

"Yes. The Teflon coating is on the outside of the suit fabric. Under the microscope the coating shows scratches exceptionally well. If we can locate the tool, we may be able to do a positive identification based on bits of the coated fabric picked up by the tool, and also by comparing the patterns of the scratches in the fabric and burrs on the tool. Of course, there should also be a lot of blood inside any crevices in the tool."

"Unless they cleaned it," Softhousen interjected.

"Right," Evan agreed.

"How about the print on the piece of the glove that was in the knot?" asked Mercedes.

Evan smiled. "Ah. It's a beauty; as clear as if it were in a textbook. It's only a fingertip—I'd say the upper quarter of a regular print." He scanned the Polaroids of Kelly's fingers. "I don't think it's Kelly's. There are 15 points of identification—all merging of ridges—on the glove. I'll print Kelly's fingertips, now that we have them, to rule her out. If we get a suspect, we have more than enough to do a match.

"The blood samples all look like they're Kelly's, so far. The floor samples are bits of all sorts of stuff: linoleum, steel filings, Teflon from the suits, flakes of paint, Tyvex fabric, chewing tobacco. It's all what you would expect to find in a factory. I'll keep looking."

"Did you find anything in Kelly's cubicle?"

"It's the usual desk paraphernalia, and a few file folders. She didn't have much. I haven't looked through it yet. I'll bet her prints are everywhere—but so what? We know it was her desk. I'll give it a once-over anyway to see if there is anything unusual, and what's in her files. I'll work up an inventory and append it to my report."

Softhousen opened the morgue door. "I've got to get back to Winsome to meet with the night shift supervisors. Thanks for staying late and going the extra mile on this. It's a good start. Now we need a suspect."

Evan followed Softhousen out.

In the hallway, after the morgue door shut, Softhousen growled, "Christ! Why does she do that? She knows I don't give a rat's ass about emissivity."

"I don't know," Evan cheerfully lied. "See you in the morning."

* * *

As she munched her last McNugget Mercedes removed her coat from Kelly.

She admired Kelly's naked body as an entomologist would admire a rare butterfly. Kelly was an almost perfect cadaver, exceptionally beautiful, even in death.

Neither the stench of formaldehyde, the deathly stillness, the chilled air, the lime-green color of the cold concrete walls, nor the blood-stained linoleum floor intruded into Mercedes' thoughts. She loved being in the morgue at night, alone, with a fresh cadaver. It was when she did her best work.

She tied a surgeon's paper mask over her nose and mouth, then clipped a small tape recorder to the waistband of her green scrubs, donned a headset, and pressed the record button.

"Subject, Kelly Kissimmee. External examination: a normally developed, well-nourished female in her early twenties. Muscle development and definition are excellent." Mercedes stopped and checked Kelly's chart. "Six feet two inches tall, weight one thirty-five. External chest is unremarkable."

She paused. Larry would have interrupted her and said that Kelly's external chest was quite remarkable. "What's really remarkable is his one-track mind," she thought. How could men ever do anything productive when all they thought about all day was having sex with sixteen-year-olds? She imagined Larry, naked, having sex with Kelly's corpse, and snickered at her power to manipulate him. But

Larry wasn't a necrophiliac. He was just an example of the average aging male; automatically turned on by the secondary sex characteristics of post-pubescent female homo sapiens.

Delicately holding a scalpel, Mercedes carefully began her Y-incision through Kelly's unremarkable chest, and said, "Let's see what else we can find."

Chapter 18

NIGHTMARE

Irma's slender knife easily cut through the Gouda cheese on her maple cutting board, producing two thick slices. As she fixed a "weed sandwich" (as her friends called anything healthy), she absentmindedly turned on the tiny color TV on her kitchen counter.

Large chucks of fresh avocado lay atop a field of bean sprouts, topped with blood red tomatoes, then mayonnaise, and a dash of mustard, all carefully tucked between two slices of lightly toasted honey wheat bread, now lined with Gouda cheese. A large cold jar of sun tea supplied the libation. Irma's mouth watered in anticipation of undoing the damage caused by the hamburger at lunch. A quick sip of tea, then both hands grabbed the sandwich and lifted it to her waiting taste buds. The sandwich stopped, inches from her open lips, and she stared at the TV.

"...In local news: At 7:56 this morning the TV-1 newsroom scanner picked up this extraordinary radio traffic on a frequency often used by emergency personnel at Winsome Semiconductor Corporation in Albuquerque."

A beautiful aerial shot of Fab 13 filled the screen.

There was a burst of static, then, "ERT leader to base." Steve Reddy's excited voice came through with exceptional clarity.

"10-4 ERT leader. Go ahead." Irma immediately recognized Sergeant Smith's deep, confident tones.

"We've got a dead girl hanging from the rafters in the interstitial above Litho near the back stairs. Send the nurse right away."

"Ah, that's a 10-4." The radio transmission ended.

"We understand from sources within Winsome that 'ERT' stands for 'Emergency Response Team,' and the 'interstitial' is an area above the clean room. The Emergency Response Team is trained to respond to chemical spills and other emergencies.

"In addition, our TV-1 helicopter steadicam obtained this footage at 11:47 this morning." The video clearly showed two police officers loading a black body bag into the APD morgue van at the Winsome dock.

"TV-1 has attempted to contact Fab 13's manager, Charles Chen, several times today. He has not returned our calls. We spoke briefly with several other Winsome personnel. All we know at this time is that Winsome has not denied being the source of the radio transmissions, nor have they offered any explanation concerning what appears to be a body bag being loaded into an Albuquerque Police Department morgue van. Was a young woman murdered at Fab 13 this morning? Did she commit suicide? Was it an industrial accident? Could her death have been the result of terrorism or sabotage?

"The Albuquerque Police Department public information officer has had nothing to say except, 'No comment.'

"The national news media picked up this story this afternoon. It is speculated that this strange death may be responsible for the enormous drop in the price of Winsome's stock today. The loss to Winsome stockholders is estimated at over fifteen billion dollars.

"In other news, brown bears are once again descending from the Sandias into the backyards of Albuquerque..."

Irma turned off the television. She was tired, and hungry as a bear. She sank her teeth into tomatoes, avocados, mayonnaise, and cheese, closed her eyes, and savored the fresh, natural taste.

Steve, she thought, must be dying of embarrassment at the moment. Chen's silence was not helping. It was fanning the flames of speculation in the media. She must meet with Chen and the Fab 13 public relations manager tomorrow.

She quenched the flames of her thirst with a huge swig of ice-cold tea.

*   *   *

Lying on top of her sheets, Irma stared at the sunset's shadows on the exposed vigas—the unpainted wooden beams—which supported her roof. She couldn't stop herself from thinking about the phalanges of Kelly's living, skilled fingers. Those fingers had held books, calculators, a cello. Those fingers had helped Kelly to attain her considerable mathematical and engineering skills. Those fingers had excelled at basketball and volleyball. Irma was sure those fingers were part of Kelly being a wonderful and loving person. Now Kelly was gone—erased—and those fingers were mutilated. All that was left were disgusting, bloody bits of meat. Irma shuddered in horror.

A thought seared through Irma's consciousness: Where were the rest of Kelly's hands—her palms? She knew they were going to find them, and it would be someplace strange: inside a machine, or someone's locker, or the cafeteria. Oh God! Irma thought of the hamburger she had eaten for lunch, turned over onto her stomach, buried her face in a pillow and shrieked in horror.

Waves of nausea threw her from her bed. She staggered to the bathroom, sagged to her knees, and retched into the toilet. Sweat soaked her body. The dry heaves came, and would not stop. She cradled her chin on her hands, on the rim of the toilet, and was too weak to move—to do anything except retch, and retch, and retch. "Oh, please God, stop," Irma prayed. Her stomach muscles ached from the involuntary contractions. Finally, she could stand it no more: the pain in her gut, and the stomach acid burning in her nose, mouth, and throat. She cried and retched, and retched and cried. She wept for Kelly, and Kelly's beautiful, soft, talented hands. Irma's tears dripped into the vomitus in the toilet, and she did not care. Her arms did not have the strength to lift a hand to flush.

At last, the convulsions ended. Her exhausted body drifted down from the toilet, the smooth floor tiles caressed her flushed skin, and she lay, panting. Slowly her strength returned, and she rolled her forehead back and forth on the cold, hard tiles, cooling her sweaty brow. "Feels good, feels good," was all she could think.

She must have fallen asleep on the tile floor, but was now shivering and naked. Specs of dried, crusty vomit burned into her face, arms, and chest. Irma pulled herself to her knees, and found the strength to flush the toilet. The noisy, familiar rush of water was soothing. She felt better—weak and drained, but better. She stood slowly, carefully, in the dark bathroom. Without turning on the light, she soaked a wash cloth in warm water, then slowly washed. Feeling clean was so much better. She turned on the light, brushed her teeth, and gargled with mouthwash. The mint taste, reeking of alcohol, overcame the biting acidity in her mouth and the stench of vomit. She ran a brush through her hair, and was back in the land of the living.

The alarm clock next to the bed read 8:00 p.m. She had an hour to get some sleep. She lay down gratefully on her clean, dry sheets, and closed her eyes. But her mind refused to rest. Faces flashed briefly—people she had casually passed in Winsome hallways; had seen working in the clean room; had eaten with in the cafeteria. It could be any of them. There were so many. Where were those faces between 6:00 and 7:00 this morning? Any one could have come into work an hour early, gowned up, found Kelly, and then...Irma would not let herself think of what had happened next.

Why? Why do this horrible thing? How could Kelly have an enemy here, at a new job, in a new state, so quickly? They were so far from the west coast, from California, from Cal Tech. Could someone have followed her from there? It must be a man. A man who had a problem with women, who had been rebuffed by one woman too many…or had been emotionally battered by a psychologically tormented mother—a mother who'd had nowhere else to turn—except to violence—except to beat the male child who was the evidence of her betrayal.

Could it be a woman? Could one of the sisterhood do this to another woman? Perhaps it was a jilted competitor in a star-crossed Lesbian lovers' triangle. Any woman could be jealous of Kelly's athletic and musical gifts, beauty, and brilliance. But could such a complex relationship have happened here at Winsome, so quickly? No, probably not.

It must be a stalker from school—from Cal Tech. *Did someone follow Kelly from California?* How could this stranger have so quickly and thoroughly breached Winsome's security? Most likely it would be a classmate; an engineer. Someone smart, but with so much rage.

Irma forced her eyes shut. She had to rest. Stop thought. Focus on a favorite memory: a butterfly on a summer's day, a mountain stream, gurgling water, dappled shade, mossy rocks, dreamy sky, puffy clouds, golden aspen leaves drifting down, feeling peace. She drifted off to sleep.

Even in sleep her mind rejected rest. Irma dreamed.

Roiling up from the valley far below, cold fog enveloped the happy stream, the mossy rocks, the butterfly, and quaking aspen—a quiet, shrouding mist. An ephemeral image gradually coalesced into a graceful, slender being—a ghostly angel, an ice princess with long blond hair, dressed in white, glided nearer, across frozen water. Gracefully balancing on one skate blade, with arms above her head, the apparition began to spin. The mist cleared—and cold, black, flat ice mirrored the spinning woman, upside down.

Irma screamed and screamed and screamed a silent scream; too frightened to move, voice paralyzed—a helpless shriek of hellish horror. She could stare, all she could do was stare.

A ruddy haze obscured the scene. When the redness cleared. Irma saw a wet, rotating, splashy fountain, spouting swirling streams of blood. Irma traced the spurting to its source, and...the skater had no hands! The severed arteries in the skater's wrists formed the fountain nozzles. The skater gaily spun, oblivious to her ghastly wounds—the fatal loss of blood—and did not stop her inertial dance of death.

Irma's hands were paralyzed at her sides. She could not warn this angel, could not help, could not reach out, and could not stop the suicidal spin. Irma tossed from her stomach to her back, then to her side. The skater's holographic image slowly vanished into the night.

Finally, just as dreamless sleep soothingly enveloped Irma's mind, the wretched loud bleep of her alarm clock shattered her unconsciousness.

Punchy, exhausted, she staggered out of bed, splashed cold water on her face, and dressed. She stumbled through the front door and fell into her little black car. The Miata started itself and maneuvered out of her dusty driveway.

Top down, the cool evening air flowed around her as she drove. An ostinato chorus of cicadas sang in the sturdy arms of ancient cottonwoods and accompanied her motion through the night. Her mind cleared under the black sky and eternal desert stars.

"Catharsis," she thought, and knew she was healed. Her unconscious had forced her to face the worst and her fears were swept aside. Exhausted, she was stronger, and would not be sick again. She was ready for the 10:00 p.m. meeting.

Chapter 19

ZWITTER IONS

They arrived together. Irma paused in the hall and watched Larry sign in and get a visitor's badge from the guard. She looked at him quizzically, but he said nothing as they walked to 307. Their steps were slow. They were both tired.

Chen sagged against the hallway wall outside of the meeting room, waiting for the night shift supervisors to arrive. Dark circles ringed his eyes—he had aged ten years since morning. When he saw them he straightened. Irma watched Chen will himself to move out of his fatigue and to pay attention to the matters at hand—to do what had to be done.

He spoke to both of them. "Litho began getting high particles on the TW's, the test wafers, this afternoon. The techs narrowed it down to the develop tracks. Then we ran an LPC, liquid particle count, on the bulk developer liquid. It comes from another tote with a pumping system. The counts were extremely high. We put some of the developer on slides and looked at it with an optical microscope a few minutes ago." He handed Softhousen and Irma each a high-resolution color print.

Irma asked, "What are those red doughnuts?"

"Blood cells," said Chen.

Softhousen wrote down "bulk develop" and "blood."

Chen continued, "We think the rest of Kelly's hands, the palms, are inside the developer tote."

"They are still in the tote?" asked Softhousen.

"Yes. We can see something at the bottom, but haven't fished whatever it is out yet. I left instructions not to touch it. As you requested, the police are to handle all evidence."

Softhousen opened his flip phone and stabbed at it with his forefinger. "Yeh, Evan? They think they've found the palms at Winsome…Have them page Miss Laches when you get here…Thanks."

He turned to Chen, "The fun never stops, eh?"

Chen did not respond.

"So, that's everything that was missing from her body?" asked Irma.

"I guess so." Chen was weary. "The Litho bulk systems engineer, Fuller Linksland, can help you figure a way to get them out. He should be here in a moment."

Irma took stock of herself: no reaction. She was numb to the finding of a beautiful girl's body parts in strange chemicals, and was horrified instead at her lack of feeling. "What's wrong with me?" she thought.

Chen stared at their images, mirrored in the dark hallway windows, and spoke quietly. "This is another flush-out sort of cleanup. Not as bad as the others because there's no gold involved, and the developer is already a soapy solution. It more or less cleans up after itself. We can install filters at the coaters, to catch any blood cells which may remain in the tubing after a purge. The developer contamination is maybe only $150,000 in actual damages."

Softhousen wrote down "developer—$150K," then asked, "Why so much? All you have to do is flush out the tubing and install filters, right?"

"Yes," Chen patiently explained, "but the chemicals we use are all ultra-pure, and precisely formulated. That means they contain practically no particles or chemical contaminants, and are mixed in precise and repeatable ratios. It is expensive for the manufacturers to meet these requirements. A gallon of developer costs one hundred dollars. In addition, everything the chemicals touch in this factory—the pumps, tubing, and filters—must also be ultra-clean and made from high-purity plastics and stainless steel. Those parts are expensive. What may look to you like a twelve dollar filter probably cost us twelve hundred dollars. Also, the coater-developers are the most numerous machines in the fab, and we will need to install expensive filters at each one."

"Why so much emphasis on purity and precision, if it's so expensive?" asked Irma.

Chen paused before speaking. "I think you know about airborne particles already. We don't teach this in the introductory classes, but liquid particles can be just as deadly. A liquid particle—usually just a solid particle suspended in one of the liquids we use in the manufacturing process—can stick due to a combination of electrostatic, chemical, and mechanical adhesive forces, such that it cannot be rinsed off of the surface of the wafer by any normal means. Organics, such as blood cells, are a particular problem."

Irma asked, "Why?"

Chen stared at the wall for a moment, marshaling his thoughts. "Okay. Organic electro-chemical adhesion: a molecular charge is caused when there are either not enough, or too many electrons in a portion of the molecule. Biochemistry is rampant with chemical groups having these charges. For instance, blood cells have amino acids in their DNA. Amino acids exist as a Zwitter ion, meaning they have both negative and positive charges in the same molecule.

"To illustrate the electrical charges in DNA, consider how DNA is analyzed. Enzymes are added to chemically chop up the DNA. The enzymes are specific to known functional spots. This means they chop it up the same way every time. Electrophoresis is then used to separate the gemished—chopped—samples into bands. The pieces move at different rates through the media as they are motivated by the electric potential that is placed across it. Dark bands are caused because the chopped pieces have different electrical charges and so are moved to different locations. Since each person's DNA is unique, unique bands are yielded from this procedure. Finally the media—the paper strips showing the bands—are placed next to each other and visually compared. If the bands line up, it's the same person. My point is not to lecture you on DNA analysis, but to illustrate that the organic segments of the DNA molecule have different electric potentials which are readily seen.

"So charged molecules; the amines, sulfides, acids, and bases which are in organic particles—in this case, blood cells—have many sites of functionality which offer many ways for the organic material to electro-chemically interact with doped silicon surfaces. These multiple interactions are difficult to break simultaneously with soap during washing. It's like having chewing gum, different types of glue, and different kinds of paint on the bottom a pair of shoes. One cleaning method won't work for all of them. So it's almost impossible to remove organic contamination—like blood cells—from silicon wafers without mechanically scrubbing them…"

"Which will damage the wafers!" Irma interrupted. She had overheard an engineer say that the last mechanical wafer scrubber was being removed from the factory, and good riddance.

"Exactly," Chen nodded. "We would have to kill the patient, that is, destroy the wafers, in order to save them. It is better to eliminate the particles instead. Prevention is the cure."

"Zwitter ions…" Softhousen mumbled, expressing no enthusiasm whatsoever for the wonders of organic chemistry.

Chen turned, faced the detective, and spoke through clenched teeth. "This person really knew how to hurt this factory. He damaged every area in the clean room. He thought it out. He planned it. He's cost us millions of dollars. He's traumatized every person in the building. He caused damaging publicity. And, he's killed, possibly, two of our employees. It's up to you to catch him."

"I know that," said Softhousen, defensively.

In spite of law school, which had trained her to use gender-neutral speech whenever possible, Irma also preferred to think of the person who had wreaked all of this havoc as a man. She did not correct Chen's use of the male pronoun. "Nine out of ten criminals are male, anyway," she thought.

Chapter 20

FRANK LEATHERS

Three women and two men came into the room. They wore slacks and polo shirts—not jeans and tee shirts—and expensive white leather walking shoes. Irma noted the unwritten Winsome dress code: managers and supervisors didn't wear ties, but dressed just a little better than techs and operators. Irma concluded that these were the Diffusion, Lithography, Etch, Thin Films, and Sort supervisors.

A very fit-looking fellow strode in carrying a radio. He wore faded jeans, a wide leather belt with Leatherman and flashlight holsters, and a blue work shirt with "Fab 13 Facilities" and "Frank" embroidered over the pockets. He was thirty-five years old, Irma guessed.

"Frank Leathers, night shift facilities lead," he said with a big warm smile. Irma smiled back, looked at his six foot three inch frame, and shook his huge hand. True to his name, the hand was so calloused that it felt like a warm baseball glove. He carefully gave her hand only a light squeeze.

"Woah!" thought Irma. "I would pay this guy for a date!" A clean calloused hand was sensuous to the max. Then she noticed the wedding ring on his other hand.

An older fellow—at least forty-five, she guessed—drifted into the room. He wore baggy jeans and a large, loose, blue tee-shirt. He was muscular through the chest and had a telephone-pole neck that made Irma think, "ex-football player." His wavy black hair, going silver at the temples, terminated in a perfectly round bald spot on top, like a monk's. He shook her hand politely. "Fuller Linksland, bulk systems engineering," he said in a husky tenor voice, soft and precise.

As Irma introduced herself, she felt some sort of strangeness about Fuller. Not only was he older than most Winsome engineers, but he was quiet and watchful. It was hard to pin down her feelings. Partly, he wasn't dressed properly; more like a fab worker, not an engineer. She could see he had just come from the fab by the patterned crease in his forehead left by the elastic of his hairnet. Below his bald spot his hair was a mess. "Fab hair," they called it—matted from sweat and mashed down under the helmet of a bunny suit—badly in need of being rinsed and brushed.

After everyone was seated, Chen explained that he had decided to meet with only the supervisors, or "sups" ("soops," he said) rather than having a shift-wide meeting which would include all of the technicians and operators. He implored everyone to keep the situation as low-key as possible. The sups could then meet with their own small groups and individuals throughout the night and ask whatever questions Softhousen wanted to have asked. They would meet again with Softhousen and Irma at the end of the shift—tomorrow morning at oh nine-hundred.

Chen emphasized the absolute confidentiality of everything, then he and Softhousen reviewed the events of the day in chronological order, including the death of Mary Martinez.

Softhousen concluded the recitation, "...and we checked the fingerprint found on the screwdriver with Kelly's prints. It's a perfect match to the left thumb. Her file prints also match the ends of the fingers which were found in the machines. The print on the screwdriver doesn't prove anything except that she touched it without gloves on, somewhere, sometime. But there was also a piece of helmet plastic found on a metal strut near the floor in the chase which matches a gash in her helmet. Healthy, athletic young women just don't fall over without a reason. Most of what we've seen so far is consistent with nitrogen suffocation."

Violette Steppe, the night shift Lithography supervisor, spoke up. "When did the last contamination—the developer—occur?"

"Based on the particle test wafer data logged into the SPC database, our best estimate is around noon—possibly a little before," Chen replied.

Irma whispered to Softhousen, "SPC is statistical process control."

"And the murder, or accident, occurred when?" asked Violette.

Softhousen replied, "According to the medical examiner she died at approximately 07:00. Her hands and neck had to be cut at approximately 07:40 for Mary Martinez to notice the blood dripping on her from the ceiling at 07:45."

"And the service chase where you think she suffocated?" Violette persisted.

"The one in CVD with the LN2 tank," said Irma. "Chemical vapor deposition," she whispered to Softhousen.

Polly Immid was the night shift diffusion supervisor. Her initial look of shock was gradually wearing off. "You think this person worked last night, found Kelly's dead body, carried her up a ladder into the interstitial, strung her up, cut her hands off, and then spent the rest of the morning contaminating the high vacuum equipment and bulk delivery systems?"

"Exactly," affirmed Chen.

"Then why did we have conductivity failures in Diffusion starting at 5:00 a.m.?"

There was a moment of silence.

Excellent question, thought Irma.

Softhousen answered. "It's possible that there was a plan to sabotage the equipment all along. Let's say the perpetrator got started with Diffusion at 5:00 a.m., and then just happened across Kelly's lifeless body. It was a fortuitous circumstance. The perp seized the opportunity to combine sabotage and terror by using Kelly."

141

Irma hated the word "perp." She thought it was crude. And, if that was really the way it happened, the criminal would have to be a very self-assured, intelligent, and uncaring person. Self-assured and intelligent in order to be able to interrupt an apparently well-thought-out plan of sabotage in order to take advantage of Kelly's accidental death and to insert spontaneously improvised terrorism using Kelly's body. Self-assured and smart and creative. That, Irma could believe. But who could possibly be so uncaring as to cut off the hands of a tragically dead, beautiful girl, and drain her blood? A man who hated women, Irma answered herself. It had to be a man who hated women. No one else could be that depraved.

The night shift Thin Films supervisor was Ian M. Plante. Everyone called him "I. M." He asked, "Isn't it just possible Kelly was murdered? She could have been forced to breathe the nitrogen from the LN2 boil-off."

"That would be extremely tricky. Nitrogen is colorless, odorless, and tasteless. The killer could easily wind up killing himself." Perry startled everyone. He had arrived late and had come in quietly through the rear door.

I. M. turned to Polly. "Wasn't there Visqueen up in CVD during shutdown? I also think I remember seeing a ladder leading up into the interstitial from that chase."

Polly nodded. "As I recall, there was."

"What's Visqueen?" Softhousen hated to ask.

Frank Leathers explained. "It's just a brand name for that milky-white plastic you see painters use. We get it on huge rolls and use it everywhere during shutdowns, to surround work areas—to keep construction debris and particles isolated."

Softhousen nodded, and scribbled "Visqueen = plastic." This investigation was expanding his vocabulary, whether he wanted it to or not.

"I've pulled the construction Gantt," said Perry. "It shows additional scrubbed exhaust hookups were being installed there. The work was to be finished this morning, and the ladder was probably still up when Kelly died. The ladders are usually the last things to go."

"So it had been removed by the regular workmen by the time we got to Kelly?" asked Irma.

"Probably," said Frank Leathers. "I'll find out tonight when it was taken out."

"Nothing so far in sort, right?" Tad Inkfales, the sort supervisor, looked unconcerned.

"No," Chen confirmed. "It's a separate clean room, and the probers are not very sensitive to contamination. I hope we're safe, there. But it could be one of your people who used to work in the fab. Also one of your folks could have noticed something—someone strange in the parking lot—anything. We need your help."

"How did the blood get through the Litho ceiling in only five minutes?" asked Tad. "It would take a lot longer than that in my apartment."

Frank turned in his chair and faced Tad. "The ceiling in the clean room is covered with HEPA filter boxes, powder-coated honeycomb aluminum ceiling panels, and fluorescent lamp fixtures, all resting on a standard suspended ceiling tee-track grid. Nothing is sealed. The idea is for the higher air pressure in the fab to blow back up into the interstitial through all the little cracks in order to keep the dust out. However, the capillary wicking and surface tension of liquids, and gravity, are more than enough to overcome that small amount of air pressure. Liquids run right around the panels."

Tad nodded.

"So, what questions do you want us to ask?" said Polly.

"We need you to approach every one of your people—the operators, technicians, and engineers." Softhousen paused.

"Also the FSE's—field service engineers, who work in your areas. Everyone," Chen added.

Softhousen continued, "Just outline the two deaths. Don't go into great detail. Don't talk about the hands or the blood. If someone has already heard about them, don't deny it, but just move on to what we need to know.

"We need to know if they saw or heard anything strange, or any strange person. Get a description of what everyone did and where they were last night—especially from 05:00 to 08:00. Confirm their whereabouts with other folks. Generate time lines for each employee showing where they were and who they were with. Note any conflicting stories on the time lines. We need a very accurate, detailed report from every one of you on each one of your people by tomorrow morning."

I. M. whistled. "Whew! This is going to take all night."

"This is first priority," said Chen. "With Diffusion, Etch, and Litho down, you're not going to run much product anyway."

Polly spoke up. "This is putting us into the role of the police, you know."

"I know," said Chen, "in a way it is. But this is a lot less Draconian than having the police interview every Fab 13 employee. This is our least intrusive option. Also, let's not lose sight of the fact that this is gross misconduct. This person—probably an employee—has sabotaged this factory. They have put all of our jobs, and our lives, at risk. This happened on Winsome property. This is something Winsome has a right to investigate."

Irma nodded. "Legally, in court, whatever you hear can't be used. It's hearsay. So your conversations are just background information gathering. It's not your job to make someone confess."

Softhousen nodded vigorously. "If anyone starts acting weird, back off. All we're asking is for you to ask a few questions and see what reaction you get. Write anything unusual down immediately after you speak with the person. Keep it informal. Be friendly. Be sure everyone knows you are interviewing everyone else, so they don't feel they are being singled out for persecution. You know your people: which ones are shy, and who hangs out with who."

"Tell your employees not to touch any evidence they may find," Irma directed. "Page me right away, and I will call APD. Are there any more questions?"

There were no more questions.

"We would like a brief verbal summary, and your written employee time lines at 09:00, tomorrow morning, here. Thanks, everyone," said Chen.

Irma knew the shift supervisors often worked sixteen-hour days. They were tough. None of them even raised an eyebrow about being asked to work this overtime.

Winsome made it clear that whiners would not be promoted. Even if it was a significant personal hardship, even if it shortchanged their wedding anniversaries, their children's birthdays or school plays, none would complain merely because of sixteen- or eighteen-hour days.

The sups left quietly. They would work hard all night, and be back, dutifully, reports in hand, at 9:00 a.m.

*   *   *

Irma drove home, stripped off her clothes, dropping them onto the floor, and crawled beneath the sheets. As soon as her head touched the pillow, she was asleep.

Chapter 21
DAY TWO

Irma barely opened her eyes and squinted at the clock on her nightstand. Its green numerals glowed 5:00 a.m. She muttered into her pillow "Why so early?" and rolled onto her back. Her vigas were painted with a faint-but-vibrant, pinkish, pre-dawn glow, urging her to greet the day.

She got up. After washing herself with a damp cloth, she pulled on clean shorts, jogbra, socks, and sneakers. Her mountain bike was waiting in the foyer.

"This is the new Irma," she told herself. "Murder or no murder, I quit my old job so I could exercise, so I'm going to exercise." Then she was out the door and pumping down a dirt trail beside an irrigation ditch, deftly weaving around fibrous green piles of horse hockey.

The cold morning air streamed passed, causing her eyes to water and goose bumps to form on her arms and legs. Sunrise was painting a brilliant orange border above the dark browns and greens of the Sandias.

She pumped hard, really hard, and shifted to her outside gears. The dark little piñon pines in the naturally landscaped back yards bordering the dirt path flew by. The ditch veered suddenly to the right, and in the growing light she took a full speed banking turn in the opposite direction, down a forty-five degree dirt slope onto the wash of an arroyo. Its sandy bottom led from Corrales up to a broad plateau—the eastern edge of the vast West Mesa, which separated the watersheds of the Rio Grande and Rio Puerco rivers.

The floor of the arroyo steepened as she climbed. She twisted her grips and alternately downshifted, back, front, back, then front, until she was on her innermost chain ring and cone gear. She pedaled quickly and smoothly, careful not to loose traction, and cast back and forth, searching for the firmest route through the sand. Other mountain bikers had gone before, and she had the benefit of following their tire tracks—barely discernible amidst footprints and the wide patterns made by four-wheelers.

Halfway to the top of the mesa she broke into a fierce sweat. The arroyo narrowed to a crevice. Finally she could pedal no further. The last fifty feet was a jumble of huge caliche boulders. Irma dismounted, leaned her bike against the earthen wall, clambered up the nearest boulder, and leapt from boulder to boulder up to the top of the mesa.

Once on the broad plateau she ran—faster and faster. She weaved from side to side, dodging sagebrush, until the edge of the precipice at the eastern rim forced her to a skidding stop.

A diamond tiara sunray broke above the northern foothills of the Sandias and rewarded her effort. Irma grinned, then laughed and stretched her torso backward, her arms skyward, and lifted herself on her toes as high as she could, her body now fully bathed in sunlight. At her feet lay the adobe homes of Corrales in earthen camouflage, the light green algodones, and the black water of the broad Rio Grande. On other side of the river swept a broad valle—a gradual slope of detritus, leached from Sandia granite through the ages—where the lights of Albuquerque still twinkled.

She was alone, isolated in time and space, between earth and sky, between life and death, in the desert. She belonged to the light and air. It was another glorious New Mexico morning.

Chapter 22

CONFLICTS OF LAWS

Softhousen, his hands in his pockets, leaned nonchalantly against the wall next to the pay phone in the Winsome security lobby. He was clean-shaven and wore a lightweight tan sports jacket, dark blue pants, and a clean, unwrinkled white shirt. His top shirt button was open, his navy blue tie loosened and askew. Irma had to smile. He looked exactly like a police detective was supposed to look in the morning. She wondered if he ever buttoned his shirt and straightened his tie.

"Good morning detective."

"Morning, counselor."

Larry even smirked a little! Irma was delighted. She was beginning to think they might become friends.

As they entered the cafeteria Irma spied Chen sipping coffee at their semi-official murder investigation table. When he saw them he stood. "No clear winners from last night," he said softly as they approached.

"You mean no suspects?" asked Softhousen.

Chen nodded. "But at least we haven't discovered any more sabotage…"

"…or body parts?" Irma added.

"No. Go get some breakfast, and we'll talk."

Irma purchased her usual bagel, green chile cream cheese, and extra-large cup of gourmet coffee. Larry kidded her: hers was designer coffee—just as overpriced as the designer water sold in the little plastic bottles. In contrast, and displaying common sense, his tray held bacon and eggs and straight black coffee.

Irma grinned, "Did you ask for extra cholesterol and caffeine?" as they sat.

A very fit, forty-ish woman with gray-blond hair and piercing grey eyes strode purposefully toward their table. She held herself perfectly erect, like a model.

"Nice posture," thought Irma. The clothes indicated that the newcomer could not be a clean room worker: a simple flat gold necklace adorned her lightweight gray short-sleeved summer sweater; black slacks with a shiny black belt emphasized her slender waist; and black leather shoes with one inch heels did the same for her long legs. The shoes were the real giveaway.

For the health of their feet women in the clean room wore walking shoes. Any sort of heel—even only an inch—added a touch of glamour. It separated the office women from the operators and technicians.

Female operators called the office workers "carpet dwellers." The carpet dwellers could wear makeup, nice clothes, shoes with heels, and fix their hair. Under a bunny suit, jewelry and clothes didn't matter. Hair was a lost cause. Of course, a good body could always be discerned, but, overall, the carpet dwellers were more attractive to men. This woman was, without question, a carpet dweller.

Irma ended the analysis of her boss. "Detective Softhousen, this is Lindley Meddlar, Fab 13's human resources manager, my supervisor."

Softhousen rose and politely shook Lindley's hand. His eyes widened at her hard fingers and strong grip.

Chen acknowledged Lindley with a curt nod. He spoke to Softhousen. "We need to have Lindley fully involved in your investigation. The human resources people here speak with all of our employees on a regular basis, are the custodians of their records, and deal with any and all personnel issues. They may be able to help us develop a list of suspects."

Lindley met Softhousen's eyes with a firm stare. "I regret having been occupied with auditing startup yesterday. Charles briefed me last night. This is the first time we've ever had to deal with anything like this. I believe it's a first for the industry."

Irma could tell that Larry was impressed with Lindley. She was a no-nonsense attractive woman who would look you straight in the eye. She was a model of Winsome corporate culture; a paradigm of the "Winsome type of woman."

Lindley whispered to Irma, Softhousen, and Chen. "I'm not certain of the legal issues with doing this, but we can provide APD with confidential information about our employees. I have already started looking through employee records for suspects."

"We need to develop that list as soon as possible," Softhousen urged.

Irma quickly glanced around them. "This can be a tricky issue, legally." They were alone in the corner of the large cafeteria. The thick carpet and acoustic-tiled ceiling made it a quiet, pleasant place to eat. Winsome's employees were keeping a respectful distance from the factory manager and his guests.

Irma continued, softly. "Winsome has a duty to provide a safe work environment for its employees. That includes ensuring, as much as possible, a crime-free workplace. But we do not want our employees' Fourth Amendment right to be free from unreasonable searches and seizures, or their personal privacy, to be violated."

"I certainly have a right to investigate this crime!" Softhousen exclaimed, but kept his voice low. "No one's under arrest, or being detained."

"Of course," Irma turned to the detective, "I agree. But we need to take care not to disregard the privacy of the one thousand, nine hundred and ninety-nine employees at this site who are innocent, in order to find the one who is guilty. Let's not lose sight of that."

"Let's not lose sight of Kelly's dead, mutilated body and industrial sabotage worth tens of millions of dollars,"Softhousen responded. "Yesterday you were talking about cooperation."

Chen nodded.

Irma backed off. "Look—like so many other things in the law, there is a balancing act going on here. There are competing policies. Of course Winsome has a duty to cooperate with a police investigation. Of course Winsome has a duty to its employees to see that dangerous people are removed from the workplace. But these duties must be balanced against our employees' rights to privacy. We can't lose our heads and wiretap every Fab 13 employee."

"I said nothing about wiretaps!" Softhousen snapped.

"That was only an illustration. I wasn't suggesting…"

Chen cut in, "Why can't we divulge information already in our files?"

"That's my recommendation," Lindley agreed.

"You mean education, age, time with Winsome, pay—the things that are in an employee's personnel file?" Irma asked.

Lindley lowered her voice until it was just audible. "Yes, of course, but we have confidential files as well. They include counseling reports from MHCS—that's Winsome's Mental Health Counseling Service. The MHCS Trust Line is part of the health care benefits package we provide to all of our employees. They can call the Trust Line any time, twenty-four hours a day, and receive free counseling over the phone."

Irma looked at Lindley in astonishment. "We keep secret records of our employees' mental health counseling?" Irma had carefully read the employee handbook when she was hired. It stated that employees could look at their personnel files at any time. Lindley's statement about secret files contradicted the handbook's implication of openness. Handbooks could be held in court to be legal documents—contracts between corporations and employees!

"Breach of contract," and "fraud" echoed in Irma's mind. It was a breach of the employment contract implied by the handbook for Winsome to keep secret files on its employees, and it was fraudulent to recruit employees with the understanding that they could inspect their files after being hired, when, in fact, they could not. In civil law it was called "Fraud in the Inducement." Irma felt frightened. Up to this point she had believed Winsome to be a perfectly honest and straightforward company. She had thought it was one of the best.

"We don't have secret files on all personnel, just the ones who come to our attention," Lindley said without a trace of defensiveness.

Irma's brain skidded to a stop. Her boss apparently thought this was good policy! Irma hesitated for a split-second, then shifted into cross-examination mode. "Exactly how does someone come to your attention?" she asked, her voice even.

"Through violence or anger at work, homicidal or suicidal ideation, a drug problem, or a run-in with the law."

"Ideation? You mean their thoughts?" asked Irma.

"As expressed to the MHCS counselors, of course," said Lindley.

Softhousen interrupted, excited. "You know which employees have threatened to kill people?"

Irma ignored Larry. "You mean MHCS reports these things to Winsome human resources?"

Lindley explained. "The MHCS Trust Line counselors are actually in Los Angeles. They serve all of the Winsome fabs in the United States. It's a toll-free phone call. An employee doesn't have to give her name, but he or she must give their Winsome i.d. number in order to receive counseling.

"The Trust Line has a current Winsome employee database, so each employee's name, employment status, and work site can be found instantly simply by entering their i.d.

number. The counselors also have the phone numbers for every site's human resources department. They simply use the database, find the employee's work site, and then call human resources to report problems."

Now Irma's fear turned to horror. In addition to being in breach of the policy stated in the employee handbook, Winsome had arranged with the MHCS telephone counselors to intentionally breach therapist-patient confidentiality!

Irma hid her reaction. Lawyers called it "courtroom demeanor" —a euphemism for a poker face.

"And these counselors are all in California?" Irma asked, calmly.

"That is correct," Lindley replied. "As I said, Los Angeles."

Irma pulled out her pad and scribbled, "California— place of the tort—most significant contacts—right to privacy." This was "issue-spotting." Irma and every lawyer in the west knew that in 1972 California, by voter-adopted initiative, had placed a right to privacy in its constitution. That measure had been motivated by public fear that California corporations were breaching the privacy of California citizens.

Legally, the analysis was simple. Since the MHCS counselors and Winsome's corporate headquarters were in California, they were both governed by California Law. Apparently Winsome had contracted with MHCS to divulge employee secrets in violation of the California constitution—in violation of California's strong public policy. A court anywhere could hold Winsome and MHCS guilty of conspiring to violate those rights.

Irma even knew the cite. California Business and Professions Code section 2960(h) specifically prohibited "[w]illful, unauthorized communication of information received in professional confidence" by mental health counselors. Winsome's Mental Health Counseling Service was violating that law. Wow.

Since Fab 13 was in New Mexico, and there was no right to privacy in the New Mexico state constitution, this was what lawyers called a "conflict of laws." It happened often when the parties to a legal dispute resided in different states.

There were two approaches. First, the court in whichever state the parties chose to sue could apply "the law of the place of the tort." "Tort" was the five-dollar word lawyers used for civil wrongs—things like negligence, breach of contract, intentional infliction of emotional distress—stuff you could sue for. Torts included the "civil side" of criminal law as well: assault and battery, wrongful death, and conversion (theft). In this case, California was the place of the tort because it was where the counseling, the duty of the counselor to maintain therapist-patient confidentiality, and the breach of confidentiality had actually occurred.

Second, if the state chosen for the lawsuit favored a more recent approach, it could apply "the law of the place of the most significant contacts." "Significant contacts" could include where the parties resided, where they worked, or the location of the corporate "nerve center" (corporate headquarters). It was a broader test.

But the significant contacts test also pointed to California, since the principal business entities involved— Winsome and MHCS—were both headquartered in California and operated under California law; the place where the illegal contract between MHCS and Winsome had been agreed to was California; the location of the therapist—the "principal tortfeasor"—was California; and the counseling, the duty, and the breach of that duty—all of the elements of the tort itself, except the harm to and location of the employee—had occurred in California.

Of course it could be argued that the location of the victims was significant in that their expectation of privacy would be based on New Mexico, not California, law. Irma frowned. She thought this was a weak argument because the employees' expectations could also be that Winsome's corporate actions were occurring under California law, since that was where Winsome corporate policy was made. Also, New Mexicans could not reasonably believe that New Mexico law should govern the actions of a California therapist.

She concluded that under either the "place of the tort" or the "most significant contacts" tests California law would govern. It didn't matter whether suit was brought in New Mexico, California, or in any of the other states where Winsome had factories. California law would govern, and Winsome would lose.

People without legal training generally knew nothing of how the courts resolved conflicts of laws. Irma clearly remembered how surprised she had been in law school to learn that the courts of one state could apply the laws of another. But it was true.

Irma said nothing. Conflicts of laws was not a legal principle to try to explain in the heat of the moment. "There are posters all over Fab 13 with pictures of jumping dolphins which advertise the Trust Line, aren't there?" she asked.

"Yes," Lindley responded.

"And the posters say, "Life isn't always carefree, but you may speak freely and confidentially with Trust Line counselors," don't they?"

"Yes, but page sixty-one of the employee handbook mentions that Trust Line confidentiality may be breached in case of an emergency."

"Breached by and to whom? Where is 'emergency' defined?" asked Irma.

Chen broke in. "Debates concerning Trust Line policy can occur off-line. We need to decide upon a course of action."

"Off-line" was Winsome code for "You're wasting valuable meeting time with something you can discuss later. Shut up." Irma and Lindley looked at Chen, then at each other. They shut up.

"Who keeps this secret file?" asked Softhousen.

"I do. It's usually in a locked file drawer in my desk, but I have it with me." Lindley placed a handsome leather briefcase on the table and pulled out a slim file folder.

"That's it?" asked Irma, incredulously.

"I keep a Word document which summarizes the original files. It's just an alphabetical list of employees' names, the dates they contacted the Trust Line, the nature of the crime or threat—suicide, homicide, or whatever—and the action taken to protect Winsome's rights."

"The nature of the crime!" Irma was incredulous. She remembered a case from 1992, *Donaldson v. Lungren,* where the California Court of Appeals had performed a search and had discovered that suicide was not a crime in the criminal codes of any of the fifty states. Irma had thought it remarkable, and was pleased, that every state legislature in the United States had decided that depressed, suicidal people had enough problems to overcome without being branded criminals.

But ah, the wonders of the law. One day, several years later, Irma was entertaining herself by looking for modern cases citing *Blackstone's Commentaries* (that famous 1803 tome of the English common law—the legal bible of frontier America), when up popped *Wackwitz v. Roy.* In *Wackwitz* the Virginia Supreme Court had affirmed that suicide was still a "common law crime." That meant that though it had been written out of the laws of Virginia, because Virginia still revered English common law, suicide was still technically a crime. It was in the very odd status of being a crime without a punishment.

In wacky *Wackwitz* the Virginia Supreme Court had affirmed that in order to commit the common law crime of suicide, one must be of sound mind. Astounded at the blatant irrationality of a modern court holding that only sane people could commit an insane act, Irma dug deeper. *Black's Law Dictionary* said that in old England being of "sound mind" meant being able to care for oneself, i.e., being able to get up in the morning, bathe, eat, and go to work. A very straightforward and sensible definition of sanity, Irma thought, quite unlike the prevarications of modern psychology.

So, in England, if someone was so mentally incapacitated that they could not feed and clothe themselves they were presumed to be too far gone to be able to form that essential element of crime, the *mens rea*—the "guilty mind" or "criminal intent." Thus, only a sane person could commit any crime, including the crime of suicide.

Why punish the successful suicide? You can't punish someone who's dead. However, Irma knew there were other consequences that flowed from suicide being classified as a criminal act. For instance, in *Wackwitz* the immediate family of the suicidal person was legally barred from suing for wrongful death, because that death had been caused by the criminal act of the victim. Thus, in Virginia, a shrink could not be held accountable for his patient's suicide unless the patient could be proved to be "of unsound mind."

Irma had to laugh. Psychology-and-the-law was turning out to be just like religion-and-the-law. The United States Supreme Court's no-law-respecting-an-establishment-of-religion decisions were described by one of her Constitutional Law professors as "an intellectual train wreck." The Supreme Court had refused for two hundred years to define the term "religion." An entire trainload of cases had been decided by avoiding the issue at the heart of the matter. Now, in Wackwitz, common law policies based on the common law definition of "unsound mind" were being promoted by the Virginia Supreme Court. But evidence was going to be presented by expert witnesses— shrinks—who completely rejected that definition. Irma shook her head in dismay. Once again, an elite group of judges were refusing to decide an issue at the heart of the matter. "What is mental health?" was the question. "We don't know," was the answer from the courts.

She knew the reason for this intellectual disaster. The judges were afraid that by wading into social controversies they would promote the fragmentation of society through disrespect for the courts. So their decisions were an intellectual game of dodgeball.

But Irma thought this legal loophole should be closed. It insulated shrinks from malpractice. *Wackwitz* also stated that suicide was still a non-statutory common law crime in the states of Alabama, Massachusetts, North Carolina, South Carolina, and New Jersey. Suicide should be completely de-criminalized, immediately. The common law crime of suicide was an unjust anachronism. Doctors— psychologists and psychiatrists—just like anyone else, should be held accountable if they were negligent.

Lindley was absolutely wrong about suicide being any sort of threat, Irma thought angrily. First, there was no such general crime as "threat." But the word "threat" was spoken reverentially by the legally illiterate as if it were some sort of crime. Saying "I'm going to dump a truckload of manure on you tomorrow!" was only a crime if it put the aggrieved party *in reasonable fear of immediate bodily harm.* Speculative, future harm was nothing.

Anger was still allowed in the U.S., and supported by the First Amendment right to free speech. Of course there were limits. You couldn't yell "Fire!" in a crowded theater. There were specific statutes that prohibited threatening politicians in office, threatening school personnel, stalking, and using foul language. And you could always bring a civil suit for intentional infliction of emotional distress against your loudmouthed neighbor. (Though IIED was tough to win.) But there was no general crime of "threat." And, thought Irma, that was a good thing. People should be able to verbally express their feelings, even anger. Better that than the alternative: physical violence.

And, there was no such thing as a right not to have someone die on one's property. If someone just happened to hang themselves from a tree outside your house, assuming no intentional infliction of emotional distress, there was no cause of action. There was no lawsuit against their estate. Any "right" which Lindley assumed Winsome might have not to have its employees die on its property was nonexistent. Lindley was not in touch with legal reality.

Lindley's assertion that depressed, suicidal people were "criminals" or "threats" was simply that ages-old prejudice: anyone who could be labeled as different would be labeled as different and branded a heretic. Apparently that prejudice was alive and well at Winsome, and embodied in Lindley Meddlar.

Chen looked at his watch. "Almost time for the 9:00 a.m. meeting with the night sups. I want the three of you, after the meeting, to compare Lindley's MHCS list against the lists of those who had access to the clean room during shutdown. Sally Sue is preparing those right now. She will meet you at 10:00 a.m. in 313." He turned to Softhousen. "Will that be acceptable, detective?"

"Yeh. Thanks," Larry nodded.

Chapter 23

TRANSPARENCIES

The meeting with the sups was a disappointment.

They had worked hard all night questioning their operators and technicians. Each brought meticulously detailed timelines that showed their employees' whereabouts during the preceding evening. But the timelines revealed nothing except hard work. There were no substantial inconsistencies from one worker to the next, and the workers' verbal reports revealed nothing—none of them reported seeing any strangers or strange behavior. The sups could not recommend a single suspect.

News of Kelly's strange death had not elicited much emotion from any of the night crew. None had known her. She was simply too new. Mary Martinez' death, on the other hand, had brought forth anger and tears of grief. Everyone in the building knew and liked Mary. There were pointed questions about how she could die while taking a safety shower. Drew Goode, sitting at the back of the room, fidgeted.

Perry stood up. "Tonight, please tell everyone that we are pursuing a vigorous investigation of the Mary's accident in the shower. Let everyone know we are soliciting volunteers to be on a corrective action team."

Irma understood this Winsome strategy. The quickest way to quell discontent was to put an upset employee on a team to fix the problem. Everyone got the point after volunteering for the first time. It was often hard work, on overtime. The message was, "Put up or shut up." If you wanted to help fix a problem fine, but if not, quit whining and get on with your regular work. This policy cost Winsome some overtime pay, but paid big dividends in constructively turning complainers into problem-solvers.

The people on the team got recognized when they fixed the problem: the extra work showed up on their annual reviews as an accomplishment. Everyone came out ahead, and problems were solved. It was a brilliant solution.

The night shift knew about the blood that had dripped on Mary from the ceiling, and about Kelly's severed hands and fingers. Too many people had seen. Word had gotten around. But, so far, no one had quit or threatened to quit. The terrorism had not worked. "Except it terrorized me," Irma thought. She would never forget her nightmare.

Chen collected the time lines and gave them to Irma. He thanked the supervisors for their hard work, asked them to continue to keep their eyes and ears open, then told them to go home and get some sleep.

Only Irma, Softhousen, and Lindley were left in the room.

Sally Sue's cowboy boots came in through the doorway.

Softhousen stared, first, at the boots, then at the long brown hair, and then at everything in between. Irma watched him carefully. She even thought she could detect his blood pressure rising in the color of his cheeks. While an undergraduate Irma had named this male response the "sexual charisma effect." Apparently Sally Sue could cause the effect.

Sally Sue briefly held up the sheets of paper she had brought. "This is a list of all of the employees who had shutdown access, arranged alphabetically by last name, grouped by job description: supervisors, engineers, operators, clean room technicians, and facilities technicians. There is another list of all of the contractors with access. There are also lists of all current clean room personnel, regardless of shutdown access, grouped the same way. Please give me a call if you need anything else." Her boots left, gracefully.

Softhousen almost imperceptibly, sadly, shook his head. "He knows he's too old for her. His libido has no place to go," Irma mused. Getting old was not only hard on women.

Lindley got up and turned out all but one of the room lights, then returned to the end of the table. She fanned out the overhead projector transparencies of her confidential files and slapped the first one onto the projector's glass surface. "I thought I would start with the employees who have a mental disturbance which might cause them to hurt Kelly. I've marked them with green x's."

A number of names on the list had green x's.

They read the first name Lindley had marked.

<u>Name and MHCS contacts</u>:
x Allen Abrams, facilities technician, f/d

12/03/99	depression due to crib death of his child and pending divorce
12/07/99	"
12/10/99	"
12/13/99	divorce + possible alcoholism
12/22/99	" + guilt + possible domestic violence + referral

William Ace...

"I flagged Abrams because of the indication of possible domestic violence. Depression and guilt can lead to violent acting out," Lindley was matter-of-fact.

"He's been violent at work?" asked Irma, incredulously.

"No, of course not. He would not still be here if he had. But he expressed some violent fantasies about his ex-wife. It's best to be proactive. The human resources department tries to anticipate problems." Lindley was condescending.

Irma winced. "His 'violent fantasies about his ex-wife' were expressed to his therapist?"

"That's right."

"In the course of a confidential therapist-patient relationship?"

"That's what we want our employees to think." Lindley smirked. The system was working exactly the way it was supposed to.

"Isn't a major benefit of confidentiality in counseling that it encourages people to verbally, rather than physically, deal with issues like anger?" asked Irma.

"Yes, of course. Another major benefit is that it alerts us, in advance, to problems. That's how we found out about the Abrams threat."

"So speaking one's innermost thoughts to a counselor, which is what one is supposed to do, can result in being labeled a 'threat' at work?"

"Of course."

"So therapist-patient confidentiality is a joke?" Irma kept her voice even. She wanted to scream at Lindley.

"I'm sure you, as an attorney, are aware of the *Tarasoff* case. It provides *carte blance* for psychotherapists to divulge threats of violence to others." Lindley had taken a college course in employment law.

Irma dug in her heels. She, too, had studied *Tarasoff.* "It does no such thing! It is a holding limited to immediate threats of harm, likely to be carried out, which are directed toward specific individuals. The warnings are to be carefully conveyed to the police or other professionals, *not to employers!"* Irma was outraged. She had strongly disagreed with *Tarasoff* from the second she had started reading it in law school, and now it was being misinterpreted in exactly the way pyschiatrists, in their *amicus curiae* briefs to the California Supreme Court, had said it would be.

"Furthermore," Irma continued, *"Tarasoff* is a California Supreme Court decision. It is primary, binding legal authority only in California. It is not binding in New Mexico, or in any other state."

"Well then," Lindley shrugged, "it should be. The MHCS counselors are in California, so Tarasoff binds them. If they choose to call us here in New Mexico, that's their business. The Winsome corporate legal department has okayed what we're doing."

Irma stated, "Well, they're wrong. Succeeding California cases have made clear that *Tarasoff* is a very limited holding, and that it does not apply to hot line counseling services. Don't you realize that thoughts of violence are extremely common, especially during divorce? None of us are angels."

"Winsome has a duty to protect its employees," Lindley responded.

Both Irma's lawyer's and woman's instincts told her that looking at people like this was wrong—not just an unconstitutional invasion of privacy, a violation of the common law right not to have private facts publically disclosed, a violation of Winsome's employment handbook, a misinterpretation of the seriously flawed *Tarasoff* decision, and a violation of therapist-patient confidentiality under California law, but it was also morally wrong. It was wrong and irrational.

It was irrational to determine possible murder suspects by using hearsay garnered over the phone by some Jung-reading do-gooder who had never met the person face-to-face. These psychologists in L.A. were making career-changing phone calls about real people they had never seen in Albuquerque—real people who had done nothing wrong except to call a "professional" they were supposed to be able to trust, for help.

It was morally wrong, regardless of the legal and scientific status of the act, to betray people's trust—to hurt them when they had let down their guard, when they believed that they were speaking to a member of a helping profession. It was morally wrong, and dangerous.

Irma remembered the Columbine Colorado High School shooting. According to *Time* magazine, as part of his psychotherapy prior to the shooting one of the shooters had been prescribed an antidepressant. Instead of being protected by doctor-patient confidentiality, the boy's prescription had been disclosed to the Marine Corps. He was labeled "a nut" for life and denied admission to the Marines. The boy had apparently dreamed of becoming a Marine for most of his few years. His "therapy" had shot down that dream. Did the boy feel that his dreams had been unjustly shattered? Did he feel betrayed by his "helper?" Could that betrayal have turned him into a murderous sociopath?

Irma remembered a John Travolta movie, *The General's Daughter*. In it an exceptionally beautiful, intelligent, and talented female officer engaged in an insane series of acts after having been repeatedly raped by fellow officers at West Point. The rapes were not what caused her insanity. As the plot evolved, her psychiatrist asked Travolta the question, "What's worse than rape?" The answer: *betrayal*—betrayal by her father—a loved one—one she trusted—her "helper." Her father, the General, had refused to prosecute the rapists "for the good of the Army." For the General's Daughter betrayal was the last straw, the unforgivable sin. In psychological terms, betrayal engendered "cognitive dissonance" too great to be overcome. It caused a "psychosocial crisis" in the mind of the General's Daughter.

Wasn't "Do no harm" a fundamental principle of medical ethics? But, thought Irma, apparently not of psychology and psychiatry. So what if betrayal of the client forever foreclosed the trust necessary for the formation of a "therapeutic alliance" with a therapist?

Thank god the Columbine shooter had been prevented from having military training, Irma thought, bitterly. After all, then he might have taken a gun into a school and shot someone.

She hated shrinks. As an attorney she had always been able to find one who would contradict another one on the witness stand for money. Scientifically, they had a lousy track record. People with really serious problems, like child molesters, were hardly ever cured no matter how much time they spent with a shrink. And it was likely that people with less serious problems cured themselves. Irma believed psychotherapy was little better than a religious fad. But she usually bit her tongue. She was a minority of one. Most educated people these days worshiped the "science" of psychology.

"What does 'f/d' mean?" asked Softhousen.

Lindley replied, "Front end of the week, day shift. 'f/n' means front end, nights, 'b/d' is back end days, 'b/n' is back end, nights, and 'd/s' is day, salaried personnel, like the engineers and admins who work Monday through Friday, five days a week."

"And 'referral?'" Irma asked.

"People with serious problems are referred to a local counselor, here in Albuquerque, by their supervisors."

"By their *supervisors?*" Irma couldn't believe it.

"Generally there is no further contact with the Trust Line after that. We have good counselors in Albuquerque, and people prefer to speak with someone face to face. Our employees can go to these counselors for an hour every week, for a year or two, if it's needed. Winsome has excellent mental health benefits."

Irma thought, "Except for completely ignoring therapist-patient confidentiality and stereotyping-the-hell out of people who have done absolutely nothing wrong."

Softhousen spoke up. "Look. Let's just whip quickly through all your overheads. Then we'll go back and hit the most likely candidates in detail."

Irma shook her head in disgust.

"Fine," said Lindley. She placed the next dozen foils on the projector just long enough for them to scan the marked names.

They read in silence. Each time Softhousen wrote a name in his notebook Irma winced.

Lindley left the projector on, still showing the last foil, and turned on all of the lights.

"Perry Nerrid was in there!" exclaimed Softhousen.

Chapter 24

PERRY NERRID

Lindley shuffled back through her foils. She placed Perry's on the projector.

<u>Name and MHCS contacts:</u>
x Perry Nerrid, site safety manager, d/s

12/22/97	depression and anger due to divorce
12/25/97	" + suicidal ideation
1/6/98	"
1/13/98	" + family history of suicide by mother
1/19/98	" + witnessed murder of father by mother and mother's suicide + referral
2/15/00	" + anger at "useless psychological concepts" after 2 years of counseling
2/23/00	" + anger due to MHCS call to Winsome HR being divulged to his supervisor
3/1/00	" + angry questions concerning legal issues of confidentiality, and the effect on his Winsome career
7/1/00	"

"Whoa! This guy's loosing it," said Softhousen.

Irma spoke to Lindley. "'HR' is Human Resources?"

"Of course."

"How did he find out that the Trust Line counselor had called Winsome?"

"After his Christmas, 1997 call threatening suicide, I had Chen, who's his supervisor, talk to him and refer him to a counselor in Albuquerque."

"You told his *boss* about his suicide 'threat?'" asked Irma.

"We can't have an employee, especially a manager, killing himself at work. We probably saved his life." Lindley was smug and self-congratulatory.

Irma thought Lindley and the Winsome Human Resources Department were idiots. Paranoid, delusional, idiots. They perceived depressed, suicidal people as the enemy. It was an incredible injustice, and a stupid policy. Truly suicidal people were almost always dangerous to themselves, not to anyone else. Anyone could have "suicidal ideation"—even Lindley. Perry's mother committed suicide! The only way he could "deal with it" was to think about it!

Lindley had probably permanently alienated Perry and made him, justifiably, madder-than-hell. But Irma held this back. Instead she said, "Yet, after two years of counseling, he still seems to be extremely upset. His last call to the Trust Line was just four days ago. Is Perry an example of successful counseling?"

"He is a man with some real issues with anger, like so many men," Lindley's voice held a trace of concern.

It sounded to Irma like fake feminist compassion. She had heard it before. Lindley belonged to that school of feminism that thought of men as beasts first, and people second.

"Much of his anger apparently stems from his childhood," Lindley continued. "He admits coming from an abusive home. His mother was probably a battered spouse. It is typical for children who have been abused to suffer PTSD—post traumatic stress disorder—characterized by intrusion, constriction, hypervigilance, hyperarousal, anger, and depression. In addition, they often suffer from suicidal, and possibly homicidal, ideation. When Perry was a child he may have repressed this anger. So, in a sense, his expression of anger is an uncovering of repressed feelings and learning to be whole again—he is developing a fully integrated personality. It is a desirable therapeutic outcome."

Irma thought that really pissing off an employee was *not* a "desirable therapeutic outcome!" She had heard this psychobabble before. Shrinks on the witness stand often claimed their clients had suffered psychological damage. She had cross-examined them: "What behaviors can be measured which prove that someone suffering from 'intrusion' is different from anyone else?" The response was that these diagnoses were determined by the shrinks' "clinical intuition."

Irma fumed. Their argument was that psychologists had magic powers (i.e., "clinical intuition") and therefore were the only ones who could make these determinations. Witch doctors said the same thing. Their patients were inhabited by an evil spirit ("intrusion,") and the witch doctor was the only one who had the powers (the "clinical intuition") to see the evil spirit (the "intrusion") and cast it out (by forming a "therapeutic alliance.") So, psychologists defined the disorder, they claimed they were the ones who could see it, and they had the power to cure it as well. Irma had learned that this type of false reasoning was even called "the witch doctor fallacy."

A shrink's goal was apparently to develop a "coherent narrative"—strung-together psychobabble that sounded good to other shrinks. Psychobabble was intellectual mush: ill-defined words obfuscating every-day concepts. For instance, "hypervigilant and hyperaroused" apparently meant something like "nervous," "thin-skinned," "jumpy," "touchy," or "waking up on the wrong side of the bed."

In Irma's courtroom experience, psychologists and psychiatrists generally had no provable facts and, what was more frightening, couldn't collect scientific data which might show whether they could predict human behavior any better than any normal person. Their reliance on "clinical intuition" was a tip-off that they knew nothing about science. It was shocking to hear Lindley affirm the false prophecies of psycho-wisdom.

Softhousen raised his eyebrows. "Well, he had me fooled. He really seemed like an alright guy."

"Fortunately, most of these people are able to keep their work lives and private lives separated," Lindley spoke analytically. "We wouldn't know these facts were it not for our special relationship with the Trust Line. Perry acts like such a good employee at work that we fear he may be suffering from multiple personality disorder, as well."

"So, when someone is doing an outstanding job, it can be grounds to suspect that they are seriously mentally ill," Irma summarized.

"Of course," Lindley agreed. "And, you're right about MPD being a serious mental illness. Except now it's called dissociative identity disorder—DID for short. DID is quite serious."

Irma spoke earnestly, "You're saying that Perry did not bring his private life and problems into work. Instead you did; you brought his private life into work by telling Chen, his boss, about confidential conversations he had with his Trust Line counselor. Aren't you aware that work is often a refuge for people from their personal problems? Now you've taken that refuge away from Perry. His personal problems are here!"

"We were responding to a perceived emergency, which superseded his personal concerns," said Lindley, professionally. "The good of the many had to prevail over the good of the one."

"The good of Lindley must prevail over the good of the one asking for help," Irma thought. Now Lindley had absolute power over Perry's career, and she was ruining it. Irma tried to remain calm. She liked Perry. An unwelcome thought intruded: it might be a good idea for Irma to kill Lindley. Irma immediately hid this thought. "This emergency was perceived over the phone, by a counselor with no personal knowledge of Perry, a thousand miles away from here?" Irma could not keep a trace of anger out of her voice.

"Those counselors are highly trained. They have Ph.D.'s in psychology. It's best to take suicide threats seriously. Of course, there may now be some transference of Perry's anger toward his parents and himself to Winsome because of Chen's intervention. That, too, may be therapeutic."

"You *want* the employees here to be angry with Winsome?" Irma, and every other lawyer in the world believed in maintaining a professional standard of behavior at work. If you didn't, you risked being shot by your client. Professional boundaries were one of the keys to staying alive.

"We're like a family. Winsome management is often in a parental role. I'm sure you've heard of tough love," Lindley expounded.

"Yes, *with children*," Irma's voice was acid. "You've stated that the dynamics in Perry's family led to one of his parents being murdered, and the other committing suicide. Do you really want to bring those dynamics into work?" Irma kept herself from adding, "Are you nuts?"

"It's up to Perry to maintain the proper interpersonal boundaries at work. If he cannot, he will be fired. We have strict rules concerning harassment and stalking." Lindley remained unperturbed.

"So, it's okay for Winsome MHCS counselors to violate their ethical boundaries and the commitment of their profession to therapist-patient confidentiality, but it's not okay for employees to choose to disclose their counseling as they see fit?" Irma's eyes flashed in anger.

Lindley was not fazed. "Since Winsome has contracted to pay for the MHCS hot line, the MHCS counselors have both an ethical and contractual duty to Winsome. Those commitments, especially our financial control, outweigh any minor therapist-patient obligations MHCS counselors may develop toward our employees individually. Winsome's contract with MHCS simply supersedes our employees' rights to privacy."

"And Winsome employees are not told their confidentiality is secondary?" asked Irma.

"Of course not. If we did they would not use the Trust Line and we would not be able to track unstable employees." Lindley sniffed. The benefits of the policy were obvious. "You can see from this situation, where we have a murder at Winsome, how valuable knowing our employees' psychological diagnoses can be."

"That remains to be seen," Irma observed. "But back to Perry. Chen isn't a trained counselor. He's not Perry's therapist. He's in a position of authority, and he controls Perry's future at Winsome." Irma was still doing her best to remain as calm as possible. She was infuriated at Lindley's smugness. Perry had a perfect right to be angry at Winsome. Really angry.

"This guy looks like a *numero uno* wacko to me," Softhousen offered.

Irma spun in her seat. This was her turf. "Detective, if you go around arresting innocent people, you will destroy any case you may eventually develop against the real criminal. A good defense attorney will tear you apart. You'll be accused of making 'random arrests.' Every bit of this is hearsay. You can't use it in court."

"We'll see, counselor. We could subpoena the Trust Line counselors as witnesses, or take their depositions in L.A. Their narratives of their patients' counseling can go to what you counselors call *mens rea*—motive. A shrink can testify in court as to a defendant's mental state. And as experts, they can give their opinions. I didn't say I was making an arrest, but this guy goes on my short list of suspects. He certainly knew the victim."

Irma said, as evenly as she could, "All I'm saying is, someone who's divorced, or whose parents fought like a cat and a dog should not be labeled as a 'potential criminal.' They shouldn't be ratted on by their therapist. It is fundamentally unfair. It is bad public policy. Excuse the vernacular, but people don't like to be treated like shit. There is free will. People are not just reacting to their parents for the rest of their lives. To paraphrase Nietzsche, 'Freud is dead,' and so is all of this neo-Freudian nonsense. We are supposed to believe in a presumption of innocence in this country. We are supposed to assess people on their actions, not anyone else's, not their parents'."

"Calling a MHCS counselor is certainly an action," argued Lindley.

Irma was loosing her cool. "But it's not a criminal action. Legally what Larry said, *mens rea*—motive—is only relevant as it applies to criminal acts. A criminal act must occur before the assessment of *mens rea*. You are putting the cart before the horse. Seeking help from a therapist is not a criminal act. In fact it's just the opposite. It's likely to be someone who is actively trying not to do something untoward. It is absolutely wrong to criminalize therapy."

Lindley shrugged her shoulders. "But murder is a crime."

"And after the police make an arrest, then a psychological assessment may be ordered by the court." Irma felt her internal boundaries failing. Her urge to kill Lindley was getting stronger.

Lindley responded with absolutely sincerity. "We aren't in a court of law. As a private entity Winsome may choose to prevent violence by looking at motive first. It will be useful in this investigation—you'll see. Look at what Perry witnessed in his family: murder and suicide, in his family of origin! One of his role models murdered the other one, and then his remaining role model committed suicide. He's learned how to commit murder directly from his parents.

"Someone who has decided their own life is so worthless that they become depressed and suicidal has no reason not to murder, do they? What's to stop them? They aren't afraid of any legally imposed death penalty, since they've decided to kill themselves. They certainly don't belong at Winsome."

"So you're recommending firing everyone who, according to a Trust Line counselor, has ever had 'suicidal ideation?'" Irma asked.

Lindley nodded, "If it were completely up to me—of course."

"You're admitting that psychotherapy is worthless?" asked Larry.

Irma turned toward Larry, grateful for his question.

Lindley shook her head sadly in the affirmative. "We simply don't have the medical knowledge to diagnose and cure all of the chemical diseases of the brain."

Irma felt ready to explode. "So exactly what good does therapy do?"

"It warns us of psychopaths."

Irma barely restrained her anger. "The Trust Line counselors have remarkable powers! Predicting that Perry is going to commit suicide, presuming he hates women enough to murder Kelly, presuming his socialized internal restraints have completely broken down, and presuming that he has no religious, moral, or ethical beliefs. That's quite a feat of mind reading! What do we do now? Why don't we just execute him? Why even bother with evidence and a trial? With your extraordinary powers, we can eliminate the cost of having a legal system!" Irma shut up. She had lost it. She had just made the mistake of being completely honest and disagreeing with her boss.

Lindley smiled patronizingly. "Good points. You're right, I can't read his mind, but it's quite likely that Perry has a deep-seated fear of women, coupled with repressed anger at himself and at women.

"He may have been emasculated by his father's abuse of his mother. As a small child he could not protect his mother whom he loved from being battered. All he could do was impotently witness the emotional and physical carnage taking place around him. He could do nothing to protect himself from hearing the heart-rending screams of his mother as his father beat her. Emasculation leads to deep-seated, irrational, generalized anger, which may be directed at anyone, including us, including Winsome, including you. I should think you would be concerned for your own safety, at least."

Irma frowned and bowed her head in frustration. She now had an extremely strong urge to jump across the table and strangle Lindley—but "successfully repressed" it, as Lindley would say. Instead of killing Lindley, Irma said, "How much of what you just said can you prove? Isn't emasculation a rather passé Freudian concept? How sexual is a pre-pubescent child? And isn't the real problem in the situation you describe helplessness, which is gender-neutral?"

"Helplessness is part of emasculation." Lindley replied.

Lindley was an idiot, a parrot that could not think for itself. Time to fight sound-bite with sound-bite, thought Irma. "Or emasculation is part of helplessness."

"The order of the words is not important," Lindley stated. "Every time Perry closes his eyes, every night when he goes to bed, he probably recalls the screams of his mother and the angry snarling of his father. In order to protect itself the mind represses and dissociates. These self-defense mechanisms may have caused Perry's superego to have become so isolated from his id and ego that Perry sees himself as if he were outside of his own body.

"This is a form of learned sociopathology. Perry may know the difference between right and wrong, but he is so detached from himself that the rational part of his mind no longer takes responsibility for the parts of him that act and feel. In essence, he feels pain and anger, but watches these feelings from afar."

Irma wanted to scream, "This is all unprovable horse shit!" But she thought of a better tactic. "It sounds like you have taken a number of courses in forensic psychology."

"I have."

"Have you ever counseled Perry?"

"No."

"Are you close friends?"

"No."

"Have you talked with him in depth at any time?"

"No."

"Do you know any of his family?"

"No."

"Do you know any of his teachers?"

"No."

"Are you familiar with his scholastic record?"

"No."

"Do you know any of his friends with whom he went to school or grew up?"

"No."

"Do you know what he does with his free time?"

"Only what he's reported to the Trust Line counselor," replied Lindley, impassively.

"Lets look at some of these other suspects." Softhousen stopped Irma's cross-examination. He got her point: Lindley knew nothing about Perry as a person. To Lindley Perry was merely a psychological label.

Chapter 25

ELLEN RENCH

Ellen Rench was on the list.

<u>Name and MHCS contacts</u>:
x Ellen Rench, Lithography technician, f/n

11/11/99	depression and sleep disorder
11/15/99	" + loner, lack of male and female friendships
12/3/00	" + workaholic
1/13/00	" + family history, raised by single mother with four step-brothers
1/17/00	" + raped by all four step-brothers from age 12 through 18 + referral

Lindley had spoken with Ellen's Trust Line counselor several times. She remembered the conversations well and dispassionately related Ellen's story.

Ellen grew up with an alcoholic mother and four older stepbrothers in a dying steel town in Pennsylvania. Both her birth father and stepfather had run off; she couldn't remember either one.

All four stepbrothers became sexually attracted to her when she reached the age of twelve. She was long-legged and had short blond hair, blue eyes, and a tomboy's athletic good looks. She also had four miscarriages before she graduated from high school. Ellen figured each stepbrother was responsible for one of them. She couldn't remember how many times they had held her down and taken turns raping her. Sometimes two of them penetrated her at once, in different ways—they were creative rapists. It happened almost every day for six years. Six multiplied by three hundred and sixty-five—it was over two thousand rapes.

They took her whenever they felt the urge. Her mother was either not at home or slumped in an alcoholic stupor in front of the blaring television. Ellen's screams never brought her mother to her room. Not once. Her stepbrothers seemed to enjoy her screams, so she eventually stopped screaming. But it didn't help. They kept raping, and raping, and raping her. She never reported the gang rapes to anyone. She thought her stepbrothers would kill her if she did. They would finally tire and leave her alone after she became torn and bloody inside, outside, and at her wrists and ankles. She fell asleep soaked in their sweat and semen, and her own blood. Her mother washed the sheets.

Ellen wore long pants and oversized, long-sleeved sweatshirts to hide her wounds. Maxi-pads soaked up the blood. She stayed after school every day for as long as she could. Everyone thought she was weird for voluntarily coming to detention, but she studied hard and made good grades. She also worked at night and on the weekends washing dishes at a restaurant. But she had to go home to sleep. She had nowhere else to go—it was the only home she had. She hoped her stepbrothers would finally get enough, would get tired of gang raping her—but they never did.

Ellen joined the Air Force on the day she graduated from high school. Her stepbrothers made a point of gang raping her every night after that. The last time was the night before she took the bus to boot camp. At first light, she was gone. She left her blood-and-semen-soaked sheets behind.

The Air Force tests showed she had an aptitude for electronics. They trained her and assigned her to a service depot in Alaska. At the end of her tour she responded to an ad in *Stars and Stripes* and got a job as an equipment technician with Winsome Semiconductor Corporation. She was assigned to Fab 13 in Albuquerque.

Ellen had never had a boyfriend. And, she admitted to the Trust Line counselor, she had not had a Lesbian relationship either. In fact, she had no close friends at all. She just felt no attraction. The love stories she saw on TV and in the movies seemed fake. The Trust Line counselor reported to Lindley that Ellen felt like she had never had a home—she never wanted to see her mother or stepbrothers again.

Lindley summarized Ellen's conversations with Trust Line. Ellen was sexually conflicted and socially isolated— she hated men for obvious reasons, and she hated women because her mother had betrayed her by not protecting her.

Ellen at age twenty-nine was completely celibate "and another sociopath," Lindley concluded. "She is probably our most dysfunctional employee—even worse than Perry—extremely dissociated—a personality disorder— borderline schizophrenic."

Irma wept inside for Ellen. She'd heard similar stories, though not as bad, from angry women in law school. "Last time I checked being celibate wasn't a crime. We have no proof that she's done anything criminal yet, do we?" asked Irma. "So she is not technically a sociopath."

"Of course not. I stand corrected," said Lindley with a gracious smile. "She is a potential sociopath. Although celibacy is not a crime, it is evidence of serious psychological dysfunction."

Once again, thought Irma, psychobabble was squarely against public policy, and no one cared. Both popular religions and the law promoted celibacy. Fornication and sodomy, though widely practiced, were still crimes. Yet shrinks used celibacy against their clients, to prove they were nuts. The irony was that this sort of institutionalized psychological schizophrenia promoted "cognitive dissonance."

Lindley added that Ellen worked as much overtime at Winsome as she could, and it was a lot. She routinely put in eighty hours a week. The supervisors considered her to be the top technician at Fab 13. Though Ellen was complaining of depression and of having trouble sleeping to the Trust Line counselor, she never let these problems show at work. On the job she was always professional, enthusiastic about working at Winsome, and polite. Lindley concluded that Ellen also had dissociative identity disorder because she "hid" her problems so well.

"Ellen is dysfunctional because she is acting responsibly and morally!" Irma wanted to say. Apparently Ellen was "dysfunctional" because she was working her ass off for Winsome. Ellen was "dysfunctional" because she was struggling heroically to be a constructive, valuable, member of society, in spite of her continuing, heartbreaking loneliness. Ellen was "dysfunctional" because she had perfectly understandable fears due to her horrific family. Strangling was too good for Lindley. It would be much more satisfying if Irma were to kill her boss very slowly.

"If she weren't so high-functioning," Irma observed, "you might be able to find an excuse to fire her."

"Yes, it's too bad," agreed Lindley. "But if she starts emoting at work, you can be sure that we will find a way to let her go."

"Emoting—you mean showing her feelings?"

"That's right. Inappropriate displays of emotion are characteristic of an incipient psychotic break."

"So people who show their feelings at work are nut cases," suggested Irma.

"Well—I would never put it that crudely. But they certainly can be a danger to themselves and others. So the answer is—yes." Lindley was not afraid to speak the bare truth.

"Tell me something," said Irma. "Do you think you would ever recommend that Ellen be promoted to a position as a supervisor where she could influence other Winsome employees' careers?"

Lindley said, sweetly, "Of course not. Her past will be quite difficult to overcome."

"Regardless of her skills and accomplishments?" prompted Irma.

"She is *dissociative*, as I said. It's all an act," Lindley affirmed.

"Fixing machines and successfully accomplishing engineering projects are merely an act?" asked Irma.

"Of course. What other interpretation is possible?"

Irma wanted to say, "Perhaps those things indicate that someone is working like a dog for Winsome, that they love their job, and that they are worthy of promotion and recognition." But instead she asked, "How about recommending her for a job at another semiconductor company?"

"We generally find a way of letting other employers know about these people. We do it *sub rosa*—under the table." Lindley furrowed her attractive brow. "When another company calls and asks for a recommendation on a former employee like Perry or Ellen, we will say something like, 'You may wish to obtain additional background information.' That statement is always true, and it lets the other company know that the person they're considering has a skeleton in their closet."

"Just wondered. Thanks." This time Irma successfully hid her outrage. Her fantasy had changed. Now she imagined shooting Lindley in the back with a shotgun, in the parking lot, at night. But Irma wasn't sure whether it would feel better to blast an enormous hole in Lindley's heart, or to shoot her in the back of the head and blow her brains out through the front of her face. Either way, nothing of any value to Lindley, or society, would be lost.

Chapter 26

GOING POSTAL

Irma's image of Winsome was rapidly changing. Her initial impression that Winsome was making a real effort to be a positive influence in its employees' lives had become a certainty that Winsome—via its human resources and legal departments—was destroying anyone who did not fit its faddish psychological stereotypes. Winsome trainers called this psychological effect a "paradigm shift."

"One more thing," Irma added.

"Please," said Lindley, politely.

"Why not just cut an employee loose if they quit and look elsewhere for a job? Is it really necessary to let the next employer know about their psychological problems, *sub rosa*?"

Lindley was thoughtful. "We feel some social responsibility. We don't want an employee, even a former employee, going postal and hurting anyone else." It was clear that Lindley was proud of her role in protecting society from bad people. "As you know, there is always the potential for a lawsuit, and Winsome is a very, very deep pocket."

"And keeping a former employee from getting a good job will help?" asked Irma.

"As I'm sure you know, when employees end up hurting people at work employers are now being sued for negligently hiring employees without investigating their criminal backgrounds," Lindley explained. "The next step is for the preceding employer, the one who fired that employee and has knowledge of their aberrant psychological background, to be sued for failing to publicize that information.

"Also, an ex-employee who can't get a good job will have very little money to hire an attorney and sue Winsome for breaching their confidentiality. And as they unsuccessfully look for employment their legal option to sue will completely snuff because of their increasing poverty and the running of the statute of limitations. There is very little risk to Winsome for us to err on the side of caution."

Irma, added, helpfully, "Of course. Not hiring an attorney because of dire poverty and ignorance of the law are not reasons to postpone—what attorneys call "toll"—statutes of limitations. And, if Winsome is successful in keeping its policies secret, the fired employees will never know why they can't find work."

"Exactly," Lindley smiled. It was clear to her that this policy was helping Winsome to be in control of its own destiny—to exercise its corporate free will.

Irma decided it would be pointless to explain libel, slander, Title VII, the Age Discrimination in Employment Act, and the Americans with Disabilities Act to Lindley. In Lindley's view, "risk of foreseeable harm" overwhelmed all other considerations, including the simple courtesy of seeing Perry and Ellen as human beings with failings. Irma gave up. Attempting intellectual interchange with her boss was a waste of time. "Thank God none of the people on your confidential list have 'gone postal' yet." Irma agreed.

"Yes, thank God!" said Lindley, fervently.

"But even though it hasn't happened, you never know when it might. People are so unpredictable. Of course a mere violation of employee confidentiality is much less important than the risk of someone 'going postal,'" said Irma.

"Yes, that's right." Lindley was enthusiastic. "Better safe than sorry. The DSM-IV—that's the American Psychiatric Association's Diagnostic and Statistical Manual,

Fourth Edition—calls it the Intermittent Explosive Disorder. It predicts that people will behave unpredictably."

"And that makes so much sense!" Irma gushed. She just had to see how far Lindley would go. "I have seen the DSM-IV. We should permanently label the people who explode intermittently, or who have the potential to explode intermittently, as having a disorder. Any man who occasionally loses his temper obviously has a brain disease."

Lindley shook her head in violent affirmation. "Yes. Men, in general are quite disturbed and violent. They violently persecute women. You know every year in the United States men murder nine out of ten women."

"And if that were true every woman in the U.S. would already be dead," thought Irma. She knew that stupid statistic. Every year during law school, after its November release, she had made a point of looking at the FBI Crime Report. While it was true that men were responsible for nine out of every ten murdered women, they were also responsible for nine out of ten murdered men. In fact, Irma thought, men probably murder nine out of ten dogs, and nine out of ten cats. In fact Men committed ninety percent of all violent crimes, including assault and battery and armed robbery. Men were simple more violent than women. There was no gender war. Women weren't being singled out for persecution.

There was one statistic especially damming to women. Women murdered the majority of the living, loving, breathing, babies. Women were the champion baby killers. Of course the feminists in her class had said that it was perfectly understandable, due to "post-partum depression." But many of the children were murdered by their mothers years after childbirth. It was obvious that both men and women felt homicidal rage.

What about suicide? Irma had memorized the numbers of suicides in the United States. Every year 26,000 men and

5,000 women committed suicide. This, too, indicated that men were simply more violent than women—even when it came to killing themselves.

But Irma knew it was best to agree with her boss. "Nine out of ten women is an absolutely outrageous statistic. Men are beasts who don't deserve to live," Irma lied.

"Hey! That's unfair!" exclaimed Softhousen.

"Shut up!" Irma and Lindley said in unison.

Softhousen cringed and began doodling in his notebook. An old dog might be able to hold its own against one cat, but not against two.

"That's right, men are beasts who don't deserve to live." Lindley glowed with enthusiasm. "I have a copy of the DSM-IV at my desk. You are welcome to borrow it!"

"Thanks, I will," Irma gushed. "It really gives you quite a lot of power to have so much scientific insight into what other people, especially men, are thinking, doesn't it?"

"We bring in psychologists as consultants to help train all of our supervisory employees to identify the men who may 'go postal.' I think it is our most helpful training." Lindley was responsible for this proactive program.

"And don't forget about Ellen Rench," Irma interjected.

"Of course not. We must be vigilant against the occasional, very rare, violent woman, as well."

Well, Irma thought, at least Lindley was making an effort to be an equal opportunity idiot. "Do most Winsome HR personnel know about the DSM-IV?"

"Oh yes. Many of us either majored or minored in psychology. It is an excellent background for people in the helping professions."

Irma tried to identify exactly how being on Winsome's list of nut cases was being helpful to Perry and Ellen, who appeared by their actions at work to be excellent employees. She wondered how getting stabbed in the back by Winsome, *sub rosa*, would be helpful to them when they needed to find another job.

One of Irma's most vivid law school memories was the first thing her criminal law professor had said in class: "There is no such thing as thought crime in the United States. Your thoughts are your own. This is a free country. You are free to think anything, absolutely anything, you want to think. It is not a crime to even think about committing a crime. Here you are judged by your actions, not your thoughts. Thoughts—motives—are only relevant legally as they pertain to criminal actions."

How could Perry deal with his parents' murder and suicide without—what did shrinks call it—"mirroring" thoughts of murder and suicide himself? How could Ellen ever come to terms with her anger concerning her awful family without honestly expressing the horrible void in her life, the anger, the distrust that she had learned from her family? Irma couldn't imagine, *couldn't imagine* how Ellen felt. Winsome encouraged employees to talk to counselors who they said were warm, who they could trust. What moral right did those counselors have to violate that trust?

Perry and Ellen were "high-functioning," normal people who'd had some traumatic things happen to them. Okay, some *very* traumatic things had happened to them. But don't very traumatic things happen to everyone? People's children drown and die in car crashes. Soldiers see their buddies step on land mines. People have children crippled by birth defects. Every single person on the planet has parents, siblings, or spouses who will die—possibly slowly and agonizingly from cancer after first having contracted Alzheimer's disease. Do these things make everyone go postal?

Irma screamed the answer to herself, "No! This is pseudo-scientific psychological nonsense!" Psychologists *wish* they could understand, predict, and control everyone. That's their role. People want to feel great all the time. People wish there were "experts" who could fix their feelings the way surgeons fix gunshot wounds. People want to believe the march of technology has also fixed the angst of the human condition. Every human being on earth was going to die. Their parents and siblings were going to die. Their children and pets were going to die. Thoughts of death were not happy thoughts—and death was inevitable.

Irma knew she felt best when she dwelled on her own free will—when she believed that she would succeed or fail, have good relationships or bad, based on her actions, not on an external assessment of her thoughts by a shrink, or by a shrink wannabe like Lindley.

In college, Irma had become terribly depressed during a psychology course. She had begun wondering how many feelings she repressed as a child, how many secret parts of her brain she would never be aware of, and how all of this Freudian, Jungian, Adlerian, Reichian, Horneyan, and Rogerian stuff was wrecking her relationships with men.

Finally, in desperation, she began to think for herself. She discovered the source of her self-doubt: it was the intellectual mush she was being fed in class. She checked the index of every psychology text she could find in the library. Free will was erased as surely as if it had never existed. Free will—"belief in the efficacy of the self"—was missing from psychology. Instead of free will shrinks believed in B. F. Skinner and "operant conditioning." Irma knew to a certainty that she wasn't a rat in a maze, a pecking pigeon, or a salivating dog.

Shrinks believed in chemical brain disease. There was lots of evidence that the neuroleptic drugs shrinks fed their patients to "counteract chemical imbalances" actually damaged their patients minds—sometimes permanently. Irma had found dozens of books in the library written by Ph.D.'s, M.D.'s, and others, warning the public against the debilitating effects of psychiatric treatment, psychobabble, and drugs. She recalled some of the authors: Eve Bargmann, Peter Breggin, Bonnie Burstow, Phyllis Chesler, Lee Coleman, Lindsey Coombes, Gerald Coles, Robyn Dawes,

Seymour Fisher, Roger Greenberg, Martin Gross, Margaret Hagen, Ken Kesey, Joan Levin, Dianne McGuinness, August Piper, Ronald Leifer, Lou Marinoff, Jeffrey Moussaieff Masson, Robert Morgan, Jonas Robitscher, D. L. Rosenhan, Alan Scheflin, Peter Schrag, Nicholas Spanos, Thomas Szaz, Don Weitz, Sidney Wolfe, and Jay Ziskin.

Irma believed, passionately, that her belief in free will was essential to her mental health. She thanked God for her revelation. Free will was affirmed in the Bible, in Genesis, where it was a choice between good and evil. In a philosophy text Irma discovered that the Danish philosopher Søren Kierkegaard had championed free will without requiring a belief in organized religion. Irma decided, for herself, that she needed no elaborate religious or philosophical underpinnings for her belief in free will, other than that it was absolutely necessary for her mental health. Free will was her leap of faith.

Winsome encouraged its employees to speak their thoughts in confidence to a counselor. Then Winsome corrected any illusion its employees might have that they would be assessed on their good actions at work by having their supervisors confront them with their bad thoughts! What Winsome was doing was anti-therapeutic, unethical, illegal, and, if Perry was any indication, really pissing off its employees.

There is a saying. One of the most precious rights we have is the right to be left alone. Irma closed her eyes and assessed her feelings. She felt powerless to stop the corporate psychological juggernaut being driven by idiots like Lindley. There was outrage. There was frustration. There was anger. She found an expression that perfectly described how she felt: she felt like going postal.

Chapter 27

KISSIMMEES

Softhousen's beeper, lying passively on the table, suddenly buzzed and scooted around like a thing possessed. He chased it with both hands, grabbing it just as it fell off the edge—a successful snag. After scowling at the little liquid crystal display, he reached for the speaker phone and punched in a number.

"Softhousen," he said.

"Larry, it's officer Stewart," said the phone.

"Chewey, go ahead."

Irma was afraid to ask how officer Stewart had acquired the nickname "Chewey." From the background noise it sounded as if Chewey was in a car.

"Yo. We've just picked up the Kissimmees. We're en route."

"When you get to Winsome have the guard desk page Miss Laches," Larry ordered.

"Should be there in twenty minutes."

Softhousen punched the off button. Irma checked her watch and mentally added. They would be at Winsome by 10:30. It had been an early flight from California.

Softhousen was impatient. "So that's it? Our only two suspects so far are nut cases? Enough on them." He asked Lindley, "Do you have anything on Kelly's two friends, Troy and Tracey, that the Kissimmees mentioned?"

Lindley pulled a fistful of folders from her briefcase. "I brought all the summer hires' files." She quickly searched, then opened two of the folders. "Troy Gannet is an environmental engineer from Miami of Ohio. Tracey Siggs is an electrical engineering major from Virginia Polytechnic Institute. They both have excellent academic records— 3.9's—and are well rounded in their college pursuits, though we have no psychological information on them. Most universities won't release students' mental health records," she said regretfully.

"That's a shame," said Irma with great sincerity.

"It would be wonderful if the university counseling services would do psychological profiles on all of their students and share them with us," agreed Lindley. "We're working on it. Hopefully they will realize what a benefit it is to society for the semiconductor industry, in particular, to have a stable work force. You know that Winsome is the leader in the new technologies which are forming the backbone of the national economy for the new millennium."

Irma interrupted, "That is so true. Along with this new technology should come a new set of rules. Quaint notions of privacy and employee's rights are just impeding progress."

"Absolutely!" Lindley was enthusiastic. "In fact, college counseling information should be made available to all hiring employers. It would definitely improve the national economy. I believe the colleges will come around, eventually."

"That might also save Winsome a great deal of money in MHCS fees," Irma suggested.

"That's another benefit, definitely. We just wouldn't hire those people," Lindley agreed.

"Isn't it possible that Troy and Tracey both could have sociopathic backgrounds, or, at least, personality disorders?" Irma couldn't resist asking.

Lindley frowned. "If we only had the resources to do extensive background checks on their families. I have asked for the money, but those investigations are quite expensive. I'm afraid we will have to have an employee 'go postal' before we will get an adequate budget."

"This may be it. This may be your postal employee," Softhousen observed.

Irma decided that Lindley was clinically paranoid. She couldn't resist prodding to see just how paranoid. "The internet could be used to provide a means of instantaneous access to everyone's health insurance records. That way, anyone who wanted to subscribe to the health insurance records database—including other insurers or employers—could see if an employee had received counseling."

Lindley was enthusiastic, "Absolutely! In fact, that's already in place. Health insurance companies routinely share that sort of information with each other. I believe all Fortune 500 companies—especially those who self-insure—should have access to those insurance databases as well.

"But I have to admit that there has been some bad publicity. A female lawyer needed counseling after a divorce and complained to the New York Times that a subsequent insurance company denied her health care coverage. The new insurer had accessed her insurance records and had found out that she had mentioned suicide during her post-divorce counseling. They denied her new coverage on that basis."

Irma shook her head sadly. "It would be such a benefit to society for large companies to have unlimited access to everyone's mental health records. I can't imagine why an attorney would publicize her own counseling like that. Things work much more smoothly when it's all done behind the scenes, don't they?"

"They certainly do!" said Lindley, fervently. "People who are labeled by shrinks as being dysfunctional need to embrace the fact that their brains are diseased. They need to come to terms with being different than the rest of us. That lady lawyer should have just accepted the fact that she is mentally handicapped," Lindley was resolute.

"Yes!" Irma placed her palms firmly on the table. "If more people embraced their serious mentally illnesses and the inevitability of their own dysfunction when they come from dysfunctional families—even though they seem to be able to function adequately—and either self-committed themselves to mental institutions or sought psychiatric therapy, we might eliminate crime against women in this country!"

Softhousen pulled a wooden pencil from his sports jacket and held it rigidly between both hands. His teeth were clenched.

"Anyone who has a brain disease, especially men, should spare no expense—quit their jobs—leave their families—whatever it takes to get well," stated Lindley.

The pencil broke in Softhousen's hands, but he said nothing.

Irma glanced at the pencil without reacting. "Of course. Medical emergencies always come first. It will be expensive, though," she mused. "Is it worth the cost? The counseling is expensive, and many more psychiatrists and psychologists will have to be trained."

"Psychiatrists and psychologists have my greatest respect. They are so highly trained in the science of human behavior," said Lindley, reverently, "that they are worth every penny of whatever the market will bear."

Yes they are expensive, thought Irma, but they are seldom worth a cent. Numerous marriages were blown apart and thousands of people lapsed into deeper depression because of their counseling. There was case after heartbreaking case where patients committed suicide under the care of a shrink. Dredging up every painful, embarrassing, hateful, sexually inappropriate, angry moment in one's life, and then using all of that garbage to justify placing a "brain disease" label from the DSM-IV on a patient was not the way to mental health. One could spend years wallowing in one's own psychological feces, feeling like hell, pitifully depending on one's shrink for absolution. The shrinks even had shrinky labels for their toxic treatment: "psychiatrogenic" or "psychotropic" counseling which resulted in "learned helplessness." That was counseling which made people worse.

"We should spare no expense," said Irma. "Anything we can do to reduce the number of violent men will be more than worthwhile, even if most of those men are bankrupted in the process."

"The financial concerns are certainly secondary to women's safety," Lindley agreed.

"But it does seem a bit unfair that insurers can communicate this sort of private information amongst themselves, behind the employee's back, don't you think?" Irma asked.

"Insurers have a right to define the risks they insure against. I'm sure you know insurance is a contract into which both parties may freely enter. An insurer may investigate preexisting conditions. People often lie about having had counseling, and that denies the insurance company information they should have about that particular preexisting brain disease…"

Irma interjected, "…and anyone who doesn't like it has a right to self-insure. That is completely fair, especially for their children." Irma knew that "self-insurance" was a ridiculous, unreachable option for any but the very wealthy. Only large corporations had the resources to self-insure. Health insurance was a monopoly. It was play their game or risk financial ruin at every turn of the road, and watch the disease and death of one's children.

"Absolutely!" Lindley smiled. "A patient's reluctance to divulge their counseling history may be somewhat understandable, though. In the early days, the 1950's and '60's, there was quite a social stigma attached to seeking help from a mental health professional." Lindley oozed compassion.

"Really? I wonder why?" Irma asked.

"Counseling was a new form of medical treatment. It was treated with skepticism. Now it seems rather silly. Counseling is so widespread," Lindley explained.

Irma nodded in agreement. "But thank God we have it as a tool which predicts that depressed people, or those from bad families, or those who have bad life experiences, may go postal, so that we can eliminate them from the workplace."

"Thank God!" Lindley nodded.

Irma reflected on the hundreds of Vietnam veterans who had been prisoners in the POW camps in Hanoi, who were now doctors, lawyers, businessmen, and political leaders in the United States. No doubt Lindley thought they were sick people who should be whimpering and crawling to a psychiatrist. They and been through the worst kind of prolonged, brutal, dehumanizing trauma. It was wrong for them to be doing so well.

Irma tried to think of a more satisfying way of killing Lindley than by shooting her with a shotgun. Repeatedly stabbing her would be personally satisfying in a way that merely pulling the trigger of a gun would not. Stabbing involved physical exertion: the up and down motion of the arm. In fact, it would be wonderful exercise—great for her abs.

But, there was still something very liberating about the explosion, the smell of gunpowder, the spray of blood and bone, and the instant death caused by a shotgun. A double barrel 12-gauge, Irma thought, would be best; loaded with double-aught buckshot. Firing both barrels at once—the kick would be brutal and the buckshot would go clean through Lindley's skinny body. Irma recommitted herself to the gun. Holding it firmly against her shoulder would minimize the bruising caused by the recoil.

"But do you think this widespread use of counseling, where people are encouraged to voice their most violent thoughts, even if they are only passing fantasies, in any way encourages people to voice things they would not otherwise have mentioned prior to this era? Do you think our societal preoccupation with this voicing of dysfunctional thoughts in any way encourages people to have dysfunctional thoughts and behave in dysfunctional ways?" asked Irma.

Lindley looked perplexed. "Hmmm. So you're asking if counseling can become a self-fulfilling prophecy and actually encourage dysfunction?"

"Exactly." Irma wrote "self-fulfilling prophecy" on her pad.

"You're confusing cause and effect. The cause of a person seeking counseling is dysfunction," Lindley patiently explained. How simple it really was.

"But isn't the nature and definition of a self-filling prophecy that what appears to be "the effect" can subtly turn out to be "the cause?" It can either cause "the effect," perpetuate "the effect," or exacerbate a small problem and turn it into a big one. Don't psychologists believe that we all have the ability to pick up the non-verbal cues which are given out unconsciously by others?" Irma continued.

Lindley sat back in her chair and placed her hands behind her head. "Of course. But psychologists are trained to not interfere with their clients. They observe passively."

Irma actively wrote down "passive observation," then said, "If they really wanted to observe passively wouldn't they use an intercom, a mechanical voice, and observe from another room through a one-way mirror so they couldn't be seen?"

"Of course, experimental psychologists used to do that," said Lindley. "Now we have moved on. Being in the client's presence is part of experiencing their world. However psychologists do ask carefully edited, neutral questions which do not reveal their own biases."

"But isn't it inevitable they will non-verbally communicate their unconscious desires to their patients? They must have unconscious parts of themselves, mustn't they?" Irma scribbled "non-verbal communication" on her pad.

"Perhaps psychologists have unconscious parts of their minds. But they know themselves better than most of us. Many of them have been through psychoanalysis." Lindley's voice held a tinge of awe when she spoke the word "psychoanalysis."

"So, people who have been psychoanalyzed have a smaller unconscious than the rest of us have? Can this be shown by any sort of empirical test?" asked Irma.

"All of this is silly. It sounds like something an experimental psychologist would say." Lindley said the word "experimental" with disdain. "No one has ever seen the unconscious, and we don't know where it exists, physically, in the brain. Clinical intuition requires personal interaction."

Irma was certain she finally had Lindley cornered. "So the concepts 'the subconscious' and 'repression' are used by psychologists only when they are convenient? When they apply to others? Are they merely hypothetical constructs?"

Lindley was mildly outraged. "Those ideas have helped millions of people! They are quite useful."

Irma wondered how much Perry and Ellen were being helped by having their "repressions" evaluated by Winsome, instead of their actions. "Let me finish my thought," said Irma. "By definition, a person cannot be aware of that which is unconscious?"

"That's true."

"Therefore, psychologists cannot be aware of the unconscious cues they are providing to their patients."

Lindley was unperturbed. "I'll have to think about that. The point you're making seems to have more to do with semantics that it has to do with the real world."

"Perhaps it has more to do with sound reasoning. It is a simple syllogism: All people with functioning minds have a subconscious. Psychologists are people with functioning minds. Therefore psychologists have a subconscious."

"Psychologists believe reason cannot always be trusted. Our feelings are our best guides," said Lindley, smugly.

"Either people in general have a subconscious, or they don't. They can't have one only when it's convenient. You're saying determining whether psychologists have a subconscious is a matter of feelings?" Irma wrote "FEELINGS!" all in caps, on her pad.

"Feelings and dreams. Sigmund Freud discovered the unconscious mind, largely through his work with dreams," Lindley explained.

Irma felt like giving up. Now Lindley was relying on an appeal to authority. After all, if Freud said it, it must be true. It was difficult—impossible—to have a rational conversation with someone who didn't believe in reason. "Our feelings are our best guides. Wow! This meant that a group of people who "felt" that someone was guilty of a crime were justified in holding a lynching. Apparently Lindley's job was to "lynch" Winsome's employees—to destroy their careers with information given under a false promise of confidentiality.

Irma tried to get her point across one last time. "Don't you think people seek counseling also when they experience the kind of unhappiness that we all experience during a divorce, or the loss of a loved one?"

"Well, of course…" Lindley admitted.

"Then if they voice some violent fantasies which we all probably have but usually don't talk about, and also have an unhappy childhood, they get branded as someone who is "dangerous," who "may go postal." Is that fair?"

"Fairness has nothing to do with it," Lindley stated, firmly. "We feel it's a matter of survival, of protecting innocent people from being killed by someone who goes postal."

Irma spoke softly, "California law requires both therapist-patient confidentiality and adherence to the American Psychiatric Association ethical canons."

"Well," said Lindley, "You should know that laws like that are simply ignored. Even if they were not, how many employees in New Mexico are going to know to look them up? We can count on their ignorance of the law. Also, Winsome is not a member of the APA, our HR personnel are not counselors, nor are we in California, so those laws don't apply to us here in New Mexico."

Irma thanked God, for the millionth time, that she was an attorney. She would never, under any circumstances, use Winsome's Mental Health Counseling Service, now that she knew the way the information was misused internally, or could be divulged and misused by insurance companies, succeeding employers, and the police.

Softhousen glanced up from examining Troy and Tracey's folders. "I don't see anything incriminating in their records. We'll have to actually talk to them."

Irma's pager went off. She glanced at it and dialed the security desk.

"Smith. There is a couple here at the desk—the Kissimmees—accompanied by an APD officer."

"Please give them temporary badges. I'll be right there." Irma punched the off button.

"I'll have Troy here for you at 11:00, and Tracy at 11:30. Will that be alright?" Lindley asked Softhousen.

"Yeh," he grunted.

Lindley excused herself to round up Troy and Tracy as Irma and Softhousen left to go to security. The hallway walls passed quickly. At the Fab 13 main entrance two slender white-haired people stood awkwardly next to an APD officer.

Softhousen stuck out his hand as he approached them. "Detective Larry Softhousen."

"John Kissimmee. This is my wife Susan," the old fellow replied. They warmly shook Softhousen's hand.

Irma introduced herself as politely as she knew how. The Kissimmees started to smile, but as soon as she said her name, they pulled back and remained distant. Irma felt hurt. She really wanted to be nice to these people. But apparently her role now was to be a corporate attorney. She was the enemy.

As they walked back down the immaculate hallways Irma asked if the Kissimmees had been provided breakfast on their flight. They said they wanted to talk, not eat. Irma led them to the meeting room.

The door to 313 clicked shut and they all sat down.

Mr. Kissimmee asked, "Do you know the cause of death yet?"

Softhousen spoke carefully, "We normally do not release a cause of death, or speculate publicly, until we receive the formal report from the medical examiner. So this is preliminary and could change. I trust you to keep it completely confidential. A premature release of this information could not only prevent us from catching the criminal, but it could weaken our case in court. A defense attorney could make it sound like we were floundering around, guessing, ready to arrest anyone just for the sake of making an arrest. Do you understand how important it is to keep this confidential?"

Both of the Kissimmees nodded.

"It appears right now that Kelly died of nitrogen suffocation as part of a project she was working on in the clean room here at Winsome," Softhousen explained. "However, there are also strong indications of criminal activity, and we don't know if the suffocation was accidental or not. That's where we are."

"So it's possible that her death was accidental?" asked Mr. Kissimmee.

Softhousen replied, "Yes sir. That's possible. We haven't ruled it out, yet."

"Is anyone under arrest?" Susan Kissimmee asked.

"No. We have leads and evidence, which, of course, we are pursuing as we speak."

"But no arrests?" asked Mr. Kissimmee.

"If we rush things and arrest the wrong person, once again, it could weaken our case against the real criminal later. It could make the real arrest look like just one of a series of false arrests," replied Softhousen. "We want to get this person."

Mrs. Kissimmee seemed lost in thought. "What is Winsome's position on all of this?"

Irma was thrilled. This was her first chance to be a corporate attorney under fire. "We are fully cooperating with the investigation. We can't have criminals running around Winsome. It puts everyone here at risk."

"And the nitrogen?"

Irma summarized what Perry had said about the nitrogen and not feeling like suffocation. She held back the information about shutdown, the plastic sheets, the power outages, and Kelly's not having attended any of the shutdown planning meetings.

John Kissimmee suddenly looked angry. "It sounds like something that could have been anticipated. A very dangerous thing for a college intern to be around..." He waited for Irma's response.

Since she didn't know what to say, she said nothing. But she thought Mr. Kissimmee was right. Perry hadn't prepared Kelly adequately. From what she had seen, the shutdown was too complex to have an inexperienced, unsupervised college student in the clean room. But she couldn't say what she thought. It was her job to be Winsome's attorney, not the Kissimmee's.

"Well?" asked Mr. Kissimmee, angrily.

Irma would have to have a meeting with Perry, Winsome's general liability insurance carrier, the excess insurance carriers, and Chen as well, to decide how to handle the Kissimmees. She wrote a quick note to herself.

She cleared her throat and looked up. "Uh, I'm not a technical person. Winsome needs to finish its investigation as well…"

"And you're not going to blame Winsome under any circumstances! Isn't that right?"

Irma thought she had better also include Winsome's chief corporate counsel in the meeting. It would have to be a teleconference.

She tried to keep her tone as reasonable as possible. "Mr. and Mrs. Kissimmee, it's a bit early to start assessing blame, before we know all of the facts. We have no idea how much of this is due to any criminal activity…"

"…or Winsome's negligence!" interrupted Mr. Kissimmee.

Irma sighed. "Or any possible negligence on Winsome's part, you are right."

"How are we supposed to get the facts?" asked Susan Kissimmee, on the verge of tears.

"The Albuquerque DA's office has a victim-witness coordinator, Miss Joy Harper, who will stay in touch with you," answered Softhousen, acting as peacemaker. "She will keep you informed of how the case is progressing and the court dates." He handed them one of Joy's business cards. "We will take you to the DA's office today to meet her."

"What about Winsome?" Julia asked Irma.

"I am your contact," stated Irma, simply. She pushed her card across the table.

Mr. Kissimmee was still angry. "I suppose you won't tell us anything."

Irma was a soothing as possible. "There are a number of things I can tell you. I'm sure Winsome is insured for the deaths of employees at work. I don't have a copy of that policy, and don't know its exact terms, but I will get the name of the correct insurance person for you. They will be able to answer specific insurance questions. There may be other benefits that are due to you as next of kin through the normal employee benefits process at Winsome. The person to contact for those questions is Lindley Meddlar." Irma wrote down Lindley's name and phone number and gave it to Mr. Kissimmee. "In addition, I will do my best to have the appropriate people contact you first, so you don't have to track anyone down. If there are any problems or other questions, please call me."

"You mean, any problems besides having our daughter negligently killed?" asked Mr. Kissimmee.

Susan Kissimmee started to weep. Irma choked up and could say nothing.

"And where do we get a lawyer?" Mr. Kissimmee continued.

"The New Mexico State Bar Association has a lawyer referral service. Just a moment." Irma tried to surreptitiously dry her eyes while she extracted an Albuquerque phone book from the shelf below the windows. She copied down the number and gave it to them. "They can refer you to an attorney."

Softhousen raised his eyebrows.

Mr. Kissimmee looked surprised. "Are you advising us to get an attorney?"

"No, I'm not. It is unethical for me to give you any legal advice. I can tell anyone, though, about the referral service."

Julia stopped crying. "Why is it unethical…?"

"The legal system in the United States has a strong policy of separate representation. It is a conflict of interest for me to represent you in any capacity since I work for Winsome."

"But you just told us to get an attorney," said Susan.

"No I didn't. I would tell a stranger on the street about the lawyer referral service, if they asked."

Softhousen looked apologetic. "You understand that a police investigation is confidential, even from the parents of a victim, don't you? I'm sure you want to help us catch the criminal. The best way to do that is to let us get on with our investigation. I've actually told you more than I should."

"And Kelly's…body?" asked John Kissimmee, bravely.

"Please contact the Medical Examiner." He wrote Mercedes' phone number on one of his cards. "She is legally the official custodian."

Irma felt as if she were sharing the Kissimmee's thoughts. They were both on the verge of panic, and felt angry and helpless. They could do nothing for Kelly now except to let people who didn't care about the real Kelly— the police—do their jobs.

"Custodian!" It sounded as if Kelly were a piece of trash. The next step was to get more people who didn't know Kelly—the lawyers, Winsome human resources staff, and the insurance company—involved. None of them cared about Kelly either. They cared about their jobs. Irma turned her head to the wall and held back her tears. She also knew that an attorney might do them absolutely no good. It depended on whether the Workmen's Compensation statutes in New Mexico absolutely barred suits for wrongful death against employers. Had Kelly's death occurred "in the ordinary course of employment?" If a subcontractor had negligently placed the visqueen over the air returns, they might have a chance of getting around the Workemen's Comp bar, and at least being able to sue the subcontractor.

There was a knock at the door. Irma quickly rose and slipped out of the doorway into the hall. As she closed the door behind her a very intense, dark-haired young man examined her face.

"Troy Gannet," he said. "Lindley Meddlar told me to be here at 11:00."

Irma thought quickly. She didn't want a murder suspect meeting the victim's parents. "Please go down to the cafeteria. We'll meet you there in five minutes."

"Oh…sure."

As Troy walked away, Irma opened the door and found Softhousen shaking the Kissimmees' hands.

Irma asked, "Do you have a place to stay?"

Softhousen answered for them. "After they meet Joy Harper, we're taking them to the Albuquerque Hilton. They can rent a car from there and go to another hotel, or stay there if they want."

Irma nodded. She wished she could help, but even offering to pay the hotel bill would probably look like a Winsome bribe. "I'll walk you to the entrance," was all she could think to say.

The four of them walked in silence to the security desk where Chewey was waiting.

"Goodby," said Irma.

The Kissimmees walked out into the bright New Mexico sunshine without shaking her hand.

Chapter 28

INTERNS

Irma and Softhousen found Troy sitting in the corner of the Winsome cafeteria, tapping his fingers on the table. They all bought drinks and returned to 313.

"So you met Kelly during new hire orientation?" Softhousen asked Troy as they sat.

"She's hard not to meet, you know? She's so attractive and outgoing. She was interested in environmental engineering, too," said Troy.

"The two of you had that in common?" Softhousen confirmed.

Troy answered breezily, "She was really more into the safety side, but environmental and safety kind of fit together..."

"Did you meet her the first day of the class?" Softhousen flipped open his notebook.

"I'm pretty sure—yeh, I'm sure. They did this introduction thing, where they went around the room and everybody had to introduce themselves. She sat in front, on the left. It was hard not to notice her...You know what I mean," said Troy.

Softhousen wrote something in his notebook. "You became friends?"

Troy's face saddened noticeably. "Yeh. Tracey and me and her."

"You met Tracey in the class, too?"

"Nah. We met on the flight to Albuquerque. We both changed to Cattle Car Airlines in Dallas. We had seats next to each other."

"Cattle Car...?" asked Irma.

Troy shifted in his seat and looked at Irma. "It was pretty funny. It's that airline that flies around the southwest part of the United States. They don't have assigned seats. So the plane was late and we're all milling around the gate, you know, trying to be first in line to get decent seats, and someone starts mooing like a cow. You know, 'mooooooh,' a pretty good imitation. Pretty soon there are people laughing, and everyone is doing it. Like seventy people all going 'mooooooh, mooooooh, mooooooh.' It was the funniest thing I've ever seen. Even the guys in business suits, 'mooooooh.'

"So I was standing next to Tracey, and she's going 'mooooooh,' and I'm going 'mooooooh.' The ticket agents were all as red as tomatoes. They didn't know what to do. It was a spontaneous mass protest; anarchy in action at a gate in the Dallas airport! The people walking past were laughing their heads off. The stewards, stewardesses and pilots from other airlines who walked by were laughing. Everybody was laughing except the Cattle Car Airlines personnel.

"The people coming out of the plane were frightened for a couple of seconds, but then they figured out what was going on and they joined in, 'mooooooh, mooooooh, mooooooh.' Then we had over a hundred people doing it. Everybody kept 'mooooooohing' until they started boarding. It must have gone on for five minutes."

Irma put her hand to her face. She couldn't hide her huge grin. She knew exactly which airline it was.

"And that's how you and Tracey met?" Softhousen continued.

"It was a very 'moohving' experience," said Troy, with a straight face.

"The flight to be here to work at Winsome?" Irma verified.

"Yeh."

"And you're still friends?" asked Softhousen.

"Me and Tracey? Sure, why not?"

"So, what did you do the first day of orientation?" Softhousen wrote briefly in his notebook.

"You mean what did they cover in class?"

Larry was patient. "Not the class. What did the three of you do? Did you go out to lunch or dinner together?"

"Yes, I think we sat in the cafeteria at lunch and talked about our schools and Winsome and how easy the intro class was...stuff like that. After class we went to Ranchitos, you know, the Mexican food place in Corrales, for dinner."

Irma butted in, "Just the three of you?"

"A coupla' others from the class came too."

"Do you recall their names?" asked Softhousen.

Troy pursed his lips in thought. "Zipper Wiles, Sherry Bota, and Trees Algodones."

Softhousen quickly wrote down the names. "So there were six of you there."

"That's right, six."

Irma also wrote down the names. "Have you all kept pretty tight? Do you still get together?"

"Yeh, sure."

"Did Kelly have a boyfriend—someone she met in class maybe?" Softhousen's voice was neutral.

"I don't think so. She seemed pretty conservative about stuff like that. You know—cautious."

"So none of the guys were..." Softhousen's voice trailed off.

"Friends, just friends. Kelly was intense. She was really into Winsome. She wanted to ace her project and learn everything there was to know about semiconductor manufacturing."

"How about the others who were there?" Irma asked.

There was a knock at the door. Irma quickly slipped into the hall.

"Tracey Siggs." A smiling, slender, redhead held out her hand.

Irma introduced herself, then said, "Tracey, I'm sorry, we can't speak to you right now. Could you have lunch with us at noon, in the cafeteria?"

"Sure."

Irma slipped back through the door and returned to her seat next to Softhousen.

Softhousen was still questioning Troy. "How did you spend yesterday? Was it your first day back after the Fourth?"

"Uh, I'm preparing a summary of this year's air emissions legislation, and how it may affect Fab 13's emissions limits."

"So, you were working on that in your cubicle?" Softhousen persisted.

"Yeh, at least I was around the environmental engineering group's cubes all day. I had to get some numbers from reports other people had done."

Irma broke in, "Have you worked in semiconductors before? Do you have any experience running any of the equipment in the clean room?"

"Nah. Environmental engineering is sort of a mixture of law and engineering. I've had a course in end-of-pipe treatment systems—you know, scrubbers and fluidized charcoal recovery units. We played around with working models in the lab. Also, Miami has a good set of analytical laboratory instruments which we work with—mass spectrometers, residual gas analyzers, gas chromatographs, flame ionization detectors, x-ray fluorescence detectors, Geiger counters—stuff like that. But only the EE's get to work on the semiconductor equipment. But I've seen it—nothing like what Winsome has here. It's a bunch of old stuff."

Irma looked at her watch, then at Softhousen, then at Troy. "Is there anything else—anything you can remember about Kelly or anyone who knew her, which may be relevant to her death?"

Troy thought for several seconds, then looked up. "No...no. I have no idea why anyone would do something like that."

Irma wondered if Troy secretly belonged to that environmental action group. What was it called? "GreenWar" was its name. Environmentalists could be pretty militant...similar to those right to life folks willing to kill people. "Does Winsome Semiconductor have a pretty good reputation, environmentally?"

"Basically. I think they had some cleanup issues with some land they purchased in California. You know, superfund site stuff. But they inherited that problem from the previous owner. Other than that, Winsome's reputation is good. From what I've seen Winsome tries to cross all the T's and dot all the I's of what's required. The only problems here have been some acetone in the wastewater discharge, fugitive solvents, smelly stack emissions, NOX from the boilers, and high water consumption. But, none of it's really serious. I think they are trying to comply. They have cooperative research and development agreement— CRADA—projects with Sandia Labs and Los Alamos Labs to reduce the water consumption and air emissions. I don't know all of the details."

Irma remembered Lindley's point about not having information about the students' families. "Anyone in your family, or any friends involved in semiconductor work?"

"Nah. They think it's pretty neat though. My family has a web site on the Internet. My friends from high school are all doing different stuff. Most of them are still in college, and don't know what they want to do, but I don't think any of them are doing anything having to do with semiconductor manufacturing."

Irma had no more questions. "Thank you."

"Yeh. Thanks," said Softhousen. "If you remember anything at all, in addition to what you've told us, please contact Miss Laches or me."

Softhousen and Irma slid their business cards across the table.

Troy nodded, picked up their cards, and walked out.

After the door shut, Irma turned to Softhousen. "Seems like a decent kid."

"Yeh."

"Lunch?"

"Yeh."

*　　*　　*

Irma spotted Tracey sitting at their unofficial murder investigation table. Irma introduced detective Softhousen. Tracey stood up and shook his hand.

The three of them got lunch and Irma and Softhousen went through the same litany of questions they had asked Troy.

Irma felt old, looking at and listening to Tracey being questioned by the detective. It was disconcerting, but she had a persistent thought that Tracey was sixteen. Irma knew better. She had to be at least eighteen to be hired by Winsome as a college intern. It was just her appearance and manner of speaking that were young. "I really am getting old," thought Irma. Then she thought, "So is everyone else. Deal with it! Grow up!" She began fiercely taking notes.

Tracey gave the same answers they had received from Troy.

Finally Softhousen asked, as if he were just making conversation, winding things up, "Do you have any family or friends who work in semiconductors?"

Larry was subtler than Irma had thought. He was even a fair actor. Suddenly she picked up a flash of emotion—subconscious body language from Tracey which riveted her attention. Tracey had looked away for just a moment—a micro-second of panic. She'd seen it in the courtroom a hundred times. It was a 'gotcha' for the attorney doing the cross-examination. Larry was onto something.

Tracey smiled. "No, not really. My Dad and brothers are double-E's, but they don't do semiconductor equipment engineering."

"So you come from a whole family of engineers?" Softhousen verified.

"Well, not my mother. She's just a homemaker."

"Nothing wrong with that," said Irma.

"No, of course not."

"And, your whereabouts yesterday?" asked Softhousen.

"I was monitoring startup in Thin Films. My personal project is to review the shutdown and startup procedures written into the maintenance specs, meet with the techs, engineers, and operators, and then make recommendations for changes. The idea is to look for areas where Winsome can save time and money by looking at all of the equipment and personnel in a functional area as a whole—from a systems approach."

"So, you're already pretty familiar with the equipment which is used in Thin Films?"

"Sure, a bit. We have a good semiconductor lab at school, and I've specialized in thin films, especially ion implantation. I think that's why I got this position this summer."

They were finished eating. Irma stood and smiled. "Thanks for sacrificing your lunch to speak with us."

"Well, I hope it helps to find whoever killed Kelly." Tracey stood up.

They all smiled, shook hands, and Tracey left to get back to work.

Softhousen and Irma both got iced coffee for dessert and sat down.

"What do you think?" Irma spoke first.

"I dunno. She's familiar with the machines."

"She started to panic when you asked about her family."

"I didn't see that."

"I did, and I'm sure. Did you hear how careful her answer was? She never told us who her dad and brother work for or what they do—no specifics."

"You think she could have a motive for sabotage?" Softhousen took a sip of iced coffee. "She gets into Winsome as a college intern in order to cause millions of dollars of damage to help the company her family works for?"

"Maybe something like that. This industry is so competitive that just delaying the introduction of a new product, or even slowing down a product upgrade by a few weeks could give a competitor an edge." This was the Winsome company line, but Irma thought it was true.

"So these new products—the competition—can you find out who they are?"

"I think so." Irma scribbled on her pad. She was getting excited. Maybe Lindley wasn't totally off base about background investigations. Chen was the man. He could put her in touch with the head of product engineering at corporate headquarters in Silicon Valley, Santa Clara, California. She needed to find out about new products and competition and correlate that information with family backgrounds, especially Tracey's family background.

"What next? Do we interview Zipper Wiles, Sherry Bota, and Trees Algodones, or do we follow this lead? Do you think this could be some kind of conspiracy?"

"I have no more idea than you do about a conspiracy. But I think it's pretty unlikely in three weeks—these kids are from all over the country. This is still only a theory; right now we only have means and opportunity for Tracey, no real motive."

"Why don't we just fingerprint her? You've got that partial from the glove. All we need is a match."

"Come on, counselor. That's a seizure. Ya gotta arrest 'em to fingerprint 'em, and ya gotta have probable cause for the arrest, which we don't got."

Irma turned red. It was embarrassing to get lectured on the law in bad English. And it was law she should have remembered.

Softhousen finished his coffee. "But I'll call downtown and get a check through the FBI database. Maybe she was in ROTC and has been printed already."

They walked to the little meeting room next to the cafeteria where they had originally interviewed Steve, Ellen, and Drew.

Irma called Sally and got her finding out about the head of product engineering, and trying to locate Chen. Then she called HR to get Zipper, Sherry, and Trees down there every half-hour for interviews, starting as soon as possible.

Softhousen called one of his cronies at APD to find out about Tracey's fingerprints.

Chen burst into the room, "What have you found out?"

Irma explained her "slowdown" theory of sabotage.

"So Kelly's hands could just be a smokescreen? Something to send us scurrying around looking for psychopaths, so we waste Winsome's time and money psychoanalyzing every employee on site, trying to hypnotize them, and figure out at what age they were potty trained?" asked Chen.

"That's the idea," Irma said, dryly.

"Maybe the only psychology involved here is greed and old-fashioned family loyalty," added Softhousen.

Chen interlaced the fingers of his hands behind his head, looked at the ceiling, and then at Irma. "What do we need to do?"

"We need to find out the family employment of every intern or recent hire who has access to the clean room. And we only need details if they are somehow connected to the semiconductor industry. Will you okay a budget?"

Chen nodded, "Irma I want you to monitor the amount expended and to coordinate the investigation. I want a daily email with cost-to-date and a one-sentence progress report."

Irma nodded, scribbling on her pad.

Chen punched up Sally on the speaker phone. "Sally, get Lindley and Sergeant Smith here, room 313, right away."

"Yessuh," Sally drawled. Irma could see Larry's ears perk up and imagined his tail starting to thump.

"No new sabotage today?" Irma asked Chen.

"None yet." Chen buried his head in his hands for a moment. "You know, if I were in this saboteur's shoes, I would let Fab 13 repair all of this damage, just about get the fab up and running, and then hit us again and knock us down for another few weeks. A few good shots like that and we would have to think seriously about closing the place."

"Closing...?" Irma was shocked.

"This is an old fab," Chen explained. "We run only six-inch wafers. We don't run the latest processes—the multi-layer metallizations and associated planarizing on the twelve-inch wafers the new fabs are running. Fab 13 only makes money because we have a good workforce who can run the hell out of this old equipment, and because product engineering in California has been successful at re-engineering the commodity parts, like the flash memories, so they can be manufactured on our six-inch technologies. It's a constant fight to keep this place alive."

Irma was surprised. "But we are running some state-of-the-art parts, aren't we? Isn't there fierce competition from other companies who manufacture products very similar to Fab 13's?"

"Sure," Chen agreed. "The fiercest is probably with Advanced Mammary Devices—AMD. They are rushing to get their own version of the product Winsome has already developed for breast pumps to market. We are going to revolutionize breast-feeding and refrigeration in the third world. It's an enormous market which moves around so much that it's almost a full-time job for me to keep my eye on it. Winsome has been milking the profits, and now we are moving production to our commodity lines in advance of the competition.

"The Lizard lots were the first of Fab 13's new commodity shrink of the BPC—the breast pump chipset. If we can run it, this shrink will almost double our productivity for these devices. The biggest challenge for the breast sets are the deep implants they require. It's difficult, technically, to control deep implants without a lot of engineering hands-on," Chen concluded.

Larry's face was about to explode in laughter. Irma gritted her teeth and succeeded in not smiling. She couldn't stop thinking about that famous class-action suit against Dow Corning. She also remembered an article she'd read in a radical student newspaper in college. "Don't advanced breast pumps threaten companies like Fig Leaf, which export so much infant formula to the third world? Widespread use of breast pumps could seriously reduce the use of infant formula, worldwide."

"Absolutely, though I haven't heard of any real complaining by Fig Leaf, except," Chen thought for a moment, "their president, 'Babbs' somebody, I think, hates the computer industry on loss of privacy grounds."

"We'll add that to our search of family employers." Irma scribbled "infant formula co.'s" on her pad.

"Probably a good idea," Chen affirmed.

There was a knock at the door.

Lindley and Sergeant Smith came in and took the remaining chairs. Irma explained the family background investigations they needed. Lindley said, "Winsome HR can handle this, easily…"

Chen interrupted, "You may need to get some outside help. Smith has contacts with private investigators. Don't hesitate to use them. Divide up the tasks so we get this information as quickly as possible. Performance is the bottom line, not who found what. Clear?"

"Yes sir." Lindley looked a bit taken aback.

"Just do it," ordered Chen.

"Let's restrict the investigation to their family's employers, nothing else. We need to limit our legal liability," added Irma.

"And dollars spent," Chen agreed.

Lindley shot Irma a nasty look over her shoulder as she and Smith headed for the cafeteria for a quick strategy meeting.

The door swung shut quietly.

Chen got up to leave. "Okay?"

"Thanks, Charles," said Irma.

"If I can do anything else to help, let me know." Chen breezed out of the room.

Zipper Wiles grabbed the door before it could close. "Is this the place?" he asked with a smile.

"Come in." Irma stood up to shake Zipper's hand, and introduced Softhousen.

* * *

The same litany of questions with Zipper, then Sherry and Trees revealed nothing more than that Winsome had excellent taste in college students, Irma thought. They were all very bright, very hard working, very "well adjusted" (as Lindley would say), and very attractive people. Irma's courtroom intuition detected no flaws in their answers to Softhousen's questions.

After Trees left, Irma said, "Tracey still seems to be our best bet."

"Yup."

"Its strange, they all seemed to be pretty knowledgeable about each other, but none of them knew much about Tracey's family, beyond what she told us."

"I noticed. You may be on to something." Softhousen punched up Evan on the speaker phone.

"Forensics, Dinst speaking."

"Yeh. Evan. What's the latest?"

"Nothing, except the palm matches the phalanges of Kelly's right hand."

"Palm? There was only one in that tank?"

"It's called a tote."

"Yeh. Tote. So we're still missing the left palm," Softhousen confirmed while scribbling in his notebook.

"Yes."

"How about her desk? Anything?" Larry continued.

"A lot of different prints, a few of her hairs so far. Not much else."

Softhousen wrote some more. "Kelly's apartment?"

"No one's touched it, as far as I know, since you had it sealed yesterday. It should still be under guard. I was just getting ready to call you. Do you want to meet me over there?"

Irma nodded vigorously in Softhousen's direction and pointed to herself.

Softhousen nodded back. "We'll be there in 20 minutes. Don't go in…"

"…without you, right?" asked Evan.

"Yeh," Softhousen grunted.

"See you there."

Irma punched "Off" for Softhousen. "I need to be there. She would not be in Albuquerque but for Winsome."

"Bullshit counselor," Softhousen laughed. "It's private property not belonging to Winsome, and you know it. But you're welcome to come anyway. I have some discretion. You could have asked. Just keep whatever we find under your hat."

"Thanks," Irma said sheepishly. She made a mental note not to bluster Larry again.

Chapter 29

APARTMENTS

Yellow "Police Line Do Not Cross" tape crisscrossed the door to Kelly's apartment. Softhousen ripped it down. Evan meticulously dusted the doorknob, door, and moldings for prints, while Softhousen and Irma slipped on Tyvex shoe covers and pulled on latex gloves.

The manager keyed open the door. Softhousen reached in and carefully flipped a wall switch. Light splashed onto the clean white carpet, white walls, and white ceiling of the entryway.

"Another body?" Irma held her breath. But, as she walked in, her impression was "not lived in." The apartment held a tasteful, white Naugahide sofa with a white "Welcome to Winsome" introductory class notebook resting on it. A small color TV sat on a white plastic crate. A beautiful multi-hued wooden cello lay on the rug next to a music stand. Irma looked at the music on the stand: *Bach's Cello Suites*. There was a white wooden kitchen table with two white chairs.

"May I help by looking through the kitchen?" Irma asked Softhousen.

He nodded. "Look, but don't touch or move anything. Watch where you step."

The kitchen floor was spotless, and the counters were absolutely bare. Irma gingerly opened white cabinet doors and found starter sets of Corel dishes and cups, and Visions glass cookware, with much room to spare. One of the drawers held new, stainless steel flatware. A wood block held a small set of Chicago Cutlery knives. A gallon of milk, half-full, occupied the top shelf of the refrigerator. Below the milk was a Saran Wrap-covered glass bowl of sliced fruit, two grapefruit, and two boxes of Grape Nuts cereal. That was it. Irma had never seen such a clean, healthy-looking refrigerator. There was nothing in the freezer except ice cubes. Irma vowed to drink more milk.

"Ms. Laches." Softhousen's muffled voice came from the back of the apartment.

Irma walked quickly. The men were in Kelly's bedroom, at the foot of Kelly's king-sized bed. "The kitchen is exceptionally clean," she reported.

Evan and Softhousen both nodded. They were staring at the framed photographs that filled the built-in shelves along the wall.

"Notice anything odd about the pictures?" Softhousen asked.

"Give me a minute." Irma studied the shelves.

Many of the photos were of Kelly's sports teams. She did more than play basketball. She played softball in the spring and tennis in the fall. Kelly had also been a swimmer in high school. There was Kelly playing cello in front of a student orchestra. There were pictures of Kelly hiking, horseback riding, and goofing around in clown makeup. "I give up. Aside from being an amazing athlete, I don't see anything strange."

"See any boyfriends?"

Irma looked again. The swim team was coed. High school tennis was coed. The orchestra had male and female musicians. The photos of group outings had an occasional guy, but none who stood beside Kelly. In none of the 30-odd photos was Kelly next to a male. "Let me guess. You think she was Lesbian."

"You said it, not me."

"You might want to look at these too." Evan pulled a shoebox with the word PHOTOS neatly printed on it out of the top dresser drawer, and tossed it onto the bed.

Softhousen took off the lid. It was stuffed with pictures. He handed it to Irma. "You can go through these. Pull out anything unusual, or any boyfriends. Keep your gloves on."

Irma sorted the photographs into piles. 'Kissimmee family' was one. 'Sports' was another. 'Vacations,' then finally 'friends.' The sports pile soon outstripped the others. There were some men in the photos, but, again, none in physical contact with Kelly.

"So far I don't see any boyfriends—maybe some male friends, but no obvious boyfriends."

She finally worked her way to the back of the shoebox. "My goodness!"

"What?" asked Softhousen from the dresser. He was removing Kelly's panties from one of her drawers.

Irma carefully handed him a photo. "Kelly and Tracey…"

Softhousen wolf-whistled, "…taking a bubble bath."

"The photo doesn't show anything improper," Irma defended the girls, "they are both covered with bubbles."

"Yeh, but do you usually get naked and take baths with your girlfriends?"

"Not usually," Irma evaded. She looked at the only photograph left in the box and sighed, "You're right." Now Kelly and Tracey were smooching in the tub, still mostly covered with bubbles. She handed the glossy photo to Softhousen.

"Looks kinda like they're tryin' to extract each other's tonsils with their teeth," Softhousen observed.

Irma winced. That was what it looked like. It was definitely not just a friendly kiss. Two extremely beautiful young women . . . "So now what?"

"Maybe some rejection, jealousy, and anger thrown into the mix. Just like with men and women." Softhousen was staring at the pictures.

Irma thought his face was getting a little red…it was the sexual charisma effect. "Tracey said nothing about Kelly being her lover, and she didn't seem very upset when she talked about Kelly's death."

"Nope. I agree, and that looks kinda suspicious."

"But maybe Tracey thinks that revealing she's Lesbian will ruin her career as an engineer. It must be very frightening."

"Counselor, your lover gets killed, are you going to pretend you're just friends?"

"No I wouldn't. But I'm not Tracey."

"You're going to indicate somehow that you have a relationship, and can provide inside information."

"I suppose..."

"Damned straight you would. And maybe Kelly just broke up with Tracey. Maybe Kelly put her pretty hands on another girlfriend. That could have provided a motive for Tracey to cut off her hands."

"I guess so," Irma sighed. "But we're just guessing."

"Irma, look. These pictures aren't consistent with Tracey's behavior, right?"

"But there's no evidence of another girlfriend."

"Okay. It's also possible that Kelly didn't reciprocate Tracey's feelings the way she wanted, eh?"

"Sure, that's possible," Irma admitted.

Evan affected a John Wayne Texas drawl, "Well, whadduya know..." He pulled four lab notebooks out of the bottom dresser drawer and tossed them onto the bed. Each one was labeled JOURNAL in black magic marker.

Irma snatched the top one, which looked like the newest, and scanned it at legal warp-speed.

"How can you read so damned fast?" Larry asked as he took the next.

Irma ignored him. It took her forty seconds to skim twenty pages. "Got it," she said, looking at Softhousen sadly.

"What?" He was still laboring to read the first page of the journal he had picked up.

"This is her current journal. It ends at 5:00 a.m., Tuesday, July fifth."

"Yesterday morning, before she went to work." Evan observed.

Irma nodded. She showed Softhousen the last entry:

5:00 a.m., Tuesday, July 5th, 2000. Couldn't sleep and cried this a.m. Yesterday told Tracey not to call. She is too angry, and won't tell me—doesn't trust me. She was furious. Neither of us had done it before, so we're both vulnerable the same way. But she's angry and I don't understand why. I want to help, but she won't let me.

"Had done what before?" asked Evan, innocently.

Softhousen and Irma looked at Evan, then at each other.

"Oh—that!" Evan was embarrassed.

"Won't tell her what?" Softhousen asked.

"Maybe Tracey wouldn't tell her why she was so upset. She probably wanted to confide in Kelly and tell her about the plot to sabotage Winsome, but she couldn't because Kelly was so pro-Winsome." Irma suggested.

Larry nodded. "Not to mention sabotage being illegal as hell."

"That too," Irma agreed.

"Love can turn to hate," Evan suggested.

"We still don't have any evidence that Tracey killed Kelly, or cut off Kelly's hands, or sabotaged anything," Irma pointed out. "We just have pretty good evidence that they had a relationship."

"Pretty good, counselor? I'd say real good."

Irma sighed. He was right. "Now what?"

"Details. Exactly where was Tracey yesterday? We need one of those time line things for her. Who do her parents and brother work for? Can you get that information ASAP?"

Irma nodded. "Lindley and Sergeant Smith are working on the summer hires' family backgrounds. Take me back to

Winsome. We need to set up a meeting with the day shift supervisors anyway."

"You meet with them," said the detective. "You know what we need. Same as last night, focus on Tracey. Might as well also confirm the locations of everyone else. I'll trust your judgment on how to handle it so that no one gets spooked."

"What are you going to do?"

"I want to see if the judge downtown will let us pay a little surprise visit on Ms. Siggs' apartment this afternoon."

"You mean a search warrant?" Irma asked.

"All nice and legal." Softhousen began punching numbers into the phone beside Kelly's bed. "Stew, Larry. The deceased had a girlfriend...Yeh, one of those. Need a warrant to search the friend's apartment, right now...Yeh, we have probable cause for homicide...Can you send it over in a black and white? We'll meet him there." He spelled out Tracey's name and gave the assistant district attorney her address.

Irma used her cell phone to call Sally Sue to arrange the meeting.

She rode back to Winsome with the officer who had been guarding the apartment.

Chapter 30

RANCHITOS

At 4:00 p.m. the supervisors and engineering managers walked into 313. The day sups were responsible for the front end day shift operators and floor techs. The engineering managers managed the day shift salaried engineers, summer interns, and engineering technicians.

Irma quickly gave them the rundown on Kelly. But they already knew most of it, and about the contamination. She requested they develop time lines for all of their employees, including themselves, for the preceding day. The deadline was "by this time tomorrow." That gave them a full shift to do the work.

Chen walked in and added that Irma's request was the number one priority.

A few of the engineering managers stayed and grumbled to Chen and Irma that the time lines would slow down the decontamination of the fab. Chen politely pointed out that if the perpetrator were not caught, they might have even more sabotage and contamination to deal with. They all nodded. Chen was the boss, and he was right.

As the meeting broke up, Irma whispered to Chen that the police investigation of Kelly's apartment had helped to confirm one of their leads. He didn't ask who it was. "Keep after it," was all he said.

Chen's not asking about the apartment cheered Irma. It meant he trusted her to do the right thing. Chen was smart enough not to micro-manage his employees.

Irma asked Charles to introduce her to Tracey Siggs' boss. Chen looked at her with hard, tired eyes. He'd made the connection with the apartment.

"Chris Ties is Fab 13's Thin Films engineering manager. He's Tracey's supervisor." Chen spoke over his shoulder as he pulled Chris aside.

Irma explained that they needed the time lines for all of Kelly's friends, quickly, and that Tracey was one of them.

"I'll write her up first—as soon as I finish interviewing all of my people. I should have it by early afternoon tomorrow." Chris smiled.

"This is urgent," Irma stated.

Chris looked at Chen, who nodded almost imperceptibly. Chris hesitated for just a fraction of a second, then said, "I'll have her come in for an interview this evening, write her up right away, and call you when I get the results." Irma's sixth sense told her that Chris really didn't want to do this.

Chen gave another little nod, "Thanks. Take off early tomorrow, or come in late."

Irma noticed the ring on Chris' finger. It looked like he had a family. She wondered what it was like for them when he worked eighteen-hour days.

"And please don't use your cell phones to discuss anything about this," Chen advised Chris and Irma.

Irma frowned. "The TV news last night about the radio?"

Chen nodded. "Scanners." It was all he needed to say.

Finally alone in 313, Irma called Lindley and requested the employment information on Tracey's relatives as soon as possible. Lindley wanted to know why Irma was so interested in Tracey. Irma said that it looked like Tracey had a reason to be angry with Kelly. Lindley pressed her for details, but Irma demurred that it was something Softhousen had told her in confidence.

Lindley was furious, "You represent Winsome, you know, and you work for me."

"Yes, I know, but this information is not from Winsome, and Softhousen only gave me access to it with the condition that I keep it confidential. I've told you the substance. It looks like Tracey may have been angry with Kelly."

"But you won't give me the details."

"As an officer of the court, I can't."

"You mean you won't."

"I mean what I say. Ethically I cannot divulge that information without Softhousen's permission. I will ask him to let met tell you."

"Are you sure you're not hiding behind that 'officer of the court' status of yours?"

"I don't have anything personal to gain by keeping the information to myself. You know attorneys must keep things confidential. If the details got out, somehow, it could prejudice Softhousen's criminal case, which is not in Winsome's best interest, either."

Lindley slammed down the phone. "Ouch," Irma thought. Security was next. Maybe they would be more helpful. She dialed the security desk. "Hello Sergeant, it's Irma. We need to get the employment background of Tracey Siggs' family as soon as possible. Can you help?"

"Yes ma'am. Will do. I'll make some calls right away. It shouldn't take too long."

"By tomorrow, do you think?"

"Perhaps even tonight."

"Please page me as soon as you get something— anything." Irma could hear the clicking of computer keys. He was already working on it. "Thanks, Sergeant." Irma hung up. At least one department at Winsome was helpful.

Finally, she paged Softhousen. She waited for him to return her call. It looked like Sergeant Smith was going to be another friend. Was part of it the invisible bond between people who worked in law enforcement? She had noticed that even as much as attorneys were universally hated and derided, cops and attorneys got along better than attorneys and other people. There was some mutual respect. Most cops didn't want to do the crushing load of paperwork that came with a legal practice, and most lawyers didn't want to be out on the street wrestling bad guys and risking getting bitten by AIDS-infected druggies. Irma shuddered at the thought. The real world could be a little too real.

The phone chirped like a cricket on steroids. "Irma Laches," she answered.

"Yeh."

"Have you found anything at Tracey's?"

"I'm usin' a cell phone," he said. Apparently Softhousen also knew about the TV broadcast of Steve's radio transmission.

Irma looked at her watch. "Want to meet at Ranchitos for dinner? I can be there in fifteen minutes."

"You got it." Softhousen clicked off.

* * *

Irma got into her little black Miata and grinned and laughed. This was the most fun she'd had since beginning practice. She knew they were going to catch whoever it was—and it was probably Tracey. She had to admit that criminal law was "sexy." Softhousen could be crude, but her intuition told her he was a nice guy. She felt safe when he was around. Of course he was too old for her and they had too many other differences, but she was really looking forward to dinner.

* * *

The candle on the table flickered in the chilling breeze coming from the air conditioning vents high on the walls. A small water fountain splashed soothingly in the center of the room. Tall, ice-cold glasses of red Sangria refracted the flickering candlelight. Irma took a sip—it was delicious.

Freshly-made corn-flour tortilla chips lazed in a woven basket and a large glazed bowl held fiery red salsa. Softhousen deftly scooped some onto a chip and masticated slowly as an expression of contentment swept across his face. Small beads of sweat formed on his forehead.

Irma knew from long experience that this was the "salsa effect." Spicy New Mexico salsa was the best. The chiles were always fresh. In Spanish they said *"muy picante y muy delicioso"*—very spicy and very good. A true New Mexican wouldn't touch the tasteless watery stuff in the jars.

"So, what did you find at Tracey's?" she asked.

"Nothing."

"Nothing? There must have been something . . . "

"Yeh. Clothes, shoes, that Intro to Winsome looseleaf, some food."

"But nothing relevant."

"Nothing. Clean as a whistle."

"Too clean?"

"Yup. No letters, no journals, nothing personal like that." Softhousen dipped more salsa. "Except," Irma suddenly looked up, "she did have a couple more of those bubble bath photos and a Polaroid camera with a time delay. It must be the one they used at Kelly's. Nothing else."

"How about phone records?"

"We're checking. We're going to get the judge to sign a disclosure order in the morning."

"What did Tracey say?"

"She doesn't know—and don't you tell her. We left it so she won't know we were there."

"I won't. Her manager is doing a time line on her right now, and Winsome Security is tracing her family's employment."

"How soon?"

"Should be this evening. They're going to page me."

"Okay." He loaded another tortilla chip with salsa. "So how'd a nice girl like you end up working for Winsome?"

Two steaming plates of chile rellenos arrived, smothered in cheese and salsa, with refritos, Mexican fried rice, and a generous garnish of shredded lettuce, diced tomatoes, and sour cream. Irma imagined the flavors blending together into a glorious cheesy picante medley. God, she loved New Mexican food!

Irma grinned and told Softhousen about herself, then asked him about himself. She found out that he had been a Marine in an earlier life, and had a degree in criminology. It was hard to believe he had a four-year degree.

"They don't teach you nuthin' in school." He belched contentedly without excusing himself.

She thought, "At least, not too much of the King's English – or manners." But she said, "You mean of how to actually work on cases?"

"Yeh. The only way to learn it is to do it."

"Well, I would like to learn the basics, at least."

"It's like science. Ya gotta gather data, then evaluate, then gather more data."

"You're saying it's dangerous to come to a conclusion too quickly."

"If you get too narrow too fast, you're going to miss the right suspect. I've seen it happen more than once, especially with new detectives. They think it's some weird guy, some psycho."

"Like what Lindley was saying?"

"Yeh. That crap. They're always looking for some Jeffrey Dahlmer, some mass murderer. Most of the time it's somebody who's just scared, greedy, or pissed off. It could happen to you, or me. Everybody can get angry—good people too; grandparents, who've been married forever. It's a mental thing, but not all of that psychological crap that you were discussing with Lindley. It's just anger, too much anger. That kind of pure anger can happen to anyone. I've seen it. I felt like that when my ex started to screw around and she rubbed it in my face before we divorced. It doesn't matter what kind of childhood they had."

"Becoming obsessed with anger?"

"Yeh, whatever that means. Being so angry they can't see straight. Being so angry they don't see that it's a temporary problem and they don't see there are other ways out. When you think about it there ain't hardly anything in life that ain't temporary. Suicide and homicide are both permanent solutions to temporary problems. You can always go somewhere else and do something else."

"That's not always true—how about disabilities? How about people who are crippled in motorcycle accidents?" Irma asked, and she thought, "How about people who are being screwed by their employers, *sub rosa*?"

"Even there, the human mind is amazing. It adapts, it gains new skills. There's that physicist in England who's paraplegic."

"Stephen Hawkins."

"Yeh, him. People accommodate to the loss of limbs. They can learn to live with pain."

"When you say people should leave intolerable situations, are you advocating that men and women leave their spouses and children?"

"Men and women both ought to support their kids. But leaving and sending a check is better than killing somebody or yourself."

"It sounds like you're also talking about depression."

"Yeh, maybe. In the middle ages I think they used to call the anger I'm talking about 'being possessed by the devil.' In any century the fix is to stay sane. Do whatever you have to: get another job, go visit your aunt in Alaska or an exorcist, or talk to a rabbi. Whatever works. You have to keep life in perspective. Nobody's worth going to jail over—nobody. Just laugh at the assholes and leave 'em behind."

There was a muffled "wheep, wheep, wheep" from Irma's feet. She lifted her saddlebag-leather pocketbook to her lap and took out her pager. "Security," she said to Softhousen, and pulled out her cell phone. "We'll meet you at the desk in ten minutes," she said and deftly flipped the phone shut with one hand.

"Let's go." Softhousen got up and threw a twenty on the table.

Irma appreciated his chivalry.

Chapter 31

FALSE IMPRISONMENT

Winsome's spacious lobby, strewn with comfortably-stuffed, oddly-shaped modern chairs, yawned in patient boredom. Sergeant Smith expectantly stood by his desk, his hand resting on a small stack of paper. Softhousen nodded toward the cafeteria and Smith fell into step. "Any luck?" Irma asked.

"Here's the information…" employees approached, severing Smith's power of speech. They three, silent musketeers, walked the hallway floors to the small meeting room next to the cafeteria.

"Need a drink?" Irma asked before they sat down.

Smith shook his head no. "I hope this is what you need. If not, we can keep digging." He handed the thick set of sheets to Irma. "We have a retired FBI agent we call on to do things like this. She's very, very good. She was both an agent and a lawyer, by the way."

"So lawyers aren't all bad." Irma smiled. Smith smiled back.

She whipped through the report, then looked straight ahead and passed it on to Softhousen. "Wow. Tracey's father is vice president in charge of western operations for Advanced Mammary Devices, and her older brother is manager of their new fab in Pebble, Colorado. Her mother is VP in charge of overseas sales in AMD's Homemaker Sales Division. Talk about nepotism! That's what she meant when she said her mother was a homemaker."

"Yeh." Softhousen chuckled.

"Do we arrest all of them?" Irma asked.

"Hell no. We don't have a case against her family, yet. It's possible that Tracey did this on her own."

"You mean to help them out."

"Maybe to show that she could be a big-shot too."

"Did you notice Tracey's birthday?" asked Smith. Softhousen shuffled sheets of paper. "On the last page."

Softhousen read, "June 6, 1984. She's only…"

"…sixteen," finished Irma.

"I thought you said they all had to be eighteen to work here?" Softhousen asked.

"That's the policy. Somehow she must have slipped in. Some kind of clerical error—" Smith explained.

Softhousen and Irma looked at each other. They were both thinking the same thing.

"What?" asked Smith, bewildered.

"JDR," said Softhousen.

Irma explained. "Under the laws of most states…"

"…New Mexico also…" interjected Softhousen.

"…defendants under the age of 18 must be handled by the juvenile justice system, except for certain types of crimes."

"And industrial sabotage and corpse mutilation?"

"Are not mandatory adult crimes. If this is Tracey's first offense, she will get virtually no punishment, and the record of the conviction—assuming it's not a felony—will be sealed so it cannot be used against her in the future." Irma looked at Softhousen. "Do you have enough to make an arrest?"

"Not yet. We need to get her timeline."

Irma smiled at Smith. "Thanks very much, Sergeant. You've been a big help."

Smith got up. "If I can do anything else, please let me know." He left.

"Let me find out where Chris Ties is with Tracey's timeline. Would you like be there when he interviews Tracey?" Irma asked Softhousen.

Larry nodded.

After her page, Chris' return call was almost immediate. "Chris, it's Irma. How are you coming with the timelines?"

"Tracey should be here in 10 minutes."

"Do you mind if Detective Softhousen and I join you?"

"Be my guest."

"We'll meet you in 313." Irma punched off and turned to Larry. "Can you arrest her here?"

"Yeh. I can. But let's wait and see what happens in the interview."

They both bought small cups of coffee on their way to 313.

Irma carefully placed her cup on the table and sat next to the door. "Tracey's our number one suspect, right?"

"Yeh. She has the knowledge—the means—to sabotage the plant; she admitted to working in Thin Films on Tuesday—so she had the opportunity; and according to Kelly's diary she was pissed at Kelly—so she had a motive to cut off her hands. Finally, her family is totally tied up with Advanced Mammary Devices—which gives her a motive for terrorism and sabotage."

"Now we need proof."

"Yeh. And one more thing. Like you said, she's so damned young that she probably won't get any punishment from the court, and her records will be sealed."

"If she's emancipated, there's no legal connection to her parents either…"

"…which means Winsome can't get anything from them in a civil suit because Kelly is legally an adult. Her family may be judgement-proof." Softhousen reached for the speakerphone and stabbed at it rapidly with his middle finger.

"Stew, I'm leaving a message because it's 9:30 at night and all you candy-ass paper pushers are at home watching reruns. We need to find out if a summer intern who's a suspect at Winsome—Tracey Siggs—is emancipated from her parents in Pebble, Colorado. The same girl as in the second search warrant. Need it yesterday. If you want, I have a friend in Pebble who can pick it up from the clerk of court tomorrow. Page me as soon as you get in, before you start yapping with those twenty-three-year-old law school girls at the coffee maker." He punched off.

Irma smiled. Larry wished he were going to be yapping with the twenty-three-year-old law school girls at the coffee maker.

The door opened. Chris Ties and Tracey Siggs came in together. Tracey looked surprised—there was even a flash of fear—when she first saw them, Irma thought. But she recovered magnificently. Irma stood and held out her hand. "Hello Ms. Siggs."

"Ms. Laches," Tracey shook Irma's hand with a warm smile and then extended hers to Softhousen, "and Detective Softhousen."

Softhousen politely shook her hand.

Chris began his spiel, "Tracey, thanks for coming back to work so late in the evening. We're doing timelines for all of the Fab 13 employees who had clean room access on July fifth. I've been talking to everyone under me in Thin Films.

"Please describe as accurately as possible everything you did yesterday, including the times and who you worked with, starting from the moment you came onto Winsome property in the morning. Even a small detail could be very important. Please take your time, and I'll take notes."

Tracey lowered her head, then slowly turned toward Irma. "Is this like a deposition?"

Irma was caught off guard. "Well—no. This isn't a formal deposition. Depositions are usually done for civil trials, with a court reporter, and in the presence of the attorneys for both sides. There is no civil suit pending, and we are not recording this conversation. This is a criminal investigation. We are asking only about your actions at work. Winsome is asking all of its employees to help discover how the sabotage was caused yesterday."

"...and about Kelly's death," interjected Tracey.

"Yes, that too. As Kelly died while in Winsome's employ, on Winsome property, Winsome has considerable interest in her death. Winsome certainly has a right to investigate criminal occurrences on its property."

"How does Detective Softhousen's presence work, legally?"

Irma looked at Softhousen. These questions were not what she had expected. He took over. "Both the industrial sabotage and Kelly's possible murder are crimes against the state of New Mexico. As a police officer I can go anywhere and talk to anyone I reasonably believe will help to solve a crime. In this case, that means being here to talk to Winsome employees. Every citizen has a duty to cooperate in the investigation of a crime."

"So, this is like being questioned by the police?"

Chris said "No," and Irma said "Yes" at the same time. Chris nodded in deference to Irma.

"Where an officer is witnessing a conversation, I would say so," said Irma, carefully. "But, I would have to look it up to be absolutely certain."

"Yeh, probably," Softhousen reluctantly affirmed.

"Are you my lawyer?" Tracey asked Irma in a very small voice.

Now she really sounded like a sixteen-year-old, thought Irma. "No. I represent Winsome Corporation. My representation of you is extremely limited—only as an employee of Winsome. It is not in Winsome's best interest to have innocent employees falsely charged. My job is to try to obtain the best legal result, overall, for Winsome. That means from the viewpoint of what is best for the entire corporation—its shareholders. In this case it is in Winsome's interest to catch whoever did this, and to minimize, legally, all of the damage to Winsome that I possibly can. I am not your personal attorney. I can't represent your best interest because that could conflict with Winsome's best interests. Any employee who is charged with committing a crime must either represent themselves, hire their own attorney, or use an attorney appointed by the court. But you aren't charged with anything."

Tracey put her head down again. All Irma could see was her beautiful red hair. After a very long minute, Tracey whispered, without looking up, "I want to have my own attorney."

Softhousen, Irma, and Chris exchanged glances.

"If we ask Detective Softhousen to wait outside, will you speak with Chris and me?" asked Irma.

Tracey looked up. "Only if I have a lawyer."

Irma tapped her pen on her legal pad and turned to Softhousen. "Please wait outside, Detective."

Softhousen hesitated only a second. "Yes ma'am." He picked up his manila envelope, pushed his chair back, and went into the hallway. The door clicked into its strike plate.

Irma put her elbows on the table, folded her arms, and faced Tracey. "The officer is not present. He can't hear you, and we have no bugs or secret recording devices. We are asking you, as an employee, to cooperate with an internal investigation into events that caused the deaths of two employees, and have severely damaged this factory. Winsome has a right to ask its employees about these matters. We have already asked many employees about this. You are not being singled out for questioning." Irma looked significantly at Chris.

"Tracey, can you give us a description of everything you can remember that you did at work yesterday?" Chris said, evenly.

Tracey ignored Chris. "Two employees?" she asked Irma.

Irma cocked her head slightly to one side. Apparently Tracey hadn't heard. "Kelly and Mary Martinez."

"Mary Martinez?" Tracey looked bewildered. "What happened to her?"

Irma looked at Chris, then at Tracey. "She was the Litho operator who had Kelly's blood all over her. She went into the safety shower. The water was very cold. She died yesterday in the hospital, possibly from a heart attack as a result of hypothermia."

"I hadn't heard..." Tracey trailed off. She closed her eyes, sighed, threw her head back and crossed her arms.

Irma nodded to Chris to try again. He repeated his question.

Tracey opened her eyes and stared at the ceiling.

Irma said, very carefully, "So, you, as a Winsome employee, are refusing to cooperate with an investigation by Winsome into events which occurred yesterday at Fab 13?"

Tracey glared at Irma. "I want a lawyer." She got up to leave.

Irma stood quickly and beat Tracey to the door. Irma barely opened it and spoke through the crack. "Detective, please come in."

Softhousen's hand firmly held the edge of the door and pushed it open. He blocked the opening with his body as he carefully closed the door behind him. Irma walked quickly to the door at the back of the room and stood in front of it. Tracey was trapped.

Tracey said grimly, "This is false imprisonment. I am being unlawfully prohibited from leaving this room. I'm telling you I want to leave. This is against my will."

Irma raised her eyebrows. Tracey knew some law—more than you would expect a sixteen-year-old to know.

Softhousen chuckled, "Well, not really, because right now I'm telling you that you're under arrest. That's what's called lawful restraint, and your will don't matter none."

"What's the charge?"

"Before I answer that, let me tell you that you have the right to remain silent and anything you say can and will be used against you in a court of law. You have the right to an attorney, and if you cannot afford one the court will appoint one for you. Do you understand these rights?"

Tracey ran to the other end of the room where Irma was guarding the door and pushed Irma with both arms, trying to move her. Irma weighed fifty pounds more, and did not budge. Tracey swung wildly and hit Irma's temple. Like a boxer, Irma instinctively put up her hands, using her forearms to defend her body.

Tracey grabbed Irma's left wrist and pulled her off-balance, away from the door. Suddenly Softhousen was there. He produced a pair of handcuffs from his jacket pocket, swiftly grabbed Tracey's left hand, pulled it behind her back, and cuffed her left wrist.

Twisting, Tracey tried to break away and desperately kicked at Softhousen's groin, hitting his upper thigh with her foot. Irma grabbed Tracey's free arm and she and Softhousen together forced her to the floor.

"Police brutality," wailed Tracey.

Irma pressed down on her shoulders while Softhousen roughly grabbed her right arm and finished cuffing both wrists behind her back.

Larry rose on his knees and caught his breath. "Let's see, the charges are: resisting arrest, assault and battery of a police officer, assault and battery of Miss Laches, felony destruction of private property, and mutilating a corpse, for starters. If you want to start cooperating, it won't get worse. But you can add to the list of your offenses anytime you want." As Softhousen pulled her to her feet Tracey went limp and began to cry. "We've got a nice free place for you to stay tonight, courtesy of the state of New Mexico. It's even air conditioned."

Sergeant Smith came through 313's front door and quickly glanced around. He and Softhousen each grabbed one of Tracey's upper arms and half-carried her down the hall.

Chris pulled a tissue out of a box in the center of the table and handed it to Irma. "I called Smith," he explained. "Are you okay?"

Irma sat down heavily in a chair. Blood was trickling down the side of her face from her temple. She began to shake and cry. Chris looked indecisive for a moment, then sat down next to her and put his arm around her shoulder. "Its all right," he said soothingly. "The same thing happened to me the last time I had a fender bender. I should have guarded that other door."

"I was closer," Irma laughed and cried at the same time. "Ouch! It hurts when I laugh."

The front door to the meeting room opened and a bald head and blue tee shirt entered the room. "Oh, I'm so sorry!" said Fuller Linksland. He turned on his heel to leave.

Chris got up quickly. "Come in, come in. Irma was just in a fistfight."

"Oh, I thought you two…"

Irma laughed and cried again, "Ouch! No, it's not what you thought."

Fuller saw the bloody tissue. "You were in a fight?"

"Yes, occupational hazard, with someone who was being arrested."

"Arrested? We can do this some other time—tomorrow."

"No, it's over. Now is fine." Irma sniffed, then blew her nose on the bloody tissue.

"What have you got, Fuller?" Chris sat on the edge of the table. Irma jerked a clean tissue from the box.

Fuller sat down. "I've been doing decontamination stuff all day, but just now we had a little deionized water leak, unrelated. A section of two-inch diameter poly piping…Anyway, I went to get a special set of ultra-clean tools I keep in a separate toolbox in the fab for work on the DI system. It's not locked. The guillotine poly pipe cutter for three-inch pipe had some red on it. I was madder'n hell because I thought somebody had used it for photoresist drain work and had contaminated it. Then I thought about Kelly. I put it right back in the box the way I found it and locked the box. Then I came down to find you."

"So it's still in the fab?" asked Irma. She had no idea what a "guillotine poly pipe cutter" was, but made an intelligent guess: a tool that could sever Kelly's wrists.

"Yes. They said to leave evidence alone."

"That's right. You're right. We'll get APD forensics here right away." Irma punched numbers into the phone to page Softhousen as she spoke. "And you wore gloves?"

"Yes. I only picked it up briefly and looked at it."

"Great. We'll wait for APD, and you can show us where it is."

The phone chirped. Irma answered, "Larry?"

"It's me."

"Where are you?"

"I'm just down in the lobby waiting for a black and white to take Miss Siggs to the magistrate."

Irma looked at the wall clock. It said 22:30. She suddenly felt exhausted. "We think we've found the tool that was used to sever Kelly's wrists."

"I'll be there as soon as the officer shows. I'll call Evan right now. Is it locked?"

"Yes, locked in a toolbox, still where it was found in the fab," Irma explained.

"Good."

"We'll be in the cafeteria," she said.

"Okay. Meet you there."

Irma punched off.

She, Fuller, and Chris, went down to the cafeteria. She made Fuller repeat what he had told them, and this time took notes on how, when, and where the tool was found. "Thanks. You'll probably have to tell it one more time to the detective," she said as she caught a glimpse of

Softhousen and Sergeant Smith disappearing into the food service area. Two minutes later they reappeared, coffees in hand.

"Evan's on his way with all of his stuff," Softhousen said as he sat down, "so we might as well wait."

"What kind of a case do we have against Tracey, Detective?" asked Chris.

"That's just what I wanted to ask you. Did any of your folks see her doing any of that contamination yesterday?"

Chris thought for a moment. "People saw her around a lot, and talked to her, but didn't see her doing any contaminating. But she has her own toolbox. She could have easily carried around the gold and fingers in it without anyone noticing. She participates in working on all of the equipment in Thin Films as part of her job, so no one would have had any reason to suspect anything out of the ordinary."

"And the other areas…uh…"

"…diffusion, QCR, and the bulk delivery systems?" Fuller added, helpfully.

"Yeh, those," said Softhousen.

Chris continued, "It just takes a second to throw a spec of gold into a quartz tube. The bulk delivery systems are in locked rooms which are pretty isolated. But Tracey had engineering access, so her badge would have worked with the card readers to unlock those. One person could easily contaminate those totes without ever being seen." He stirred his coffee.

"But we have no direct evidence yet that she did anything." Softhousen carefully sipped his hot liquid.

Chris nodded. "No witnesses, that's right."

Irma asked Smith, "Can you get us a printout of the card reader computer logs for the QCR and the bulk delivery rooms from yesterday?"

He tore a piece of paper from Irma's yellow pad and made a note to himself. "Sure. I'll have them for you by first thing tomorrow morning."

Fuller daintily held his cup of tea with his pinky stuck out. "I know where Tracey usually kept her toolbox. I'll show you when we go into the clean room. Maybe there's some evidence still inside it."

Irma nodded, yawned, and stretched. "Perhaps some of the fingerprints Evan has already taken will match Tracey's."

"Yeh. Maybe." Softhousen sounded discouraged.

Evan rushed in, breathless, carrying his evidence and photo boxes, accompanied by a Winsome guard. "Sit down, Evan, before you have a heart attack," commanded Softhousen. "You want coffee?"

Evan sat, but said, "I'm ready whenever you are."

"Well, just let the rest of us finish our coffee. We need to be careful and awake for this part." Softhousen went on to explain that Tracey was in custody, and that they thought they'd found the tool used to sever Kelly's wrists.

Evan's eyes gleamed with enthusiasm. "Did Tracey admit to anything?"

Softhousen shook his head sourly. "She didn't say nuthin' about nuthin' except she wants to hire a goddamned lawyer. We gotta prove this one on the evidence."

Chapter 32

TOOLBOX

They were all tired as they pulled on their bunny suits.

Irma heard it as she zipped the shoulders of her suit. One of the night shift technicians was singing. It was to the tune of "On the Road Again:"

> In the fab again
> I'm just gonna go in the fab again
> Makin' wafers with mah friends
> I'm just gonna go in the fab again

Irma smiled a tired smile. He almost did sound like Willie Nelson. This was just a little part of the new, high-tech, semiconductor society Winsome was helping to build. It wasn't all bad.

Chris and Fuller waited for Irma to gown up, and then the three of them stood together, waiting for Softhousen and Evan to finish. Irma speculated about what Chen would say. . . probably something like "The time it takes for an individual to gown up is inversely proportional to their years of experience in the industry." She shook her head. This job, this factory, were changing her. Computer, manufacturing, and engineering terms were pervading her thinking. She would never be the same.

Irma's little group air-showered, then entered the clean room. Fuller guided them into Litho's yellow light.

Litho looked exactly the same at midnight as it had yesterday afternoon. Since the fab had no windows or skylights—only artificial light and temperature- and humidity-controlled and filtered air—it always felt, looked, and smelled the same. The only natural influences inside the clean room were the violent New Mexico thunderstorms.

245

Nearby thunder could be heard over the constant rushing of the filtered air.

She had overheard Frank Leathers telling an engineer that the thunderstorms also caused sudden shifts in humidity in the fab. The storms changed the amount of water vapor in the air surrounding the building from perhaps 7% to over 90% in a matter of seconds. It was more than the automatic air conditioning systems could handle. Thunderstorms caused a brief burst of high humidity inside the clean room called a "humidity spike." But this anomaly was so brief that it did not cause any serious manufacturing problems, the engineer had said.

Fuller led them to a large service chase on the far side of Litho. The wall was lined with racks of grey toolboxes, like suitcases waiting for their owners at an airport baggage area. Fuller pointed out his toolbox, conspicuously labeled "DI ONLY—ULTRA CLEAN—FULLER LINKSLAND, OWNER."

"Are these your personal tools?" asked Softhousen.

"No," Fuller's eyes crinkled—smiling inside his helmet. "In the fab, 'owner' means I'm the one who is responsible for seeing that all of the correct tools are in the box, and for keeping them clean and in good order."

"Thanks."

Evan got busy with his trusty, battered, Nikon FM2 thirty-five millimeter camera. After zooming in and out, and a dozen shots from various angles, he let Fuller pull the DI toolbox out of the rack and place it on a small stainless steel workbench. Evan quickly dusted for prints, found none, then said, "Okay. Let's look inside."

Fuller opened the toolbox. It was filled with tools just as gleaming as the day they were manufactured. There was one large orange-colored tool lying on top of an assortment of chrome-plated open- and box-ended wrenches. To Irma it looked like a giant orange crab's claw. Fuller pointed, "That's it."

"What's that?" asked Evan.

Fuller replied, "A guillotine pipe cutter for polyethylene tubing. The blade closes a notch each time you squeeze the handles, and a ratchet mechanism keeps the blade in place while the handles reset for another squeeze."

"Could it cut through someone's wrist?" Irma queried.

Fuller nodded. "I don't know about the bones, but I think so. Poly pipe is tough stuff—especially schedule 40—what we use. It whips right on through it."

"Would it also bruise someone's wrist?" asked Softhousen.

Fuller thought for a moment. "One side of the jaw is flat with a groove for the blade to pass through. The flat side just presses against the pipe. I suppose the flat side would cause a bruise on that side of a wrist."

Softhousen nodded.

Evan produced a flashlight and a magnifying glass and examined the tool, being careful not to touch it. "Oh yeh, uh-hunh, sure enough," he said, then looked up. "Looks like someone just did a quick wipedown, and left some blood residue on the blade and in the mechanism." He gingerly picked up the pipe cutter with his gloved fingertips and placed it on a clean cloth wipe on the workbench. He quickly dusted each side of the tool with a camel's-hair brush for prints. "Nothing."

"Enough blood to analyze?" asked Softhousen.

"Oh yeh," Evan said as he carefully placed the tool in a large baggie. He turned to Fuller. "We'll take good care of it, but it may be a year before you get it back. Depends on how soon the case is tried."

"Winsome will just buy me another one. No problem," Fuller crinkled his eyes again.

Evan spoke into his little tape recorder, noting the number of the bag, the location, and the time.

Chris was idly looking at the names on the toolboxes in the rack. "Where's Tracey's toolbox?" He asked.

"Right here." Fuller turned and squatted down next to Chris. He pointed beneath the rack at a small orange-and-white plastic box. It looked as if it had been made for fishing tackle.

"That's it?" asked Softhousen. Evan came over and took more photographs.

"Yes," Fuller stood and massaged his knees.

"It doesn't look like any of the others," Evan observed.

"She's the only one with a box like that, Fuller explained. "I noticed her carrying it around. I think she bought it herself, and those are even her personal tools. You can check with Security. She would have had to log it in as personal property when she first brought it into the building."

"I'll check that out," said Irma, and she wrote a note to herself on a clean room clipboard. "Why would she have had her own tools?"

Chris responded, "It takes weeks to order a set through Winsome. She didn't want to wait. She wanted to learn the maintenance routines by working right alongside the technicians. Summer interns are eager beavers."

Evan went through his inspection for fingerprints before placing Tracey's toolbox on the workbench. They all gathered around it.

"It's not locked," Irma observed.

"True," said Fuller. "I stopped her one day and asked her why she hadn't bought a lock for it. She told me that she'd never had anything stolen, and she wasn't going to worry about it until she did."

"Here goes." Evan flipped up the catches on the side of the toolbox. Inside was a tray of hand tools with a new set of Craftsman screwdrivers, pliers, Vise-Grips, metric and standard Allen wrenches in plastic holders, and different sized adjustable crescent wrenches.

"Nothing special, but a good little set," observed Softhousen. At dinner he had told Irma that he liked to restore old motorcycles in his spare time. He knew something about tools.

"The basics of what a tech usually needs," Fuller agreed.

Evan took his photos, then gave the tools a good look with his flashlight. "I don't see anything obvious." He carefully removed the tool tray and laid it on the workbench. He peered into the bottom of the toolbox with aid of his flashlight. "Oh man!" He suddenly turned his head away from the toolbox, took a step back from the bench, and handed his flashlight to Softhousen.

Softhousen looked inside. "Shit. That's her other palm." He shook his head. "Do you want to look?" he asked Irma, offering her the flashlight.

"I suppose I need to see," she said, reluctantly.

"It ain't gonna bite." Larry's voice was dry.

Irma cautiously peered inside. She backed off, closed her eyes, and turned her head away in disgust. "Oh—worms."

"Maggots," corrected Evan.

Chris and Fuller both took a quick look with the flashlight, then Evan busied himself again with photography.

Irma surprised herself with how fast she regained her composure. "Maggots are from flies, right?" she asked Evan as he worked.

"Correct," he said.

"How could flies have gotten in here—inside a clean room?"

"They get in occasionally." Fuller was matter-of-fact. "Last year we even had a few ants. What makes it clean is the positive pressure of air inside. Dust can't go against the airflow, but insects can walk or fly in if they find the right spot. We don't get very many. You have to remember that we're on the second floor of a steel and concrete building.

The insects need to climb to get up here, and there is no food inside to attract them."

"We get reports of about one insect per month. That's pretty good for a fab this big," added Chris.

Irma was amazed that Winsome cared to track how many insects per month were in the clean room. Even hospitals didn't do that.

"Let's take Tracey's toolbox, and the guillotine tool," Softhousen said to Evan, "and call it a night."

Evan yawned. "Gladly." He put the guillotine tool into a large ziplock evidence bag, placed tape across the ziplock closure, and signed his name across the tape. Then he put all of Tracey's tools back in her toolbox closed the lid, and repeated his ritual with the tape. He pulled two large white plastic bags from his evidence kit, placed the toolbox inside the bags, then sealed them and signed the tape again.

Kelly's palm, with its maggots, was still in the bottom of Tracey's toolbox. No one had touched it.

Softhousen lead the way, carrying the toolbox, as they tiredly trooped out of the fab.

*   *   *

The wall clock above the Security desk in the lobby said 1:00 a.m. as they checked out Evan's evidence kits and Tracey's toolbox.

The guard located the entry for Tracey's tools in the personal property log. Since she had signed it in, he let them take it out without looking inside. A lapse in security, thought Irma, but she wasn't going to complain.

She, Larry, and Evan walked down the winding sidewalk to the almost-deserted parking lot. Cicadas droned in the trees in the tasteful landscaping surrounding the campus.

As Softhousen placed the toolbox and evidence cases in the trunk of Evan's car he said to Evan, "I'll meet you in the lab around nine in the morning."

"See you then." Evan strapped himself into the driver's seat and drove into the night.

Softhousen spoke to Irma. "He'll go by the lab tonight and put that toolbox in the reefer. It'll slow down the maggots." Softhousen put his hands in his pockets. It was cold. July nighttime temperatures could descend into the forties.

Irma mentally reviewed the science. This extreme temperature variation was a consequence of the altitude. Since the blanket of air over Albuquerque was thin and dry it was a poor insulator. And thin dry air was not capable of holding much heat. This lack of insulation and thermal mass meant Albuquerque was subject to both rapid radiant heat loss into the night sky, and rapid heating by the sun during the day, even in the summer. But all she cared about right now was that she was cold. She folded her arms across her chest and looked at Softhousen. "Do you think Tracey did it?"

Softhousen leaned against his car, closed his eyes, and dropped his chin to his chest in fatigue. After a while he raised his head and spoke softly. "To tell you the truth, now I'm not too sure. If she weren't so smart, I'd say she's as guilty as sin, the way she acted. But she could've just panicked. Smart people sometimes don't act like normal people. And she's too damned smart to leave Kelly's damned palm in her damned toolbox, right near where we found that guillotine tool. She had to know her toolbox would be the first place anyone would look. It directly incriminates her. There are thousands of other places in this huge factory to hide—or throw away—that palm. Every bit of the rest of Kelly's hands was used for sabotage. Why save this piece? Also I don't believe one fly every month is going to get into a new floating toolbox with its latches holding the lid shut against an o-ring seal. Flies ain't that smart."

"So Kelly's palm had to be outside of the clean room at some point, in order for flies to lay the eggs on it which created the maggots?" asked Irma.

"Yep. Like maybe down where those bulk delivery rooms with the totes are located, near the loading dock. I saw some flies down there, probably because they also put garbage from the cafeteria into the dumpsters at the dock. It attracts them."

"Tracey could have taken it down there when she contaminated the totes." Irma suggested.

"Sure. But it looks like the totes were the last things to be contaminated with body parts. Why not just use this palm to contaminate another tote? Why go to all of the trouble to sneak it back into the clean room, and then leave it in her toolbox where we were sure to find it?"

"I see your point." Irma was quiet for a while. "Do you think Tracey is being framed?"

"It's possible." Softhousen got into his car and rolled down the window. "Don't worry about it. We can always let Tracey out of jail, and things usually look better in the morning. I'll be back here around ten."

"See you then," said Irma.

"Page me if anything else happens." Softhousen closed his window against the cool night air and started his car.

Irma walked the short distance to her Miata. It was right where she'd left it.

She was too tired to think of anything on the drive home except staying on the road.

Under the vigas of her bedroom once more, Irma exhaustedly stripped off her clothes and fell into bed. She did not dream.

Chapter 33

DAY THREE

Sweat rolled down Irma's face and into her eyes. The bed sheets under her legs and back were wet and stuck to her skin. Her hair was a sticky, salty mess. She kept her eyes closed, flung off the covers, and kicked her legs wildly to disentangle them from the sheets. It was cooler to lie naked, on top of the linen.

Bright light streamed into the bedroom, through her eyelids, and into her brain. The wetness of the sheets underneath her body was unbearable. She quickly rolled onto her side, opened her eyes, and stared at her clock. 09:01, it said. "Well at least I'll be there by 10:00 to meet Larry," she thought, and staggered off to perform the morning ablutions. The shower and clean clothes felt wonderful.

* * *

Irma cupped her hands, creating a tunnel between the styrofoam cup and her nose, and inhaled the smell of fresh coffee. She could not get enough. The stronger the better. Coffee smelled so good, and tasted so good, and caffeine was such a kick, that she was surprised it was not a controlled substance. She was definitely addicted. People at other tables were beginning to stare.

"You want to mainline it? Out in the car I've got a leftover syringe from a drug bust." Softhousen laughed.

Irma smiled. "When I retire I'm going to open a cappuccino shop, and live with a hundred different kinds of coffee beans."

She carefully spread an extra helping of green chile cream cheese on the halves of her sesame-and-poppy-seed bagel with a plastic knife. She closed her eyes, devoured a big bite, and savored every second of the taste and texture. "God, I love green chile cream cheese!" she mumbled, mouth half full.

"That much is obvious. Where do you get that stuff?"

"They make it fresh here, in the Winsome cafeteria."

"In the cafeteria?"

"Yes. It's best when fresh," said Irma in between chews.

She washed it down with some coffee and closed her eyes again. Now she was ready to face the day. "Do we know anything more from last night?"

"Evan should be working on the blood in that tool right now, and Mercedes and the maggot guy will be doing the palm."

"Maggot guy?"

"Yeh. What's his face—an entomologist—a bug scientist from UNM. He knows all about maggots and can tell us how old they are, and what kind."

"That's important?"

"It might tell us something. In case you hadn't noticed, we're kinda short on suspects."

"And Tracey?"

"Bond hearing right now. Her folks are rolling in dough. They hired a crackerjack paper-pusher from the biggest firm in Denver. He's licensed to practice in New Mexico too. Flew down this morning. With no priors she'll get out of jail and sue me for malicious prosecution." He sounded depressed.

"I was assaulted!"

"Yeh, yeh. But it's not much of a charge. You might even consider letting us drop it so we can make her a deal. How's the cut?"

"Fine. A little sore." She hadn't felt it until Softhousen brought it up. She bit off another hunk of bagel.

"Oh yeh, and Tracey isn't emancipated…"

"…which means her parents…"

"…don't necessarily have any immunity from prosecution for any damage she might have caused."

"You don't think she did it."

"She was fingerprinted last night. None of her prints match the one on the piece of glove from the knot."

"So, she didn't do it." Irma looked down at the table. She had been so sure…

"I've been talking to a buddy at the FBI office in Albuquerque. Most of these big companies are pretty straight shooters. The legal liability and bad publicity are so huge that it isn't worth it for them to do outright sabotage. But they'll hire a scientist or an engineer away from each other in a heartbeat," Softhousen explained.

"So you don't suspect Tracey's family?"

"Nope. There's no reason to. All of 'em are squeaky clean. Tracey's some kind of prodigy. She's already halfway through engineering school—that's two years of college."

"At age sixteen!"

"Yeh. But you know she's still only sixteen, emotionally. We scared her. And she was already halfway crazy because of the guilt from her first homosexual relationship with Kelly, and Kelly's death. How can an attractive, healthy girl's first sexual experience be with a Lesbian?"

Irma ignored Larry. That was none of his damned business. She said, "Okay. Do whatever you want with the assault charge. What's next?"

He nodded. "Can we get the rest of the time lines this morning?"

"Sure. Let me finish this, and we'll visit Sally Sue and see if she has them."

Softhousen's face suddenly glowed with enthusiasm. Irma knew it wasn't from the smell of the coffee. She unhurriedly finished her bagel.

*   *   *

Sally Sue looked up from her PC and swiveled her chair to face them. She wore shiny black cowboy boots, tight black jeans, and a cowgirl shirt—red and white plaid with leather fringes. A magnificent black cowboy hat with shiny black crow feathers adorned the wall of her cubicle.

Irma reflected: Sally never had to decide what style to wear. It was a choice of cowgirl, cowgirl, or cowgirl. Sally's closet would have cowgirl shirts in all colors, stacks of boot-cut jeans, and a floor crowded with cowgirl boots. A pile of red bandanas probably sat on a shelf.

Irma wondered if Sally owned chaps, spurs, and whips. But it was better not to let her imagination run too far. "Have any of the day supervisors finished their timelines yet?" Irma asked.

"None have come back," Sally smiled. "Y'all have a message from Sergeant Smith. He said he has some of the information y'all requested."

"Thanks, ma'am." Softhousen reached up and tipped an imaginary cowboy hat to Sally. Irma was astounded. He had never been that polite to her. Nor, to her knowledge, did he own any cowboy hats.

"Could you ask Smith to meet us in 313 with that information?" Irma asked.

"Right away." Sally swiveled attractively in her chair and reached for the phone.

*   *   *

Smith pulled a three-inch-thick stack of eight-and-one-half-by-eleven-inch sheets of paper out of a brief case. "These are the investigative reports."

Irma's eyes widened. "I didn't ask you to get this information on all of these people."

Smith paused. "Yes, I know. It was Chen who asked me to get it, then give it to you and Detective Softhousen."

"Charles ordered this?" Irma couldn't believe it. "It must have cost Winsome a fortune."

Smith shrugged his shoulders.

"How can you get this much information so soon?" asked Softhousen.

"Chen said this was a priority." Smith pushed the stack to the center of the table. "That ex-FBI lady I told you about, her entire firm was up all night getting this for us. We've got printouts of the criminal histories of every Fab 13 employee."

Softhousen picked up a printout and glanced at it. "This even includes juvenile criminal records! I can't get this much information, and I'm certified to use the New Mexico Criminal Information Network. How does this private person—this ex-FBI lady—get access to a Criminal Information Terminal? It's supposed to be restricted to law enforcement only."

Smith coughed. "I'm not sure. She said something about there being an industrial sabotage unit within the FBI. The mainframe with the information is in the same building as the IS unit, so there's no waiting if you go to one of the dedicated terminals."

Irma knew not to ask any more questions. This kind of access by a private corporation to criminal histories that were supposed to be confidential sounded illegal to her. Best to leave well enough alone. But there was one question she had to ask: "How could Winsome hire anyone with a criminal history? I thought everyone here had their background checked?"

"Well," Smith cleared his throat, "different data bases can yield different results. The investigation outfit we normally use doesn't have direct access to the FBI's secure files." He coughed again.

Softhousen nodded in agreement. "All somebody has to do is get a legal name change, and you can miss 'em. The system isn't perfect. You do a search with the wrong last name or social security number, and nothing shows up."

"I thought it was all automatic." Irma had never run a criminal history. All she knew was that criminal defense lawyers had a right to get copies of their client's histories prior to trial.

Softhousen was indignant. "Hell no. The court clerks have to do their jobs—somebody has to input the data."

This sounded like a pet peeve, Irma thought.

"Half the time the histories are full of errors or just incomplete." Softhousen was animated. "For purposes of showing a prior conviction a lot of judges won't accept anything except a certified copy of that conviction from the clerk of the court that did it. It's the only way to be sure."

Irma knew that was true. "And nobody's going to go to every court clerk in the United States in order to compile a perfect criminal history."

"Yeh, that's impossible. Even when you call and ask for them, half the time the clerks just blow you off."

"They ignore requests for copies of documents which are in the public record? I thought that was required. The system should be better than that."

"Well it's not. Now if you show up in person and stand in the clerk's office for an hour, you might get something. Asking over the phone isn't good enough. If the court is out of state, forget it. You won't get a thing."

Irma nodded as she divided the pile into three one-inch stacks. Dumping on the court clerks, who did so much of the work in the legal system with low pay and little recognition, was not getting them any closer to finding their mutilator. "Let's look at these," she said. Irma whipped through her stack. She set aside six of the histories. She reread them and announced, "A few misdemeanors. Nothing serious."

Softhousen finished a close second. He was used to reading criminal history printouts. A few of his sheets were set aside as well. "Same here, just misdemeanors." They watched Smith finish his stack.

"Here's one," Smith said, and handed it to Irma as he looked through his last few sheets. The first item in the record was a dishonorable discharge from the Army for insubordination. There were several convictions: misdemeanor forging and uttering of bad checks, and two felony convictions for embezzlement. No active jail time had been served for any of the crimes. The history noted a name change in 1986.

Irma handed the printout to Softhousen. "Looks like your typical con artist," he observed. "They'll do anything for money. They'll betray anyone—their spouse, their children, their employer—to get it. Even if they have a good job, good friends, and good prospects, they can never get enough. It's an addiction. I've nailed several of these bastards."

"Oh no! Not you too!" Irma had thought Softhousen was immune to psychobabble.

"What's wrong?" he asked.

"They have free will, just like everyone else! Embezzling money when you have a good job is not a medical problem. It is not an addiction, it's choosing to pick up a pen and write a bad check, or choosing to forge a journal entry, or choosing to take whatever action embezzles, steals, or spends the money. It's a choice!" Irma almost slammed the table with her fist.

"I thought it was like gambling. They say gambling is an addiction," said Larry.

"The muscles of the arm which put the money in the slot machine and pull the lever, or drive the car to the race track, or lay the cash on the counter for the lottery ticket, are called 'voluntary muscles' by doctors, aren't they?"

Softhousen reluctantly answered, "Yeh, I guess so."

"Damned straight!"

Softhousen was surprised at Irma's use of the crude expression.

"That means they are under the conscious control of the human brain, right?" she continued.

"Yeh."

Irma handed the printout to Smith. "Please call the FBI lady again. We need an in depth report on this person as soon as possible."

Smith immediately dialed a number and made the request. "She'll get back to us via email," he said.

Softhousen flipped back through his little notebook. "Were you able to get the computer record of who had access to the bulk chemical rooms?" he asked Smith.

Smith picked up his briefcase from the floor and placed it on the table. "Yes." He pulled out a fanfold computer printout. "We got this late yesterday. Sorry—I was distracted by all of these histories this morning. I should have mentioned it sooner."

Softhousen and Irma huddled together over the printout. Irma suddenly pointed to two lines.

07 05 00 0736 HF BULK INGRESS ENG   F LINKSLAND
07 05 00 0744 HF BULK EGRESS

"'HF BULK' means the bulk delivery room for the hydrofluoric acid?" Irma asked.

"Yes," said Smith.

"It looks like Fuller got an early start on Wednesday. That's at 7:36 a.m., right?" Irma asked, pointing at 0736.

Smith nodded. "And 'ENG' means that Linksland has engineering level access," he explained.

Softhousen pointed at the next line. "Why doesn't it show who left the room at 7:44 a.m.?"

"The bulk delivery rooms are all designed to withstand explosion and fire, because the chemicals may be flammable," Smith explained. "According to the building code the doors cannot lock from the inside—all anyone needs to do to leave is to push the door open. Since badges don't need to be scanned to get out, there is no way to track who leaves."

"Couldn't Fuller have given his badge to someone else?" Softhousen asked.

Smith rocked back in his chair. "That's possible, but not likely. All employees are required to display their own badges on their person at all times. Loaning a badge to another employee is grounds for termination."

"This printout gives Fuller a pretty good alibi for the time when Kelly's hands were cut off." Irma scanned down the list and suddenly pointed again.

07 05 00 1122 HF BULK INGRESS SAFETY K KISSIMMEE
07 05 00 1137 HF BULK EGRESS

"It couldn't be Kel..." Irma stopped mid-word. Kelly was dead long before 11:22 a.m. "So that's why her badge was missing," she said, slowly. "It gave the perp," Irma smiled at having been linguistically corrupted by Softhousen, "access to the bulk delivery rooms for the purpose of sabotage."

"The saboteur worked fast," observed Softhousen. "Whoever it was, was only in there for fifteen minutes."

"I would say they knew exactly what to do," Smith agreed. "This was a planned operation."

Irma asked Smith for a highlighter and quickly marked the entries for Kelly's badge on the rest of the sheets.

07 05 00 1159 SULF RECY   INGRESS SAFETY K KISSIMMEE
07 05 00 1207 SULF RECY   EGRESS

She highlighted the last one:

```
07 05 00  1213  DEV BULK    INGRESS  SAFETY  K KISSIMMEE
07 05 00  1222  DEV BULK    EGRESS
```

"Who has Kelly's badge?" Irma nervously wiggled the highlighter between her fingers.

Smith leaned forward and clasped his hands in front of him with his elbows on the table. He looked at Irma and Softhousen slowly and significantly. "We've started a new locator service on the badges issued this summer. This might be the time to use it."

Irma and Larry looked at each other, then back at him.

"Kelly's badge has radioactive labeling." Smith paused, "That means we can get a satellite trace on its location."

Irma and Softhousen spoke simultaneously: "Radioactive?" "I've never heard of that!"

"We are only supposed to use it in emergencies. The satellite service is extremely expensive." Smith was defensive at first, but now spoke with authority. "This is Winsome security policy, and completely confidential. Tell no one."

Irma had no doubt that Winsome wanted none of its employees to know they were wearing radioactive badges.

Chen walked in. "Smith asked me to attend," he explained. "Sorry I'm late."

"We were just talking about radioactive labeling and satellites," said Irma.

Chen sighed heavily. "I'm sure you can understand how sensitive this information is. There are radioactive isotopes—atoms with extra neutrons—of gold, cesium, zirconium, zinc, cobalt, silver, antimony, sodium, gallium, and nitrogen, which give off different frequency gamma rays. You can think of gamma rays as being like x-rays, but at higher frequencies and with more energy. They pass right through the body, and even lead, so they're impossible to shield. This makes gamma rays ideal for permanently labeling employee badges. Each new badge has a unique combination of wavelengths being emitted which may be located anywhere on or under the earth by satellite."

"Like a radioactive fingerprint?" Softhousen asked.

"Precisely," said Chen. "The badge manufacturer mixes different chemical compounds containing the isotopes into the plastic of each badge. The chemicals are dispersed throughout the plastic. Even if the badge is cut up, each tiny piece contains the same labeling, so it can still be located."

"Suppose a badge is burned?" asked Irma.

"Matter cannot be destroyed. The charred residue would contain the same elements, with the exception of the nitrogen whose compounds are reduced by oxidation in the fire and escapes as a gas. Winsome has developed software that can identify whether the badge has been burned or not by detecting the modified gamma ray signature.

"From the satellite?" Irma was amazed.

Chen nodded. "From anywhere on earth. We can also point the satellite to detect a badge being worn by an astronaut in orbit or on the moon."

"And radioactive decay…?" Irma silently thanked her high school physics teacher. What she had taught her was coming in handy.

"…changes the relative energies of the peaks of the fingerprint. In fact, radioactive decay makes each badge's pattern more unique over time, and impossible to counterfeit. Our software also accurately predicts the decay of each badge."

Softhousen finally spoke up. "Won't the badges eventually run out of radioactivity?"

Chen laughed, "Sure. Eventually. But most of the half-lives are hundreds of years. It won't be in our lifetimes."

Irma thought of a law school girlfriend who had just died from metastasized breast cancer. "Doesn't radiation cause cancer?"

Chen answered without hesitation. "There are gamma rays from outer space passing through your body right now, so we don't think so. Their wavelength is so short—less than a billionth of a centimeter—that the waves can pass through an atom without any interaction."

"But you're not certain."

"Nothing in high-energy physics is certain. Atomic particles only have probabilities of being at any one place at any one time."

"We need to find out who has Kelly's badge." Softhousen stopped the science lesson.

Chen nodded at Smith, who punched in a long distance phone number.

A voice answered, "Da. Nomer rabotadatelya, pazhaluysta." It sounded like Russian.

"English, please," said Smith.

The same voice switched to English, but was still clearly Russian. "Yes. Employer identification number, pliss."

Smith rattled off a long combination of letters and numbers.

"Pattern identification number, pliss."

Smith consulted a small notebook full of single-spaced names and numbers, and read off one of the numbers.

"One moment, pliss."

Irma imagined a Russian bureaucrat in a filthy office with dirty old wooden filing cabinets. But it probably wasn't like that at all, she thought.

"Your location is stationary…" the Russian said, and recited the latitude and longitude.

Irma, Softhousen, and Smith all wrote down the numbers.

"We will bill employer as agreed." The phone clicked off.

"Holy smokes!" said Softhousen. The whole thing had taken less than a minute. "That's finding something the easy way."

Chen smiled, "Will there be anything else?"

"Yeh. How do we pinpoint this thing once we're there?"

"Take Smith with you. He's trained to operate a miniature XRF detector with a solid-state photo-multiplier that has been optimized for gamma rays. It will take you right to it, even if it's buried."

"Where do we look?" asked Irma.

Smith pulled an aviation sectional out of his briefcase, and a clear plastic ruler. He unfolded the map. Irma and Softhousen stood up and watched as he carefully drew horizontal and vertical lines with a red pencil. They intersected in the desert west of Albuquerque.

"Oh great. Evan'll love this." Softhousen punched the keypad on the speakerphone.

"Dinst, forensics," said the phone.

"It's me. Meet us at the city landfill as soon as you can get there without bustin' no laws. Bring a coupla shovels, and one of them big coolers of Alligator Aid."

"Anything else?"

"Pick up a search warrant for the dump from Stew."

"Okay, what are we looking for?

"A winsome i.d. badge, probably buried."

"And what's the probable cause?"

"Uh…" Softhousen looked to Irma for help.

She thought fast. "Mr. Dinst, Winsome i.d. badges are the property of Winsome Semiconductor Corporation, and we have reason, based on a scientific test, to believe that our property is buried at the dump. We also have probable cause to believe that this same badge was used by the perpetrator of the recent crimes against Winsome property and Kelly Kissimmee."

Evan copied this down to present to the magistrate, and grunted, "Okay."

"Any luck on the blood in the tool?" asked Softhousen.

"Don't have the DNA result, but the type and Rh are the same as Kelly's," said the phone.

"Bye." Softhousen turned off the phone, and looked at Irma and Smith. "We'd better all drive our own vehicles. I have no idea how long this will take."

*   *   *

Softhousen led the way in his grey unmarked police car. Smith drove a white pickup truck with black letters on each door stating WINSOME SECURITY. Irma brought up the rear in her little Miata.

They turned west when they reached Interstate 40—a black four-lane strip of tar melting in the midday July desert heat, and rapidly climbed Nine-mile Hill toward the sweeping crest of the West Mesa. They passed truck after wheezing truck gasping for oxygen, slowly staggering toward the summit in the right lane. Albuquerque was just as high as Denver, Irma recalled.

Just before the crest, Softhousen abruptly exited and lead them south on a newly paved road.

The landscape was parched, wind-blown earth. Occasionally scruffy, brown, isolated clumps of desert grass waited for a rare rain to bring them back to life. The Sandia Mountains shimmered in waves of heat, to her left. Suddenly Irma's tiny Miata was dwarfed by three trash trucks thundering down this road to nowhere, passing her on the left. She struggled to maintain control in the dusty blast of their windy wake.

Irma was surprised by a sharp right turn, and then was blinded by sunlight reflecting from razor wire atop a twelve-foot chain link fence. "Technology overkill," she thought of this ferocious protection of a modest cinder block guardhouse in front of a dump.

Evan had waited for them, and was sitting on the concrete sidewalk in the shade of the north wall of the guardhouse. He stood. "Here's the warrant, and they want Ms. Laches to sign something inside."

Irma, Smith, and Softhousen gladly entered the little air-conditioned room. "Sorry for the stop, but this is a secure facility, ma'am," the armed guard said politely.

"A trash dump is a secure facility?" Irma asked.

"Landfill. Yes ma'am." He stared at the Winsome photo i.d. badge clipped to Irma's collar. "For instance, Winsome disposes of scrap wafers here. They're a trade secret."

A good, legal answer, thought Irma. "I'm legal counsel for Winsome Fab 13, and Detective Softhousen has a search warrant."

"Yes ma'am. We just need you to sign this form. The only items Winsome employees may remove must be Winsome-related, not from another company. I will need to inspect all items taken from the site before you leave."

Irma signed the form. The guard stepped outside, pointed to a map sealed in a glass case on the side of the building, and explained where they had been dumping for the last two days.

*   *   *

Sergeant Smith walked around the earthen mounds with the portable XRF detector slung over his shoulder. The detector was about half the size of a shoebox, with a handle on top. He held a small global positioning system receiver in his other hand. It displayed his latitude and longitude.

"Why can't the GPS receiver take us to the coordinates?" asked Irma.

"It can, except there is some error. Right now, it's telling me I'm right on top of the coordinates we were given, but the dump site map says it's 15 feet that way." He pointed to his left. "It's probably over there."

Smith walked to the neighboring mound of dirt and began sweeping the area with the XRF unit. Irma, Softhousen, and Evan stood off to the side. The XRF detector began to emit slow chirps. They sped up. "This is it." Smith pointed to the ground in front of him.

Softhousen and Evan dug in the hot sun. There was a burst trash bag under the dirt. Smith again pointed the XRF. It chirped happily.

After spending 5 minutes taking photographs of the hole and the surrounding dump, Evan pulled on latex gloves and worried the bag from the ground. He shook it off, being very careful to keep the burst seam closed.

"Take the whole thing," commanded Softhousen. Evan put the trash bag into a larger evidence bag, and then into the trunk of his car.

Smith did a final sweep of the area with his XRF unit. "Nothing else here," he reported.

*   *   *

In the guardhouse Evan placed the bag on a steel table and carefully arrayed its contents across the surface. "At least it's not table scraps," he said. Softhousen nodded.

Almost all of it was paper. There were water bills, electric bills, flyers from the department stores at the malls, catalogs from mail order houses, cardboard cereal boxes, and old newspapers.

Softhousen peered at what looked like little pieces of plastic which had migrated to the bottom of the bag, along with bits of wood and pencil lead from the inside of a pencil sharpener. "See if this is it," he asked Smith. The XRF began a steady squeal when brought within a foot of the plastic shards. "It looks like Kelly's i.d. was cut up into lots of small pieces, like a credit card. We'll have to try to put it back together, so a jury can recognize it."

"Not a problem." Evan said as he assembled the flash unit on his camera.

Irma pulled on latex gloves and helped Softhousen examine the bills and other papers in the bag. All of it was addressed to the same person.

Chapter 34

CHRISTMAS

Irma and Softhousen helped the Albuquerque District Attorney's Office to expedite the criminal prosecution of the employee who had cut up Kelly's badge. The conviction and sentencing had quickly come and gone, and now Irma sat in her living room on her bearskin rug in front of a warm little fire. Outside her picture window a pretty layer of white was beginning to form on the yuccas and piñon pines in her yard.

She watched the snow fall and very slowly sipped a steaming cup of Suisse Mocha, savoring as much of its taste and smell as possible. A small Christmas tree stood in the corner, its tiny lamps emitting a colorful, cheerful glow. She loved New Mexico in the winter. She had started to learn to ski. After her first lesson, she was hooked. The high mountain air was ultra-pure, the serene winter skies brilliant blue, and the colors of the ski clothing and the trees more vibrant than anywhere else on earth.

Softhousen had said, "The perp folded like a house of cards." They got a full confession. The perp was smart. But just before the end of the trial, she caved in. She decided her best bet was to offer a plea. Now she was serving a five-year sentence, and the money she had been given by Fig Leaf was in the New Mexico State Treasury. The money had been hidden, probably during some suspicious vacations to the Caribbean. Neither Larry nor even Winsome's ex-FBI agent had been able to find the accounts, but the perp had disgorged the numbers as part of her plea agreement. The State of New Mexico was $1,000,000 richer and the Albuquerque District Attorney was a very happy woman.

The money should have been forfeited to Winsome as restitution for the damage the perp had caused, but the trial judge insisted on a separate hearing and had required briefs in advance. Irma's current chore was to prepare that brief for that hearing—a Memorandum of Law in Support of a Motion for Restitution.

Winsome could have brought a civil action against the perp for the millions of dollars' damage she had caused, but she was a shallow pocket—in legal slang, a "turnip." Not even Winsome, with its army of attorneys and unlimited legal budget, could get blood from a turnip.

And it would have been terrible publicity. When a huge company like Winsome sued a former employee it looked bad. It looked like the big bad corporation was beating up a defenseless individual. It looked like Winsome couldn't screen out bad employees. But Winsome didn't need to sue the perp. Irma and Larry had gotten unimpeachable evidence on the really deep pocket behind the whole thing.

Fig Leaf was a sole proprietorship that, over the years, had specialized in selling infant formula to the third world. Its owner, Y. "Babbs" Rebreg had refused to diversify, even after becoming a millionaire many times over. He was renowned for despising the computer industry and his lawyers submitted *amicus* briefs in every anti-technology court action they could find. His special obsession was the loss of privacy through the sharing of databases by insurance companies. Computers and insurance were the twin children of the devil.

When Winsome's development of the breast pump chipset threatened his livelihood, Babbs went over the edge. Since Fab 13 was the major production site for the BPC he targeted it for destruction. He recruited a saboteur.

Irma smiled. There was a paper trail that led directly to Babbs. He had simply wired the money the old fashioned way. Then Babbs emailed the perp instructions to "sabotage and terrorize Fab 13." Evan had found the email on the perp's C: drive. The DA had been ecstatic. She had two smoking cannons to blow away the defense.

Babbs' secretary at Fig Leaf, the one who had handled the transfer of funds, also came forward. It had been difficult; she was loyal to Babbs, had been with him for years, but was even more outraged at the mutilation of Kelly's body. Irma smiled. She had been a wonderful, unforgettable witness—wracked with pain—obviously tormented to be testifying against her boss—and obviously telling the truth.

Babbs was in jail, where he belonged. His attorneys—the best—had argued insanity, and had pleaded that he be placed in a mental institution, but it had not worked. New Mexico courts were not fond of the insanity defense, and Babbs, the CEO of a multimillion-dollar company, was obviously competent.

Now Irma was going to destroy Babbs financially in a civil suit. Justice would prevail! There were no excuses—no possible defenses for what had happened to Kelly at Winsome.

Irma closed her eyes and imagined herself before the civil jury. She would first show a videotape of brilliant, vivacious, charismatic Kelly before her mutilation. The video was from the picnic. It clearly showed Kelly's taut muscles, bouncing breasts, and iron buttocks pressing firmly against her skimpy clothes, the colors of her bronze skin and blond hair blazing in sharp relief against the deep blue sky as she spiked the volleyball, destroying her male competition. The tape showed Kelly's youthful, attractive Winsome friends dancing and cheering in the background. Slow motion would be most effective, Irma thought. She would still-frame Kelly's leap above the net at the end, leaving Kelly's radiant face and fiercely blue eyes framed by her swirling blond hair in front of the jury for as long as possible.

Next, she would project Kelly's amazing scholastic record on the courtroom wall and describe her limitless future as a safety engineer, as a professional athlete, and as a musician.

Then Kelly's parents, the white-haired, attractive, slender, articulate Kissimmees, now pitifully broken, their lives destroyed, their futures holding only their own deaths, would testify about Kelly's achievements. Frank and Susan Kissimmee's wrinkled, kind eyes, brimming over with tears, would show their boundless love for their daughter—would show their hopes, their dreams, their lives destroyed by Babbs' obsession.

Finally Irma would show Kelly hanging helpless, brutally tied to the rafter, surrounded by cold, dark, demonic steel and writhing ductwork, blood dripping from her arteries—her soft, talented hands, her life, her future viciously destroyed, her blood-streaked, ghostly white, ghastly dead face framed by her bloody, sunny golden hair.

Irma grinned. The jury would go wild. It wouldn't matter that Kelly's death was accidental. The mutilation was so outrageous that the jurors might leap from the jury box, drag Babbs from his defense table chair to the courtroom floor and beat him to a bloody pulp. Irma sighed softly. She was deeply at peace. This was lawyers' heaven. With the punitives, Babbs would be penniless. His corporate empire would be destroyed.

The final figure for the damage done at Fab 13, rounding off to the nearest thousand, was an astounding $1,744,311,000. Irma shook her head in amazement. One billion, seven hundred forty-four million dollars! And she was responsible for the accuracy of that figure. She had made sure that every single cent of the repair costs were documented. None of the stainless steel and polyethylene tubing, none of the quartz tubes, none of the filters, and none of the wetted parts of the pumps or tanks could be completely cleaned of gold. They all had been replaced.

She had also included Winsome's lost profits during the time the factory was down for repairs; a single chip which cost Winsome $50 to manufacture sold for $500. Hundreds of dollars profit, multiplied by hundreds of chips per wafer, multiplied by thousands of wafers per week.

Now the factory was up and running, better than ever.

Irma lay back on her bearskin and watched the snow fall.

But in a sense, Babbs was right. Irma hated Winsome's rampant religious obsession with psychology. Of course, she would never publicly criticize her company. But she embraced Babbs cause of privacy, though not his methods. Irma believed that privacy was central to the dignity—the self-worth—the core—of every individual. The free will which privacy enhanced was the cornerstone of the law and a civilized, mentally healthy, productive society—even if the shrinks and colleges teaching psychology chose to ignore it. Irma was doing everything she could at Winsome, behind the scenes, to ensure that the privacy of Winsome's employees would no longer be compromised the way it had with Perry's and Ellen's calls to the Trust Line.

What had happened to Perry illustrated the problem. The breach of Perry's therapist-patient confidentiality did nothing to improve Perry's mental health. On the contrary, his satisfaction with his job plummeted along with his self-esteem. Perry finally lashed out at Chen and accused him of aiding and abetting a violation of California Business and Professions Code Section 2960(h). Then Perry waited patiently, but there was no corrective action and no apology from Winsome. Perry finally quit.

Before he left Perry confided to Irma that he had spoken with an Albuquerque attorney concerning conflicts of laws and had learned that Winsome and MHCS should be adhering to the right to privacy mandated by the California Constitution and California Code. Then he had used the

Internet—findlaw.com led him to leginfo.ca.gov—to find Section 2960(h).

A shrink would say that Perry had "projected," or "externalized," his "repressed childhood anger;" or that he had "decompensated"—whatever those words meant. Irma had her own interpretation: she thought Perry had a case of perfectly justified, old-fashioned outrage at being lied to by Winsome and the Trust Line shrinks. They advertised the strict confidentiality of the hot line counseling service. The non-psychobabble, English word that described what had happened to Perry was "betrayal."

He quit his job at Winsome, and, at the late age of 46, stated his intention to attend law school and write a book about the abusive use of psychology by corporations to "help" people. "Good for him!" Irma thought. She agreed completely. Chen wasn't a therapist, and had no business mucking about in Perry's, or in any other Winsome employee's internal life. And Chen would never have done it had it not been for pressure from Lindley. Chen respected his employees' boundaries, even if Winsome's shrinks did not.

Irma couldn't prove it, but she strongly suspected that Lindley's policy of violating employee confidentiality was the cause of the string of resignations that Chen had mentioned to Irma at the July Fourth picnic. Older engineers, intimidated by the boundless energy and enthusiasm of their younger compadres, seemed especially sensitive to disrespect.

After Softhousen arrested the perp, Chen assigned Irma to lead an internal investigation and to write a report about everything related to the incident. She could to go anywhere and do anything with an almost unlimited budget. She hired outside engineering consultants, and invited both the OSHA and New Mexico Health and Safety investigators into Fab 13. They all concluded, as Chen had, that there was almost no risk of nitrogen suffocation during the normal operation of the fab.

During her investigation Irma also discovered that the lack of a central alarm for the oxygen sensors wasn't Perry's fault. He simply couldn't get the money to do it. He had, in fact, proposed the hookups to Chen, but Chen had turned him down.

Chen explained the budgeting process to Irma. No corporation, regardless of its wealth, could do everything possible to eliminate every conceivable hazard. That would mean having padded walls, ceilings, and floors. Hazards simply had to be prioritized, and nitrogen suffocation was, quite properly, low on the list.

Perry had been extremely helpful in the investigation, even though he was planning to leave. He suggested a detailed *modus operandi*, became the official owner of the investigation Gantt chart, hosted the investigators, and gave Irma detailed updates and impeccably written project reports.

He also provided his original outline of Kelly's project. It included, in bold type, "**The undersigned agrees to attend all appropriate shutdown and other engineering meetings.**" A safety section clearly described nitrogen suffocation, and Kelly's signature was immediately below.

After reading Perry's report, with Mr. and Mrs. Kissimmee's consent, Irma contacted Cal Tech and conducted telephone interviews with several of Kelly's professors. It was clear that Kelly had a history of cutting classes in order to make time for extra work. She made straight A's anyway.

Apparently Kelly had been so anxious to obtain information on the oxygen sensors that she had cut the shutdown meetings just like she had cut her classes. It was a fatal mistake. But Kelly was an adult who had known the risks, and she was responsible for the actions that led to her death. Kelly was, after all, a safety professional. She should have known better.

Irma's report determined that there was, at most, slight negligence on Perry's part in not supervising Kelly more closely. But, at bottom, Kelly's death was an accident, and accidents were not illegal. Winsome had broken no laws. She recommended, however, that inexperienced personnel not be allowed to work in the clean room, unsupervised, during shutdowns. However, this was twenty-twenty hindsight – *post hoc ergo propter hoc* reasoning.

Irma thought Perry had done a good job. The day of his departure she pulled him aside, wished him well, and told him she was sorry to see him leave. She made a point of apologizing to him for the breach of his confidentiality by Lindley. He looked surprised and grateful. Perry was a good guy.

She rolled over, placed her chin on the bear's head, and wondered how many thousands of cave dwellers in the history of humanity had done the same. She was safe and warm in her adobe cave. The fire was slowly transforming fragrant piñon wood into glowing embers.

Irma had little sympathy for her boss, even though Lindley had learned the industry the hard way. Lindley had started out as a technician, and, just like Ellen Rench, and had learned all of the equipment in the fab. She had taken college courses at night, at the end of her twelve-hour shifts. Years of hard work went into her B.S. in Psychology. Then she transferred to a job as a counselor with Winsome's Human Resources department. She continued night school and earned a Masters in Business Administration. She worked hard, and was at the right place at the right time. Lindley's promotion to site HR Manager was no surprise. But she had been a con artist, and had allowed her old ways to return.

Irma wondered if Lindley's college courses had contributed to her downfall. She had adopted the con of

277

clinical psychology as her own. It was a "science" which was junk science—not science at all. It was a system of beliefs, assumptions, and ill-defined terms which were not publically acknowledged to be articles of faith.

Irma recalled the philosophy and religion classes she had taken as an undergraduate. Priests and philosophers where honest—they admitted their beliefs and listed their articles of faith. They distinguished between fact and fiction, physics and metaphysics, knowledge and belief.

Sigmund Freud's followers could not hold a candle, in terms of intellectual honesty, to Saint Thomas Aquinas. Irma fervently shared old Tom's faith in free will—which he called "the voluntary." Aquinas' *Summa Theologica; Treatise on Human Acts* stated, "Since man especially knows the end of his work, and moves himself, in his acts especially is the voluntary to be found." Irma said to herself, "Amen." Actions spoke louder than words, then and now. A man's or woman's acts illustrated the choices of their lives—and were tangible manifestations of their free will.

Irma agreed with the critics. Clinical psychology was a fraud on the American people. Its bible—the DSM-IV— was merely a voted-upon list of beliefs unsupported by science. Any of the DSM-IV's labels could surface as the latest psychological *dysfunction du jour*.

Irma thought of the labels of the past: "heretic," "witch," "warlock," "traitor," "communist;" and the labels of the present: "victim of post-traumatic stress disorder," "battered child," "member of a dysfunctional family," "personality disorder," "repressed anger." The names were different, but the meaning was the same. "We're better than you." "You're different." "You're an outcast." "You don't belong." "You're evil and we're not." Self-righteous demonization of others was alive and well in the twenty-first century. The power to label was the power to destroy.

Just when you least expected it: The Spanish Inquisition.

Irma recalled the psychological fads of the twentieth century: toilet training, hypnosis, multiple personality disorder (called dissociative identity disorder in the latest DSM, because it sounded more "scientific,") post-traumatic stress disorder, holocaust survivor syndrome, battered woman syndrome, the Twinky defense (or "low blood sugar made me kill,") urban psychosis, black rage, repressed memory, gambling addiction—an endless repetition of a denial of personal responsibility and free will. Even more were listed in Alan Dershowitz' book, *The Abuse Excuse*.

It was Lindley who decided to accept Babbs' offer of a million dollars. She didn't have a cancer-ridden mother whose medical bills she had to pay. Lindley's "disorder" was best described by an old-fashioned noun: "greed;" whose correct adjective was "criminal."

Irma turned again, stared at Bessie's blanket, and sadly thought of Mary. At least her death had done some good. In this week's Federal Register OSHA had published a Notice of Proposed Rule Making for new standards to control the temperature of safety showers.

Ellen Rench was still at Winsome, averaging eighty hours a week. Irma, try as she might, could not help looking at Ellen and thinking about her differently—more compassionately—than she did the employees about whose lives she knew nothing. She hated herself for doing it. Ellen had a right to be treated just like every other employee— neither more compassionately, nor less. But Irma knew too much about Ellen's past. Irma could not erase Ellen's two thousand brutal rapes from her mind.

What was worse, Ellen knew that Irma knew about her past. All it took was a glance that lingered a fraction of a second too long, a facial expression of pity, or a brief smile at an inappropriate time to convey a special and inappropriate bond. That had happened. One day Irma was staring at Ellen and quickly looked away. Ellen saw the expression on Irma's face. That's all it took. That message could not be erased.

Irma knew that even a "perception of disability" had been held by the courts to be a violation of the Americans with Disabilities Act. And that was another reason why breaching an employee's privacy was such an insidious thing. Once privacy was taken away it could not truly be restored without firing everyone involved. As long as the perception of disability persisted in the memory of any manager and affected that manager's treatment of that employee, the statute of limitations would not run, for the injury to the employee was ongoing. And if the employee were to quit and then apply to be re-hired, the perception of disability could resurface. Winsome was placing itself at greater and greater risk of being sued every time an employee's therapist-patient confidentiality was breached.

Irma had taken exceptional pleasure in destroying Lindley's computer files. First she made friends with the Fab 13 network administrator. He had erasure software that did more than erase the files' names—it completely zapped the content of the original files by replacing the 1's and 0's with 0's. Next, together, they utilized his search software to check every one of the 1,000 networked pc's on site. Irma watched as he completely erased everything Lindley had touched from every hard drive in the building.

Then Irma ceremoniously carried the counseling records—both hard copy and backup floppies—from Lindley's desk to a rusty, blackened, steel drum in the service yard. This ugly barrel did not belong in Winsome's world of ultra-clean technology. It was used for fire extinguisher training. She poured in a little kerosene, then smiled as she watched the flames. After the fire died, she dumped out the ashes and melted bits of plastic and smashed them to smithereens.

Irma wrote a motion, granted by the court, whereby Winsome took possession of Lindley's personal PC and backup ZIP drive floppies. Irma destroyed those in the barrel as well.

The doorbell rang—Irma's friends had arrived. She jumped up, poured rum into the eggnog, and answered the door.

Charles was first. He extended his hand. "Congratulations. I've just promoted you to Human Resources Manager."

Irma grinned from ear to ear.

Evan looked at the sky and announced, "Looks like an occluded cold front. It's going to bring a lot of snow."

Mercedes drew the wheeping pager from her belt with a tired smile.

Last inside, Softhousen looked deeply into Irma's eyes and said, "Looks like a three-dog night to me."

Irma took their coats and hugged them all. "Merry Christmas!" she said.

THE END

ABOUT THE AUTHOR

Leigh S. Gettier worked for Intel Corporation for twelve years in its Rio Rancho, New Mexico, chip manufacturing plant. Mr. Gettier has degrees in music, philosophy, electronics and law. He has worked as a professional symphonic musician and an engineer, and he now practices law in Virginia.